Fami

Family Constellations Revealed

Hellinger's Family and Other Constellations Revealed

Indra Torsten Preiss
The Systemic View Series

By the same author:
Heal Your Relationship: A New Way of Improving Your Relationship Skills
(2015)

Original titles in Dutch:
Familieopstellingen in de Praktijk (2004)
Gezonde Verhoudingen (2008)
Je Relatie Helen (2015)

Family Constellations Revealed is a translation of the Dutch best seller, *Gezonde Verhoudingen*, 2008, Archipel, Amsterdam.

© 2012 Indra Torsten Preiss
Second edition, 2015

Indra Torsten Preiss, Antwerp, Belgium.
Contact via http://www.the-systemic-view.com.

Cover photo ©: Indra Torsten Preiss
Cover portrait: Stefan Denis
Cover design: Asif Nawaz

ISBN: 1481068636
ISBN-13: 978-1481068635

For the liberation of our children

Contents

Foreword

In this book I aim to present all aspects of traditional family constellations as well as the basics of organizational and structural constellations in a thorough and accessible way. It is my duty to share with as many people as possible an understanding of this innovative therapeutic method and its power in helping people take control of their lives and improve relationships in all areas.

Family constellations are gaining popularity worldwide because they are extremely effective. They work with the fascinating process of representative perceptions as an integral part of a new therapeutic methodology.

You also will learn an organizing principle that underlies all human relationships. This holds as true for relationships with other family members as for relationships with your partner, children, friends, and work colleagues. Getting fully acquainted with constellation work offers you the way to embark on a fascinating and unique personal journey into a new, comprehensive consciousness. You will be able to experience how intimately you are connected with your ancestors and the positive forces that stream from them to you once your subconscious entanglements are resolved.

Bert Hellinger developed family constellations based on, among other ideas, the contextual therapy of the Hungarian American psychiatrist Nagy. His work made it clear how strongly people are bound to their ancestors through loyalty. Without being aware of it, people carry the unprocessed emotional loads (called entanglements) and manifest them in their lives in subconscious ways. This leads to profound (at times destructive) consequences—not only for the people themselves but those around them.

Becoming aware of these loyalties and their costs can certainly help you move forward in your life. You will recognize how strong the influence of your ancestors is on your life as well as the freedom offered when you learn to let go of entanglements. In other words this book is about positively transforming loyalty connections with parents and other ancestors.

Acknowledgments

The support of my expartner, Griet Van Doren, made this book possible. We offer thanks to our friend Diane Broekhoven for her initial advice; Bernadette Verdonck for her help with the first edition of this book in Dutch; and Bernard Samson, Marija Duin, and the Uitgeverij Archipel for the second, improved Dutch edition.

For research help I am grateful to Martin Hell, Brenda Vos, Ad Kop, and Sophie Desseyn, my former partner and mother of my oldest daughter. Thanks also to Simone Claus for her information and insight into lost twins, Pacquette Spelt for her support with the chapter about organizational constellations, and Chaja Kruijssen for help and advice regarding intercultural constellations.

My thanks go out to my teachers. The most important I note here: Hans Mensink and Tilke Deur for sharing their thorough knowledge in re-birthing-breath work and bodywork and my enlightened teachers Michael Barnett and Osho for helping create a powerful spiritual foundation in me and showing me the dimension of just being that now underpins my work and life.

Everything I learned from these people helped me become acquainted with the work of Bert Hellinger, to whom I am especially thankful. This is not only because he discovered the methods written about in this book, but also because he has always been so gracious in sharing his work. He says, "I am pained whenever people asks me if they can use something I have said or done. It's as if I have rights over insights or reality. These are my gifts, and they are for everyone. I make no claims when someone picks up on an aspect of my work and develops it further. I have received an impulse and I pass the impulse on and I am happy when others in their own ways pass it on again."[1]

In helping me fully appreciate relevant issues, I want to acknowledge Berthold Ulsamer and the down-to-earth vision he teaches in his courses for constellation therapists.

Naturally I want to thank everyone who has allowed me to cite their constellations or those who in one way or another have assisted in the production of this book—especially Els Monden, Marleen Lejon, Bianca en Luc, Micheline, Veerle (Shutra), Andrea, and all my students.

Finally I want to thank Anthony Grant and Lionel Fancis for translating the book into English, Angela Grant for copyediting, and Martin Hell and Marc Van Gastel for editing and proofreading.

The second edition comes with hundreds of little improvements to the text. This is thanks to my oldest daughter, Sarah, and the CreateSpace editing team.

Take Note

This book is based on the theory and practice of Bert Hellinger, the findings and insights of other family constellators, and my own experience with family constellations. Readers who are familiar with other forms of therapy might recognize elements of family therapy, system therapy, and the contextual therapy of Ivan Boszormenyi-Nagy.[2] Concepts such as systemic laws and systemic phenomenology are Hellinger's; they are attributed to him in this book. Where no English translations were available, the translations offered are those of the author and translators.

Throughout the book the term *marriage* is used, but long-term relationships are naturally included. Where *husband* is used, the long-term male partner is embraced, while *wife* encompasses the long-term female partner. Although heterosexual romantic relationships are used and implied, the description of family dynamics holds equally true for homosexual relationships.

When discussing actual constellations, the names of representatives are italicized but not capitalized. For example, instead of "The representative of the mother said" or "The mother's representative said," the book uses, "The *mother* said." This was done to enhance readability by avoiding superfluous repetition of the word *representative*.

I hope this book will give people the opportunity to gain insights that will help improve their relationships and that might lead to more enriched and harmonious lives. This also applies to therapists, coaches, and their patients. That other therapists and coaches will find constellation therapy as expansive and as enriching a therapy tool as I have is another hope of mine. I cannot now imagine how I could work without it.

PS: To my surprise the majority of German books on family constellations have yet to be translated into English.

That reminds me of the strong feeling I had after my first constellation. I was having a coffee in an outdoor bar in the Antwerp Cathedral's shadow and reading one of Hellinger's books when this strong, electrifying feeling came over me. I knew people all over the world had to be told about constellations and what can be learned from them! Sharing my knowledge with you is my basic drive for writing and publishing this book.

1

Introduction

What Are Family Constellations?

When I first heard about family constellations, my first thought was it was just another fad therapy. I had heard Bert Hellinger's work was enormously popular in Germany and had spread to European circles not usually open to alternative therapies. It took a lot of effort from my friends James Bampfield and Mushin J. Schilling to convince me of the deep impact this new therapeutic method offered. Reading a short description of Bert Hellinger's work then touched me in a personal way and favorably tipped the scales.

In a family constellation, a seeker (or client) presents a personal, familial, or work relationship problem for which resolution is sought. A seeker then chooses a group member from the circle of participants as a stand-in or representative for himself or herself and for each person or family member involved. For example, the seeker chooses a representative for himself or herself and his or her father, mother, or brother. He or she then places (or *constellates*) them according to his or her inner view in relation to each other within the circle (or *constellation space*). Once all representatives are constellated, he or she takes up a position with other participants in the circle to observe and open up to the proceedings.

Then the magic begins. The representatives in their respective places access perceptions of the people they are representing. The facilitator questions one representative after another and works with the representatives to help resolve the seeker's struggle so the natural flow of love can be restored. In the end the seeker takes a position into the restored constellation and replaces the representative standing in for him or her in order to allow the new awareness to sink in. This makes the seeker conscious of all the emotional entanglements he or she was carrying so those can be released.

While reading about Hellinger's approach, I became aware of unresolved issues in my own life. At the invitation of my friend Mushin, I went to Berlin to take part in my first family constellation weekend, which Marlis Grzymek-Laule facilitated.

He suggested I first experience what happens in a constellation as an observer and representative before doing my own constellation. That proved to be good advice.

This constellation group started in a circle. Everybody introduced himself or herself and gave a short explanation about the reason for participating. One of the participants was then asked to start with his constellation. The facilitator interviewed the seeker in the circle. This way the seeker was able to pose a clear theme to be explored in the constellation. The seeker was then asked to choose representatives by asking other participants to stand in for him and the other family members involved. He placed them within the circle according to his inner perceptions. Thus my first constellation unfolded before me, which I found deeply touching.

I had never experienced anything like that before in my eighteen years as a therapist. The special roles of representatives and the way in which subconscious patterns showed up as entanglements of the family system that were then transformed into healthy solutions were simply astounding and yet so elegantly simple.

From witnessing this first constellation, two elements of my own work came together. The facilitating work in personal growth I had done for years with rebirthing-breath work[1] and inner child work[2] connected with the energy work I had learned a few years before with my spiritual teacher, Michael Barnett.[3] Right away I saw the incredible opportunities that family constellations offered me as a therapist. Instinctively I understood how it worked, and I knew immediately I was going to do a lot of good work using this method. I will never forget that moment. It became instantly clear that the power of constellations lay in restoring the flow of love between family members.

Over the course of this first day, I was chosen a few times as a representative, so I had the opportunity to experience being fully involved in a constellation.

One time I was chosen to be a father, and another time I was chosen to be a son. Later on in the day, I was chosen to be a stand-in for a cancer patient. Each time I was astonished by the clarity and depth I felt about the people I was representing without knowing them or anything about their backgrounds. The only information provided during constellations is factual. That person is the father, that person is the mother, and so forth.

Once I was placed in the constellation, tuning in and sharing my perceptions worked surprisingly well for me and most of the other representatives. This fascinating effect is the basis of Bert Hellinger's work.

Family constellations did exist prior to Hellinger, but representatives were provided with character descriptions and other information. These were processed through role-playing. Issues were resolved in these early constellations, but the depth in Hellinger's work is created because there are no character descriptions. By dealing only with clear facts, character descriptions don't distract representatives in constellations based on Hellinger's work. On top of that, there is no role-playing, and every form of drama is discouraged, as this tends to cloud rather than clarify the issues.

One of the constellations that weekend left a particularly deep impression on me. The seeker was a woman who wanted to clarify the origins of her cancer. The facilitator asked for facts from her family history, and it was revealed her father also had terminal cancer.

She chose me as her father, a woman for herself, and another man to represent death. She then constellated us. I stood about six feet away from and facing the representative for death. The seeker's representative was about two feet behind me. When the facilitator asked us to tune in to our respective places, my perceptions were clear. I was drawn toward death and experienced a pull toward the representative for *death*. At that moment this was my goal, my destiny, and where I sought fulfillment. Only there, in love and silence, could I feel at peace. That was where I had to be. On my left arm, I felt a pulling sensation from my *daughter* (names of representatives are in italics), which felt very uncomfortable. It felt as if I was being prevented from doing what I wanted. I was being treated completely without respect. When I shared my crystal clear perceptions, the seeker started to cry and nodded in affirmation. The seeker's representative responded with, "I love my father. I really don't want him to die, and I really want to do everything I can to keep him alive. I would rather die myself than see him die." Through representatives expressing their perceptions, the hidden dynamic behind the seeker's sickness became visible. The facilitator worked with special clarifying statements (see "Clarifying Statements" in chapter two) until the *daughter* (the seeker) was able to let her *father* go and accept his death. At the end of the constellation, I was arm in arm with death's representative in a deep and peaceful moment of rest.

My participation as a representative in this constellation showed me with even more clarity the genius of this approach. I was able to fully appreciate that Bert Hellinger had discovered and developed an instrument that enabled hidden, underlying truths to become visible. Precisely what becomes visible depends on the theme or question posed, and this reflects what the client desires to become conscious and aware of.

> *Constellations provide instantaneously accessible images of underlying problems.*

Over the years as a therapist, I have regularly experienced intuitive realizations about patients. Conveying the merit of these insights only works some of the time. Imagine the woman in the above constellation as a patient of mine, and I want to convey to her that she chose to be sick to share her father's burden and help keep him alive. She might have been able to consider my insights and appreciate the connection, but her constellation gave her a much broader view with a clear and immediate impact that transcended the client–therapist nexus.

> *Through family constellations people can simply make their problems visible and emotionally perceivable so they can face up to them. They then become conscious of hidden patterns and entanglements.*

As a facilitator constellations allow me to withdraw respectfully and facilitate more effectively in the background. This gives both the facilitator and the client/seeker more freedom to explore issues and reach resolutions.

Over the course of the following day, I was invited to set up my own family constellation. In principle I only use techniques that have helped me in my own development, so I had to experience my own constellation if I was going to use this technique as a facilitator.

My first constellation made me conscious of a level of understanding I had not been able to reach with other therapeutic methods. I really had no idea how strong the connections were I had with my grandparents. Furthermore I had no idea how strongly the negative effects of unresolved happenings in former generations impacted people and how many generations back that could go. In my work as a therapist, I had only been going back to the time of conception. What I witnessed that weekend went back much further.

A few of my clients with seemingly unresolvable problems came to mind. At the time I wasn't able to help those clients, and considered them as unresponsive to therapy. Now I could clearly see other dimensions to be considered.

A *yes, but* attitude burdened one of these clients. An ever-present *yes, but* fixation dampened all positive experiences for this man. Back then I thought clients such as this almost beyond help.

Through my experience with family constellations, I can now make the link between this *yes, but* attitude and unresolved family issues. This particular client did a constellation revealing that his problem was connected to the emotionally unresolved death of a child in the preceding generation.

After that weekend my new experiences excited me, and I immediately began to delve into literature on the subject, which was abundant in Germany. Bert Hellinger's book *Love's Hidden Symmetry*[4] helped me tremendously. Two weeks later I offered my first family constellations. As part of a yearlong training course I was conducting called Being Yourself, which I had given since 1996, I invited the group members to work with me using family constellations. I knew full well I had limited experience in this particular method. Despite my limited experience, they were all in agreement, and I gave my first family constellation. One constellation after another offered insights into deep-seated family dynamics, and we were able to bring issues and healing processes to conscious levels that until then seemed beyond reach.

From that weekend on, I knew I was a natural-born family constellation facilitator. I have a natural talent for this technique. I possess the special attitude needed to tune in to and flow with what shows up in a constellation and to trust and utilize the information given by the representatives. Thanks to all my previous experiences and learning processes over the last twenty years, I took to it like a duck to water. Since then I have read extensively about family constellations, and I have undergone training and attended workshops with experienced and renowned family constellation facilitators, most notably Berthold Ulsamer which has transformed me into a fully trained facilitator.

Every time I have presented a theme in my own family constellation, the effects have taken weeks or even months to manifest themselves in my life. The process remains a wonder to me, and my enthusiasm has only increased.

In most cases no special follow-up is required after a constellation. The solutions that come to the surface unfold at deep levels in the participants' lives—deeper than what they are normally able to reach with their minds. Constellation work with one of my clients who was a workaholic confirmed this. The constellation gave a very clear image that his addiction had carried over from two generations back. After the constellation he rolled up his sleeves and set about to make big changes in his life. He felt defeated, however, and after four weeks of hard work, he was convinced the constellation had not brought about the desired changes.

It was only then that transformation occurred from within. He experienced a general sense of letting go, and he was able to surrender to the situation at hand. Then his inner attitude toward his work changed completely. He was able to relax more easily, and the inner pressure from his hard work diminished.

If there is need to further explore an issue after a constellation, it is beneficial to have a few individual counseling sessions. A therapist experienced in constellation work can be called upon to help continue working through an issue.

Why Does It Work So Profoundly and Precisely?

The Tao that can be told
is not the eternal Tao;
The name that can be named
is not the eternal Name.
The unnamable is the eternally real.
—Lao-Tzu[5]

According to Bert Hellinger, family constellations work at the soul level. This goes way deeper than rational thought and one's normal capacity to change. A person is born in a family and takes on the whole family system as his or her inner images. This inner image that everyone carries with him or her includes what is known as *family conscience*. Through a family constellation, this inner image of knowing becomes visible and emotionally perceivable. Apart from the many positive elements, a family conscience might also contain unresolved or suppressed elements present in a family system.

Constellations allow people clear looks at their family con-sciences and provide them with the necessary knowledge or information to dissolve or heal repressed and subconscious information stored up in family histories.

When a person constellates a family, he or she chooses a representative for each family member and gives each person a place in the given space according to his or her inner view and feelings. He or she makes a subconscious image visible. This subconscious image is given a ge-stalt. Since the representatives don't form part of the family, they are not identified with the subconscious family conscience. That allows them free access and perception of the family conscience, so this knowledge can then be shared. In this way representatives act as a kind of sensing instrument. It is not advisable to constellate a family with the actual family members because they are too enmeshed in their own family conscience.

The fact representatives can perceive independently makes it possible to bring subconscious connections or entanglements to light, along with anything in a family that is unresolved or suppressed. By working with representatives, solutions are sought and found, and the representatives are moved around into new formations until a more harmonious family constellation is achieved.

At the end of the constellation, this new family image replaces the old inner image in the seeker. Just as the old image subconsciously determined a person's life, the new image does so from then on. The resultant changes stem from the same subconscious depth and take shape in people's daily lives.

The concept of the subconscious has been around since Sigmund Freud and Carl Jung.[6] It is now generally known that what people are conscious of is just the tip of the iceberg. All that is unworked or suppressed in people or in their families is not lost but rather remains stored in the subconscious part of memory and in the family conscience, which can be likened to the biggest yet hidden part of the iceberg.

Access to these levels is not that easy using intelligence and the power to reason. Family constellations work at the deepest layers of the subconscious and bypass the analytical mind to enable people to work through unresolved and repressed family aspects. Changes result in a more harmonious state of being. People then feel better about themselves, and their relationships work better.

The beauty of a constellation is that it provides a way out of an entangled existence; relaxation, awareness, and peace become an integral part of an improved life.

Naturally the success of family constellations depends on the seeker's level of openness and how much he or she can face up to. It also depends on how he or she can integrate newly acquired knowledge and awareness. A person's involvement in the theme and how much he or she is touched emotionally are also important factors.

A constellation conducted out of curiosity or over an issue that is not really that important to the client will be rather superficial and will lack impact. This can also happen if the client remains emotionally aloof and tries to read the constellation in a rational way.

In that sense family constellations are not wonder pills to be popped in order to achieve marvelous results. Having expectations that are too high is also to be avoided. What becomes conscious and what the client can integrate is a personal journey in the growth process. Hellinger says solutions can only be found and integrated if they are in harmony with one's soul.

It is important to realize the integration of a family constellation causes changes in the life of the seeker, and these processes of change can only happen if he or she lets go of the old inner image of the family. Sometimes this can be a painful process. During a constellation people work with unresolved elements floating around in their family systems. These elements remain unresolved because they are so painful. Some people prefer to avoid these issues; it might seem to them that daily suffering is more comfortable than going through that pain. This attitude might be difficult to understand but should also be fully respected. It should also be taken into account that it takes a few months or even up to two years for a constellation to be fully integrated into a life. Therefore, it is useful to wait until a constellation starts to manifest in daily life before embarking on a new constellation.

The Knowing Field

What we know is so influenced by what we do not know
that it cannot really be said that we know anything.
—Michael Barnett[7]

The knowing field forms the basis of constellation work. Anyone fortunate enough to experience a family constellation, as a representative or the actual seeker, knows this astonishing phenomenon. Without prior knowledge representatives have access to information that normally is accessible only to the actual family members. After being constellated, they have access to feelings and knowledge of a completely unknown family.

How do the representatives know that? Where does the information come from? How does the representative sometimes reveal details even the client has forgotten?

To give a taste of what one can encounter in a constellation, just imagine you have been chosen to be the representative for the *father* of a seeker. The only information you have about the strangers chosen as the other representatives is that they are stand-ins of the *mother* (the wife of the man you are standing in for), the *older daughter*, and the *younger son*.

You have no special feelings for these people, and the seeker has not mentioned anything about character traits of these family members. One by one the seeker guides each representative to a certain spot. More perceptions are gained with the placement of each representative involved in the constellation.

You start feeling something that was not there before. You have been placed opposite your *wife*. Your *daughter* has been placed to your left side, and your *son* is difficult to perceive. You feel a lot of anger and tension toward your *wife*, and your *daughter* is standing so close that it scares you. Your *son* is placed too far away, according to your feelings. The facilitator brings another representative into the constellation—the *second daughter*, who died as a baby from sudden infant death syndrome. Without knowing what overcomes you, tears run down your cheeks, and you feel a deep pain. Suddenly you know where the anger toward your *wife* comes from; you realize you have made her responsible for the child's death.

Through the facilitator's questioning, you start to understand the *father*'s feeling of powerlessness were too much to bear. It was much easier to find someone else to blame rather than face up to this powerlessness and pain. It was easier to blame your *wife*. All the information and feelings arise in you effortlessly.

The facilitator continues to work with the constellation and presents you with certain clarifying and healing statements. For example, "You are my wife. I am your husband. I feel a deep regret over my attitude toward you." Slowly all the entanglements become clear to you. Every time something is resolved, you become more relaxed.

After a while the facilitator gives you a new place in the constellation next to your *wife*. Now you feel a profound love toward her. Your *children* are placed opposite you, and even the *second daughter* has been given her place. You feel fatherly concern and love. You are proud of your family. At the end the client steps into the constellation, replaces the representative, and repeats the last steps to end the constellation.

Hellinger explains the process of a constellation in short:
During a constellation of the family the client randomly chooses participants as stand-ins (representatives) for himself and for other important members of his family. Typically this might be the father, the mother, brother(s) and sister(s). He or she then places them, in a centered and

connected way, in a spatial arrangement in relation to each other. Suddenly something comes to light in this process that surprises him. That is to say that in the process of the constellation he or she comes in contact with a knowing that was not accessible before.[8]

The striking thing is that from the moment they are constellated, representatives start feeling how the people they are representing would feel. Sometimes representatives even feel their counterparts' physical symptoms. A power field between the seeker and his or her family members on one side and between the seeker and his or her self-chosen representatives on the other side is witnessed time and time again.

For a long time, Bert Hellinger referred to this phenomenon as "a secret." Apparently the family soul or the family conscience is able to manifest itself in a constellation. Expressed in another way, the family conscience is given a *gestalt* and a *voice*.

This is not confined to the family sphere. Organizations, teams, sections of companies, and even whole company structures can be constellated. (See "Organizational Constellations" in chapter eight.) Indeed anything that can be described as a system can be constellated. Using this definition, all forms of relationships can be seen as systems. This might be a person and his or her sickness symptoms, addiction, or money problems. Relationships that people have in an organization or the relationship between a producer, product, and customer can also be viewed in this way. Access to underlying structures through representatives occurs each time a system is constellated in a focused way. It is then possible to clearly see deep subconscious influences beyond the reach of normal conscious means.

At first a constellation might strike people as a surprising thing. It plays tricks on reasoning and makes people feel unsure and anxious. In a discussion after a demonstration of a constellation during one of my many presentations, a participant expressed concern that revealing subconscious patterns in a constellation might be too confrontational.

The woman who had been the seeker in the demonstration constellation replied, "Somehow I have known what showed up during this constellation all along, and the pain I felt here I recognize as the same pain I have been experiencing all my life. Now I am able to feel this more thoroughly, and I can see where the pain is coming from. It was very confrontational, but now I feel uplifted."

It is sometimes confronting to become aware of something one has been carrying and silently suffering from for many years. This silent suffering can stop once one has seen it and entanglements are resolved.

Sometimes a constellation makes a person conscious of something long forgotten or even something that has remained concealed for one reason or another. The following summary from my practice is a good example of a constellation in which a long-concealed family secret came to light. The representative of the *oldest son* faced the representative for the *father* and said, "I am the son, the oldest child, and you are the father." The *father* confirmed this. I asked the representative of the *second son* to say the same thing, but instead he said, "No, that isn't my father." The *father* confirmed this and said, "No, that isn't my son." The representative of one of the *daughters* began to laugh and confirmed. "No, that isn't his father." The representative for the *mother* then said dryly, "That was my revenge."

> *Constellations often bring up the heavy load of a painful fate that has been passed down through the generations. It is these frequently unspoken matters and at times taboo topics that representatives in constellations shed light on.*

The fact that representatives have access to knowledge they normally wouldn't be able to perceive has not been scientifically substantiated yet. In chapter nine, "Science and Constellations," I will present a number of theories discussing this phenomenon. Worldwide the term *knowing field* has gained widespread usage. This is a very appropriate term and comes from the well-known family constellation facilitator Albrecht Mahr.

Anyone who has experienced the phenomenon referred to as the knowing field has become conscious of a much deeper connection between people than previously understood.

It has long been known that a strong bond exists between family members. Nagy's contextual therapy,[9] which has generally become an integral part of the psychology curricula at the university level, speaks about unperceivable loyalties and balances of giving and taking in relationships. Family conscience or memory is also known in the contextual approach. Contextual therapists assume there are accounting ledgers with records of obligations and responsibilities between all family members.

A particular seeker on one of my weekend constellations was adopted as a child. The representative of her mother complained about ringing in the ears (tinnitus). The representative of the child responded, "That's me. I'm continually calling you." Afterward the client confirmed this. "My biological mother suffered her whole life from ringing in the ears."

There is no generally accepted explanation for this phenomenon. However, scientific research is now under way in Germany. The similarity with Rupert Sheldrake's morphological field[10] and the science research about mirror neurons is notable. (See "Morphogenetic Fields and Morphic Resonance" in chapter nine.)

I remember well one of Sheldrake's documentaries. He clearly demonstrated the invisible or unperceivable connection between a pet and its owner. In this experiment the dog's owner, a cameraperson, and a public notary traveled to a nearby city. A second camera constantly monitored and filmed the dog at home. The footage of both cameras was shown together in real time on a television screen. At one point the notary said, "We are going home now." Nobody knew beforehand when he was going to say this. The dog reacted at the same time the dog's owner heard these words. He woke up in his basket at home and ran to the door. A short time later, the owner, the cameraperson, and the notary drove onto the street where the owner and dog lived. The dog began to wag his tail and run back and forward to the door. While they were looking for a parking spot on the street but were still out of sight, the dog jumped up enthusiastically at the door.

This documentary made it clear the dog and owner shared a connection that existed outside normal communication channels. Many dog owners are aware of this.

Breast-feeding mothers sense when their babies are about to wake and are ready to be fed. They have experienced a similar effect. Before the baby has had the chance to cry, the mother is standing by the crib and is ready to let the baby suckle. Women have assured me the milk actually begins to flow when their babies (in other rooms) are waking up and are ready to be fed. This is also an example of communication without an observable or concrete exchange of information.

My former partner, Sophie, had similar experiences with our daughter, Sarah. We were sitting in our back garden one lovely summer's evening. Our little daughter, who was six months old at the time, was asleep in a room with the window open. My partner suddenly jumped up and said, "Sarah's crying," and she rushed inside. There was nothing to be heard outside in the garden until Sophie was at our daughter's bedside. It was only then we heard the muffled sounds of the baby crying.

Connections do exist that cannot be scientifically proven. The strong bond between mother and child or owner and dog can perhaps explain the examples given, but this is not the same in a family constellation. People in constellations feel something for strangers they don't know at all.

A representative feels as though he is constantly standing in the mist. Later on he hears from the facilitator he was representing an alcoholic. Another representative feels terrible back pain in a constellation and later finds out she is representing a person who had to undergo a back operation.

There are thousands of such examples, and it continues to happen in constellations all over the world. I regularly give supervisory constellations with therapists or coaches without the client being present. This also works and enables the therapist or coach to get a clear image of the client's situation, which can then help in further treatment.

The knowing field is also evident in constellations without representatives, such as in individual sessions. Wooden dolls, plastic figures, pieces of paper on the floor, or even different sorts of shoes can be used instead of representatives. The seeker constellates the dolls, paper, or shoes and then goes from doll to doll or one piece of paper to the next. The facilitator accompanies the seeker as he or she feels and shares the perceptions.

Employing a method inspired by Ursula Francke,[11] I also lead successful family constellations relying solely on images and the client's visualization powers. This also taps into the astonishing workings of the knowing field. Very complex constellations are of course not possible with this method, but its value has long been proved when used to complement constellations with representatives or constellations with obvious themes.

In these cases it is important the client can tune in without props and have some distance from normal identification with the family to assist in the working of the knowing field. (Read more about this type of constellation in chapter eight.)

The knowing field exists. The phenomenon is evident in each and every constellation. It even exists in a presentation with inexperienced and unprepared people who are willing to spontaneously have their families constellated.

2
The Method

What happens and is sustained through love
can only be resolved through love.
—Bert Hellinger[1]

In this chapter I will outline the process of constellations, the importance of representatives' perceptions, and the feelings that consequently arise. The use of language and communication in constellations will be explained. This includes clarifying and resolving statements and the use of rituals such as bowing. On top of that, I will explain the basics of constellation work: systemic phenomenology and the specific attitude necessary for the facilitator to conduct a successful constellation.

The Constellation

A person who wants to have his or her family constellated has to have a theme to begin with. The theme is the posing of a particular problem close to the seeker's heart that he or she wants to become conscious of in order for it to be resolved. Having a relevant theme gives depth and power to a constellation, while curiosity alone makes a constellation superficial.

After reading this book, you might realize there are certain things about your family you would like to find out more about. To attempt a constellation on this basis, which is born more out of curiosity, is not advisable. Successful constellations stem from authentic emotional involvement.

Among other things, you can constellate all kinds of relationship problems, depression, aimlessness or the feeling you have not found your place in life. Themes concerning careers and success in life and business can also be effectively constellated.

A constellation theme is defined in a short interview between the seeker and the facilitator at the beginning of the constellation. Together they look at who and/or what should be constellated to be able to find desired solutions. That could be the seeker's family members, the current relationship, or, if it is about disease, the seeker's symptoms. The seeker provides the necessary information about the family history during the interview.

Only factual information is required for a constellation. Character descriptions of family members or partners are unnecessary. Indeed they are to be avoided because they hinder the perceptions of representatives.

The avoidance of character descriptions is what gives a constellation such a big impact. Suddenly parents are present in the constellation—just as distant or argumentative as the seeker knows them to be. Sometimes representatives make gestures just like the real parents or other relatives without knowing anything about the family. Constellations are certainly not role-playing exercises.

Representatives

Once a clear theme has been decided and the necessary facts have been presented, the seeker chooses representatives from the participants present. In general male participants are chosen for male roles and female participants for female roles. If there are insufficient males, females can be chosen instead, and something such as a tie can be worn as a readily recognizable male hallmark.

Choosing representatives is always done by request, so participants have the right to refuse if it does not feel right for them to take on certain roles.

First the chosen representatives and the seeker are gathered to make sure all are clear about who is representing whom. The representatives are then asked to feel grounded in their bodies. Guided by inner perceptions, the seeker then takes each representative by the shoulder and positions him or her within the circle. The seeker determines the direction each faces.

There are no further instructions about posture. A constellation works deeply and has strength when it is done as a ritual—conducted in silence and with everyone's complete attention. Plans or drawings completed beforehand are superfluous. A constellation is a timeless picture that reveals itself in the moment. If the facilitator senses lack of attention, he or she might call a halt to the proceedings to try again later.

Once all the representatives are placed or constellated, the seeker sits in the circle around the constellation space with the other participants. This way he or she can follow everything that is being said and done. The facilitator asks the representatives to tune into the spots they occupy and open up to all perceptions that might arise.

Sometimes in constellations representatives are asked to follow any urge to move. For example, a representative might want to step a bit further away from or closer to another representative or feel the strong urge to lie on the floor. By going with the flow and perceiving, something can come to light even at this early stage in the constellation. It seems as if the constellation wants to tell a story. Something invisible and subconscious is revealed and becomes perceivable in body and mind. The client's inner subconscious picture comes to life.

The facilitator asks the representatives one by one to share his or her perceptions in a brief yet adequate way. Their positions toward each other and their answers make the underlying family structure clear and uncover possible entanglements. Entanglements are significant connections that exist between the seeker and other family members. (See chapter four.)In attunement with the representatives, the facilitator works to bring entanglements or problematic connections to light to enable a search for possible solutions. Consequently there is often a need to add more representatives. The facilitator does this according to the facts of the family and indicated entanglements. For example, the constellation might uncover a child who died young or a forgotten former partner of the grandmother, so they too will be given places in the constellation. The added representatives are almost always excluded and forgotten family members or traumatized ancestors with difficult pasts. Once they are brought in and positioned by the seeker or facilitator, they are also asked to tune in. Based on the reactions of other representatives toward those newly placed, the meaning behind their inclusion and possible associated entanglements becomes clear. To help expose the hidden dynamic in the constellation, the facilitator uses clarifying statements. (These are explained later in this chapter.)

For example, the representative for the seeker can share feelings associated with a strong connection to a sister who died at an early age or feelings associated with the painful load of a grandfather's traumatic war experience. Later on the facilitator will work with resolving statements and rituals (see further on) as deemed necessary, until the solution becomes obvious and every representative feels at ease in the constellation. By the end of the constellation, the facilitator, in accordance with the representatives, will have found the right place in the constellation for everyone.

This right place mirrors the systemic laws discovered by Bert Hellinger, which facilitators around the world continue to validate in thousands of constellations. (See "Systemic Order" in chapter three.)

When an appropriate resolution is reached, the client is asked to take up his or her own place in the constellation, replacing his or her representative. The last important steps are now repeated, and the client is asked to repeat the appropriate clarifying statements and reenact rituals such as taking a deep bow toward the parents. It is then possible for the seeker to take on the new constellation. The facilitator helps the seeker to integrate what has been seen and felt by asking the seeker to take in the final constellation image and let it sink in until he or she internalizes it. To end the constellation, the seeker will usually be asked to take deep breaths or take a step in the new direction.

The seeker needs time and rest immediately after the constellation to allow the integration process to continue to take effect. Any exchange between the client and other participants is best avoided for at least half an hour after the constellation. This is when the integration process has usually been concluded. To finally end the constellation, the facilitator makes sure all the representatives have stepped out of their roles.

The Interrupted Constellation

There are times when a constellation has to be terminated before a solution is reached. This occurs because the constellation lacks power or important information is missing. Another reason for interrupting a constellation is because a very intense climax has been reached. The early termination of a constellation can have a positive and astonishing effect. The incompletion itself invites the soul to take a big leap forward. Through this incompletion, the client's feeling of responsibility to take the next big step is strengthened and allows space for a rich learning process.

The facilitator should never give in to the temptation of wanting a happy ending or striving to work out everything to the last detail. This might be well intended but will interfere with the essence of family constellations and systemic phenomenology. (See next chapter.)

Feelings in Constellations

Once all the representatives have been constellated and tuned in to their positions, the facilitator addresses each in turn. This is usually when they reveal their perceptions and all feelings involved. The facilitator tries to ensure feelings are not unnecessarily dramatized in a constellation. It is sufficient that a representative responds in a clear, relevant way that facilitates delving into a deeper layer. In this way the group can come in contact with the layer beneath emotions.

If a representative has a strong emotional reaction, he or she is asked to breathe more deeply with an open mouth and keep his or her eyes open to remain centered. By keeping the eyes open, the representative remains in contact with the present situation. By shutting the eyes, the representative runs the risk of losing himself or herself in an inner image from the past and repeating old emotional drama concerning the person being represented. This might even be a personal drama of the representative that has nothing to do with the constellation. Finally the facilitator asks the representative to articulate what he or she feels and elicits an appropriate phrase such as "I am sad," "I feel pain," or "I feel torn." The facilitator asks the representative to indicate which other representative the feeling is directed toward or whom it actually belongs to. Representatives are generally able to do this without any difficulty.

Clarifying Statements

To ensure communication remains clear and powerful during a constellation, clarifying statements and resolving statements (Ulsamer[2]) are used. Clarifying statements are short sentences used by the facilitator, working with the representatives, to assist them to accurately render perceptions. Consider the following scenario.

On being asked how she feels, a representative (*woman*) answers, "I am furious. I am exploding with anger." She might also show this through her body language by making fists. The facilitator asks her to breathe deeply and feel whom the anger is actually directed toward. To this she answers, "Toward my husband." Whereupon the facilitator asks her to say to the representative of her husband, "I feel angry toward you." After saying this the *woman* says she feels more relaxed. She breathes a sigh of relief. This relaxation and relief indicate clearly the feeling has been effectively revealed. Any further dramatizing is unnecessary. After this the *husband* is asked how this feels for him. He says to the facilitator, "Yes. That makes sense. She is angry with me. I feel guilty. I think I have left her in the lurch." The facilitator suggests he repeat the following clarifying statement, "I have made myself guilty," and the facilitator asks him how that feels. "That's right," he responds. "I have made myself really guilty."

The body language of both representatives now displays relief. The underlying entanglement has thus been brought to light. Reactions of relief such as this often show up in constellations and point out clearly that the flow of love has been restored.

Resolving statements (see below) play an important part in the following phase of the constellation. Continuing with the case above, the *husband* says, "I'm sorry. I accept my responsibilities now, and I leave your responsibilities with you." The facilitator makes sure no discussion between the representatives takes place. All communication is directed through the facilitator. Otherwise there is a tendency for representatives to lose touch with their roles and underlying patterns.

Clarifying statements work to bring entanglements to the surface and enable them to be properly expressed. They are formulated in tune with representatives and their responses.

Typical physical responses to suitable statements are relaxation and relief. These statements are most powerful when they are delivered without emotion and are kept as brief and to the point as possible.

The facilitator works with clarifying statements and resolving statements until all entanglements in the constellation have come to light. It is usually necessary to alternate between these two types of statements to allow various layers of entanglements to be made conscious. The facilitator's aim is to make underlying origins of emotional baggage as clear as possible. This is done so people can uncover that behind aggression is helplessness and powerlessness, and behind a victim's attitude is a power struggle or a passive-aggressive dynamic.

The following is an example from my own practice. Two representatives, a *man* and a *woman,* stand facing each other. It is obvious that there is a lot of tension between them. When I ask how he feels, the *man* responds, "She drives me crazy. I am really angry with her." I suggest he says, "I feel really angry with you." The *man* does this and confirms it feels right. The *woman* also nods in agreement. Then I ask the *man* to say, "I am helpless." That also feels right for him. The *woman* begins to smile. She then says to me, "I am also so angry, and I just can't and won't allow him into my heart anymore." I ask her to say, "I am angry and close myself off out of revenge." She confirms that this feels right, and then the *man* replies, "That makes me so mad." While the *man* is saying this, a triumphant smile breaks out on the *woman*'s face. I ask the *man* first and then the *woman* to say, "We are on equal footing in our perpetrator-and-victim game." Both say this and look each other in the eye. Then I ask the *man* to say, "I wanted you as my wife, I chose you to be my wife, and I have committed myself to you." The *woman* is asked to repeat a similar statement. After saying these statements, they look at each other in astonishment. They both nod and say, "That's right." They smile at each other. The *woman* says, "Actually he is a darling." The *man* says, "I just love this woman." They move closer to each other and stand together. They are clearly happily reunited.

In this constellation it was obvious that being argumentative was their way of being nice and showing love to each other, as strange as that might seem. Love is clearly evident at deeper levels where truth is communicated and accepted. Behind their problematic attitudes were entanglements most likely associated with difficult marriages of ancestors in both families, tendencies perpetuated over many generations.

Resolving Statements

When entanglements become clear in a constellation through clarifying statements, resolving statements are used to look for solutions to these entanglements. These are also formulated to be powerful and right to the point. That way feelings or facts can be effectively expressed.

The language in these statements might sometimes seem a little old-fashioned. When I ask a representative to say to another representative something like, "I honor you. I am but a child," or "I give you my blessing," a person sometimes feels suspicious and resistant. However, it has become more and more obvious in practice that this language facilitates access to deeper meaning.

Hellinger says, "This language works on the soul."[3] The soul exists beyond time and fashion. The particular word choice in these sentences facilitates the resolution of entanglements and has a profound effect upon people. They bring back the flow of love. They are statements that have special powers and action rarely found in everyday language. Thanks to this special use of language, communication during a constellation avoids superficiality. The following examples explain how these statements work in terms of their backgrounds and effects.

A child (*son*) is standing in front of his *mother*, and the facilitator asks the *son* to say, "You are the mother. I am but a child, your second son. You are the adult. I leave your relationship problems with you. You handle that. I honor you and your fate." After saying these sentences, the *son* bows deeply before his *mother*. Upon bowing he says, "I thank you for the greatest gift you could give—my life."

The first sentence, "You are the mother," gives the mother her place. She is the mother, and that makes her position and associated responsibilities in the family system clear.

The second sentence, "I am but a child," makes the position of the child in relation to his mother clear. The word *but* is very important and is exempt of judgment. It is rather a statement of responsibility. If a child is *but* a child, he or she has no responsibility toward the parents or their relationship. This *but* allows the child to be free from everything the parents have to carry, whether the child carries an emotional load of the parents out of blind love or because the parents have relied emotionally on their child.

If the child is *but a child,* then the adults solve their own problems and take on their own responsibilities, and the child can get on with being a child and play.

The next statement, "Your second son," gives the child his rightful place among his brothers and sisters. The next statement, "You are the adults. I leave your relationship problems with you," further clarifies the responsibility.

This will differ in constellations with other themes. For example, a *child* could say, "Dad, you are the adult. I leave your pain with you," or, "Mom, you are the adult. I leave your anger toward Dad with you; you carry it. I suppose you can accept that I have a good relationship with Dad."

The statement, "You handle that," which the *child* above said to his *mother,* clarifies that everyone has to bear (and actually desires) responsibility for his or her own fate. Even emotional reliance on children by their parents actually belongs to the parents. That's how they are. It is their fate to be like that (see text below), and it is irrelevant whether the children are content with it or not. It becomes clear through the statement, "You handle that," that the parents' patterns belong to them and have nothing to do with the children. In other words it is not directed personally toward the children.

The sentence, "It is their fate to be like that," might sound extreme. However, it has a special meaning. As long as the parents are not conscious of their own behavior and the ensuing difficulties for their children, there is little or no change possible. First and foremost, it is necessary they become conscious of their attitudes before anything can be any different. They have to see and feel what is going on and what consequences and loyalties are involved, or they must realize they are burdened with attitudes and patterns that they can release. Only then is change achievable. The parents have to start this process.

The children cannot initiate or help with this process without compromising their places as children. It is best that children accept their parents as they are and assume their rightful places in the family hierarchy. They have to let go of any desire to change their parents.

41

If a child is resistant, judgmental, or accusatory toward the parents, which is not uncommon, it will emerge in the constellation. It can then be further worked on until all entanglements come to light. In this stage of a constellation people frequently discover a distortion in the balance of give and take in the relationship between parents and children. It's called *parentification*, and it means that one or both parents are relying emotionally on their children. (See "Parentification" in chapter four.)

Once the balance is restored, the appropriate statement is, "I honor you and your fate." When people honor others and their fates, they give them places in their hearts. That can only be done unconditionally. Only when all relevant conditions in the constellation have been brought to light and made conscious is it possible to really honor someone and give that person a place in one's heart. Representatives are very accurate and delicate instruments. They immediately feel if an expression or reaction is really valid or if there is still resistance. As long as resistance is felt, there is frequently still an entanglement that has yet to come to light, or more processing time is needed.

In the latter case, the constellation will stop at this point. Representatives will accurately feel when resistance has been resolved. In the case above, the *mother* feels honored and relieved with a renewed feeling of love toward her *child*. The *child* is also relieved and feels free.

The next step is to let go of the entanglement by bowing. Sometimes it happens in a child's pose with both palms raised upward. Through this ritual bow, people let go of all constraints toward their parents. They acknowledge their parents as parts of their fates and accept them as they are. By acknowledging their parents as adults with all their good qualities and shortcomings, they allow themselves to be children, and they can leave everything that belongs to their parents with them. This frees them from old baggage and enables them to open up their hearts.

The last statement, "I thank you for the greatest gift you could give— my life," expresses thankfulness. There is no better gift from parents than the gift of life; everything else pales in comparison. This makes people humble.

What actually takes place in a constellation can differ from this example. Every constellation has its own unique dynamic and requires a tailor-made response. The dedicated use of language, however, is clearly useful in evoking appropriate responses.

Rituals in Constellations

The most common ritual in a constellation is bowing before someone such as a parent. This allows tangible detachment and release from everything children carry for the parents. In this way people honor their parents and their fates as they are. Children accept them for who they are. By bowing down before the right individuals, people restore balance and order in their systems. That is a very liberating feeling.

The facilitator makes sure the bowing always takes place voluntarily and after all exposed entanglements have been resolved. Only then can a bow be authentic and have a moving and healing effect.

Many people identify bowing as a form of subjugation. Here that is not the case at all and definitely not the intention. Bert Hellinger says, "In our culture, this movement has become difficult for many people; bowing down as an act of respect is easily confused with bowing down as an act of unhealthy submission. When we bow down and pay obeisance to someone who deserves to receive our honoring gesture, the soul and the body respond with release and we feel a sense of lightness. This is a wonderful feeling to experience."[4] Something special happens in the body while bowing. According to the French physiotherapist Françoise Méziéres and the Dutch osteopath Godelieve Struyf-Denijs, a muscle chain response is activated, which leads to relaxation.[5] This only works if the neck muscles are relaxed and the head hangs loose during the act of bowing.

A bow is also enacted in a constellation to another person in the family who carries a heavy emotional load and where entanglements are present. That could be the grandfather with an experience in war or the mother's brother who died at a young age. Bowing also helps in the process of letting go and saying good-bye to a family member, thus honoring that person's fate. The heavy emotional load is left with that person.

Another ritual some facilitators use concerns the returning of burdens people have been carrying from their parents or others. This occurs through symbolically giving back a heavy load. The person uses a stone, heavy basket, or bag. The purpose is to give back acquired or usurped feelings and emotional loads to the family member to whom they belong. This symbolic returning of heavy loads facilitates the process of letting go and gaining distance in order to start anew.

As a facilitator in family constellations, I prefer to use clarifying statements and resolving statements because they help entanglements and parentification come to light more easily. In cases where it is really obvious, the return of a heavy load through the above ritual suffices. The facilitator has to make sure the return is carried out in a loving way during the ritual. Sometimes this happens with blame, which is a sign the entanglements have not yet been fully resolved, so real detachment and letting go cannot take place.

Being a Representative

Family constellations work with and through surrogate perception. That's where representatives come in. Being a representative is voluntary. It is also important to avoid any two representatives in a constellation who are good friends, in a relationship, or in the same family. Any such relationship could lead to confusion with elements from their own personalities or relationship.

Representatives are necessary to show the seeker's family system. They can be viewed as detection instruments. They give information to the facilitator, just like one might read a thermometer. Just as a thermometer does not interpret its measurements, representatives are asked not to give any interpretations of their perceptions. They have to put their own wants and wishes aside during a constellation to make room for the thoughts and feelings of the people they are representing. That might seem complicated, but after working with family constellations for many years now, I know most people have little trouble acting as representatives and adequately tuning in to sensations and emotions.

By being a representative, one acquires an incredible amount of insight. A person can experience how it is to feel "entangled" and then pass through the various phases of a constellation until a solution has been reached. Representatives can then naturally gain from this experience in their own lives. Being a representative offers a unique opportunity to develop perception skills. People learn to more clearly express feelings and perceptions. Judgments and prejudices dissolve. The images people have of themselves also undergo positive transformations.

If a person is usually somewhat anxious in daily life, that person now suddenly experiences what it is like to feel strength. If a person is normally self-assured, that person now knows how it feels to be a weak, helpless person. All these perceptions make people richer and more aware of being human.

I feel there is no better environment to learn about life. As a representative a person can learn a lot about life's complexities in a short period of time. People see life's essential beauty and learn to allow life to be expressed in all its diversity. This can include a wide array of characters—a war criminal, an irresponsible father, a loving but victimized partner, or an arrogant son.

How does it feel to be a great-grandmother working like a slave from early morning till late in the evening, the woman who felt forced into prostitution, or the oldest daughter who had to take care of everything because her mother was always sick? A person can experience all this as a representative. There are also very difficult roles—a father who had an incestuous relationship with his daughter or a young man who committed suicide—that can really touch people deeply but also challenge them ethically.

Facilitators are mindful only to assign difficult roles to people they believe can handle them. If necessary someone with more experience can replace a representative who is finding the proceedings too heavy.

By being a representative, a person learns to perceive the smallest detail and express and share these perceptions. Once in a constellation I was the most important previous true love of a woman. The relationship was allegedly doomed because of societal pressure. The seeker in the constellation had a strong relationship with the person I was representing. It was really painful for her and caused so much confusion in her life because the relationship had never amounted to anything—contrary to her expectations. By getting into the role, I found I was only attracted to men around me, and I naturally articulated this. "I think I am homosexual," I said. It was an enormous relief for the seeker to hear this. Suddenly it was all clear to her.

Another time I was the representative for *war*. I have rarely in my life felt so invincible and strong. It felt like being a force of nature— powerful and impersonal. The role made me aware that war, despite personal judgments, is a neutral power. It can be compared to the ten-

45

sion between tectonic plates that discharge explosively into an earthquake. The tension between nations can similarly discharge violence. This does not mean war has to be embraced as a natural process, since there are ways at our disposal to diffuse (or intensify) tensions between populations. We are collectively responsible for these tensions.

These examples show that representatives must put their own value judgments and preferences aside so they can allow perceptions that might go against their concepts of justice. In the example about war, my perceptions during the constellation felt totally strange to me, but they gave me a lot to think about after the process.

It is also possible that during a constellation a representative of a father can have sexual feelings for his *daughter*, even though in real life he has never had any such desire or any inclination in this way whatsoever. A woman who is heterosexual in her normal life might become attracted to other women in a constellation.

It is important to understand that all these perceptions are part of an accurate evaluation of the client's family and have nothing to do with the representative. They are, however, indispensable for the clarification and dissolution of entanglements.

Just to have the opportunity to feel and see normally taboo or unexpressed predicaments can be a fascinating learning process.

Those who have participated in a family constellation seminar for the first time and are able to experience being representatives a number of times often feel some form of fatigue. This is a sign that a lot has been learned and a lot still has to be processed.

A little exercise and movement for the whole group can work wonders in such situations. When necessary I put on music so group members can dance, move, and relax.

As the facilitator I ask the representatives to step out of their roles after a constellation. If they are not able to do this, I ask them to perform the following ritual. The representative faces the seeker, bows, and says, "I have taken on the role of someone in your family. I now give that back. I am myself again." The seeker shakes the representative's hand, thanks the person, and says, "Be yourself again, (representative's real name)."

If this does not do the trick, there are other techniques available to ensure nobody goes home with feelings that do not belong to him or her. A good warm shower at home can also work wonders. However, if problems remain, which seldom happens, the facilitator should be contacted.

What to Keep in Mind as a Representative

o Be yourself.
o Trust the feelings you sense. The facilitator can distinguish between authentic perceptions and those you contribute from your own personality.
o Perceive what there is to perceive.
o Open up to all physical reactions.
o Share in a collected way what you feel. Be brief and to the point with information when asked. If you feel nothing, then that is the truthful perception.
o Everything you notice should be expressed, even when it seems to go against your own sense of justice or values.
o Avoid your own conclusions and interpretations.
o All communication goes via the facilitator; do not get into a discussion with another representative.
o Let it be clearly known if something makes you feel uplifted or you have other physical reactions.
o When there is an important change in your perceptions or you feel you have something worthwhile to contribute, let the facilitator know by making a sign with your hand.
o When the facilitator asks you to repeat a sentence that doesn't make sense to you or is not clearly worded, let this be known.

The Therapeutic Attitude

Practice not-doing
and everything will fall into place.
—Lao-Tzu[6]

Working with family constellations is always geared toward resolutions, which usually lead to:

o   Detachment from restraining loyalties
o   Handing back carried over and copied emotional burdens
o   Restoration of the natural hierarchy in the family

A facilitator has to be very experienced, empathetic, and professionally detached to be able to conduct a successful constellation. It all revolves around surrendering to what shows up in a constellation and being able to effectively follow up on the perceptions of representatives. Even though people subscribe to what Bert Hellinger calls "systemic laws" (see "Systemic Order" in chapter three), the facilitator should avoid conducting constellations according to the book. He or she should forget all the rules and discover them again for each new constellation. No two family constellations are ever the same, just as there are no two identical families.

The facilitator must resist the temptation to search for a good resolution at any cost or search for one aligned to his or her own ideals and preconceptions. He or she may only allow solutions that spontaneously arise through the perceptions of the representatives and that the seeker wants to become aware of in terms of the chosen theme. This requires the facilitator to be attuned yet respectfully detached.

To be able to do this job effectively, a facilitator has to keep the seeker's whole family system in mind during a constellation. His or her view has to be wide and open-minded. If a facilitator lets himself or herself get bogged down in detail, that facilitator runs the risk of losing sight of the overall context.

Bert Hellinger makes a distinction between observing and perceiving.[7] By observing people look at details. The observant attitude is one of knowing and analyzing. The perceiving attitude allows the whole picture to be seen and taken in. That is an inner attitude of openness. The facilitator is therefore a part of the constellation.

He goes along with what shows up and also the manner in which it shows up. Through the experience, the facilitator's empathy and detachment, the representatives, and the knowing field, fitting solutions regarding the seeker's theme and family system arise spontaneously.

A constellation begins with a short interview in which the facilitator connects with the seeker and his or her theme. The facilitator searches with the seeker for clarity about what has to be constellated for appropriate solutions to be elicited. The communication here is solution-oriented, meaning that problems are identified but not further analyzed. Character descriptions are avoided. Only facts about the family are required. Dwelling over character and problem descriptions confines people to the superficial—the tip of the iceberg. Following that path in the family constellation context is not helpful in finding good solutions. Experience has shown that the power and depth of a constellation is proportionate to the simplicity and directness of the formulated theme.

The facilitator has an inner connection with the seeker in a constellation and works on three levels, according to Berthold Ulsamer.[8]

The first level is concerned with energy—the knowing field. The facilitator follows what shows up and allows himself or herself to be led by what comes to light via the representatives.

The second level is concerned with structure. Through experience, the facilitator knows about a healthy family structure. This level involves principles of order (explained in chapter three) and shows ways to solutions. Even though these are important, it is never advisable for a facilitator to be tempted to abide blindly by these principles. Instead each new constellation will verify these through the representatives' perceptions.

The third level is concerned with facts. These facts bind the constellation to reality. The facilitator knows about this through the initial interview with the seeker and can make the impact of these facts clear at the right moment in the constellation. An example of the third level is bringing in a *stillborn brother* after the first stage or questioning of the representatives in a constellation. From the reactions of the other representatives, people can gauge how important this child is to the seeker and the family system, if there are any associated entanglements, and how much influence these might have on the seeker.

Sometimes the seeker has insufficient information about certain aspects of the family. Maybe he or she knows a grandfather fought in a particular war but not the conditions under which he fought and what effects this might have had on him. If it seems entanglements have been detected in a constellation, a facilitator can perform an experiment with discretion and restraint. He or she clearly announces to the participants what he or she is about to do. He or she then asks, for example, for two more volunteers to represent deceased victims, dead comrades, or civilian casualties. They are directed to lie on the floor next to the representative of the grandfather.

It becomes obvious by the representatives' reactions if this experiment has any effect on the family system and/or if any entanglements can be detected. This is done so all entanglements are resolved. If the addition of the extra representatives has no real impact, then they are removed from the constellation. Experiments such as this need to be carried out with discretion. They are no substitute for reality. They are more symbolic in nature and serve only to make solutions to entanglements clear. The same applies to family secrets, unproven suspicion of abuse, or doubtful paternity. The facilitator has to show discretion and restraint here as well and make clear to the seeker that the constellation is no substitute for reality. It is always best to work with facts in a constellation. If, for example, a father's biological paternity is in question, the seeker is advised to undergo DNA testing.

Systemic Phenomenology

Therefore the Master remains
serene in the midst of sorrow.
Evil cannot enter his heart.
Because he has given up helping,
he is people's greatest help.
—Lao-Tzu[9]

Hellinger refers to his method of working and the associated inner demeanor required as *systemic phenomenology*. From here on, whenever I use the terms *systemic work* or *systemic order,* I am referring to Hellinger's work and what he has discovered in connection with it.

Many therapists want to help save the world. However, the wish, need, or imperative to help others is often a projected inner need of the therapist to work on himself or herself. In order to work in a professional manner with family constellations, the therapist has to let go of this inner need to want to help and allow it to be transformed. Behind this inner disposition, unprocessed emotional issues lurk—mostly related to a disturbance in the balance of giving and taking between parent and child.

Usually only therapists or coaches experienced in working with people are permitted to undertake training in family constellations. They must have proven track records in other fields of therapy or coaching techniques and have worked intensely on their own problems.

To become a family constellation facilitator, a person must have had his or her own family constellated in all its various facets and have been a representative on numerous occasions. Only then can he or she begin to develop the special attitude required, which differs greatly from that of other therapeutic approaches.

A facilitator has to go beyond a subconscious wanting to do good and instead be open to perceptions that emerge. From there a facilitator must assist the client in his or her growth process. This can only happen, according to Hellinger, when the facilitator empties himself or herself of personal views, prior experiences, and inner notions of emotion, will, and judgment.[10]

It is working from an "empty middle," as Hellinger calls it. This approach is both focused and unfocused, concentrated and open. By adopting this attitude, all that has to be revealed will be revealed.

The facilitator has to work in harmony with the client/seeker and his or her problems as well as with the client's family system and all it contains—all the hidden and exposed entanglements and all contingent perpetrators and victims. This means he or she cannot set himself or herself above the seeker and his or her predicament. He or she has to be able to understand and accept, for example, that even people with good consciences can be destructive and not even feel bad about it. The facilitator can only do this if he or she has discovered and come to terms with his or her own destructive side.

Another important point regarding the facilitator's posture is that it should be one of noninterference and acceptance. A person who wants to change what has shown up puts himself or herself above reality. He or she is trying to manipulate what has shown up to suit personal preconceptions. In that way the facilitator attempts to play God and wants to make the situation subordinate to himself or herself.

Only people able to subject themselves to reality and take it as it is can work effectively with family constellations. A facilitator abstains from his or her own will. This is the phenomenological attitude.

Submitting to reality also means letting go of any anxieties about the revealed reality. This can only happen if the facilitator has come to terms with his or her own shadowy side and any destructive tendencies he or she might have. If not, then he or she will be unable to help clients through their destructive and darker sides. The deepest entanglements are usually associated with exclusion, a person's darker side, death, and destructivity.

Our darker side is where to find all that has been unresolved. It is everything a person has been subconsciously carrying and everything that person tries to push away. Many therapists are afraid of their darker sides and prefer to delve instead into the darker sides of their clients. It seems safer than becoming conscious and working through their own destructive parts. Being conscious of all these issues, however, is essential for this work.

Really tuning in to what shows up has to be done without planning, judgment, and fear. Only then can people be attuned and in harmony with revealed truths and successfully find solutions.

The phenomenological attitude is also known in science. It is referred to as *empirical phenomenology*. "The basic reference in the phenomenological approach is what occurs and the way in which it occurs in our consciousness. This implies that phenomenologists refrain from, as much as possible, all uncertainties or certainties about the existence and origin of the particular phenomenon in question and from every other, more or less developed, prior view about it. Suspending all these presuppositions and prejudices, makes it possible to become conscious of the real phenomena in all its richness."[11]
—I. Maso professor in philosophy of science and A. Smaling, associate professor of science theory and methodology

An additional important aspect of phenomenology is what Hellinger refers to as "standing on the side of the perpetrator."[12] There is a similar approach in contextual therapy—the understanding of multilateral or versatile targeted partiality. "Versatile targeted partiality is the most important therapeutic attitude and method of contextual therapy...In the practice of contextual therapy, this principle of versatile involvement has to be connected with the determination of the therapist to discover the humanity in every participant, even in the 'monster' of the family."[13]

To be able to find solutions in family constellations where the themes involve abuse and violence, the therapist must be free of the conventional perpetrator–victim judgments. He or she has to be able to find a place in his or her heart even for villains who are normally demonized and excluded. If he or she is not prepared or not aware of this, he or she will not be able to adequately search for solutions to disturbances that arise. The same applies for the subconscious loyalties that the therapist brings from his or her own family system. If, for example, he or she is still entangled with a victimized mother or father, he or she will find it difficult to help a client become conscious of similar issues.

This stresses again that a therapist must work thoroughly on himself or herself first before he or she can begin to draw up the family systems of others.

A family constellation gives people insight into the background of a person's fate and enables people to redirect the flow of love through restoring the underlying order. That can only happen when the collective and personal conscience of the client are fully respected. (See chapter three.) Working with family constellations connects these two levels of consciences. Therefore, says Hellinger, "Only those who understand, recognize and internalize the laws of the collective and personal conscience of the client may become family constellation facilitators. They are then able to unite and reconcile both laws on a higher level."[14]

3

Order of Love

There is an inner orientation about what is right, that you can't diverge from without causing yourself damage. No one can get around this.
—Bert Hellinger[1]

Hellinger's principles of systemic order and his remarkable vision about the human conscience will be introduced in this chapter. The principles he reveals operate at the foundation of all relationships.

The conscience has three different dimensions according to Hellinger: the personal, the collective, and the transcendental. Three facets determine the personal and collective consciences: bonding, balance, and order.

At first glance the term *order of love* might seem strange. It could induce a strong emotional reaction in some because it seems as if it smacks of the conservative and misogynic women-at-the-sink romanticism and the blatant gender imbalance implicit in that understanding. Many public statements of Hellinger strengthen these fears. For example, when he says, "The woman follows the man and the man serves the woman," alarm bells begin to ring for many people. A real understanding of Hellinger's work can only be appreciated by going beyond the superficial.

When people appraise something superficially, they have the tendency to quickly jump to conclusions. Only when they are prepared to look deeper into Hellinger's insights is it possible to really understand what he has discovered. People can then appreciate that men and women are valued equally in all constellations. This is actually one of his basic principles of order.

The most important characteristic of systemic order is that it is not just someone's idea, but rather it is what shows up through the unfolding of family constellations. In tens of thousands of constellations performed worldwide each year, the same phenomena arise.

Time after time representatives determine, independently from each other, that certain positions and sequences in constellations feel especially good, loving, and right. The expression of solution sentences and bowing before parents are also performed because they offer real solutions, and real solutions are what the orders of love are all about.

In commenting on his own approach, Bert Hellinger says, "Therefore, I work with very little theory, actually without theory, actually only with perceptions. Certain patterns become clear from these perceptions. These patterns are not set but are part of a process. They can change and be very different from one situation to the next. That means that the therapist should remain alert to see what is really happening and not be distracted by the hypotheses or theorem that he or she armed him with."[2]

A therapist can only work systemically in Hellinger's way if he or she goes along with what becomes visible in a constellation and if he or she follows up on the perceptions of the representatives. If the facilitator wants to direct a constellation according to his or her own vision, imagination, norms, or values, representatives will not play along. He or she can only find a suitable arrangement in concordance with the representatives. The seeker's soul and his or her family conscience lead the representatives themselves. That is why Hellinger calls the profound revelations in constellations "soul images."

The use of the term soul here doesn't preclude other understandings such as a higher self, universal power, inner godliness, and any others that might apply. Each person has to find an attributed meaning that personally feels best.

All constellations confirm the existence of orders of love. The underlying patterns and systemic laws are apparently indelibly imprinted upon our souls. We feel power, love, and freedom when we are in harmony with this order. If this order is interrupted or interfered with, we encounter problems, lack freedom, and are left in misery.

It might seem that orders of love as presented here relate principally to heterosexual relationships. However, it will become clear that they apply to homosexual relationships as well.

The Story of Freedom

A disciple asked his teacher, "Tell me what freedom is."
"Which freedom?" asked the teacher.
"The first freedom is foolishness. That's like a horse that throws its rider with a triumphant whinny, only to feel the saddle girth pulled tighter."
"The second freedom is remorse. Remorse is like the helmsman who goes down with the ship, after he has sailed it onto a reef, rather than seek safety in the lifeboat with others."
"The third freedom is understanding. Understanding comes, alas, only after foolishness and remorse. It's like a shaft of wheat that bends in the wind, and because it bends where it's weak, endures."
The disciple asked, "Is that all?"
The teacher said, "Many think they are seeking the truth of their own soul, but it's the Greater Soul that is thinking and seeking in them. Like nature, it allows great variety, but replaces with ease those who try to cheat. But to those who allow it to think in them, it allows, in turn, a little freedom, helping them like a river helps a swimmer cross to the other shore if she surrenders to the current and allows herself to be swept along."
—Bert Hellinger[3]

Orders of love are apparently manifested in the form of inner soul images that have archaic depth and a timeless quality. Even so we have to assume they can transform and evolve and that they can take on other forms in different cultures. It is, therefore, important to be alert to see what is truthful in each constellation.

Hellinger's work has also changed over the years. In the mid-nineties he wanted to stop with family constellations because he was convinced he had already uncovered the most important aspects of the phenomenon. At that time themes of *National Socialism* and *holocaust* became more prevalent, so he continued on with his work to search for ways of reconciliation between perpetrator and victim.[4]

Another development in his work was the introduction of constellations without verbal communication. In this method only spontaneous gestures and physical actions were permitted. Hellinger called these "Movements of the Soul." (See chapter eight.) Family constellations have been journeys of discovery that still continue to take place—not only for Hellinger but also for thousands of facilitators all around the world.

Systemic Order

As has been already indicated, certain systemic laws have been discovered and refined over many years by Hellinger through his experience with constellations. Systems theory[5] underpins Hellinger's work, but he also relies upon Ivan Boszormenyi-Nagy's ideas. Nagy's contextual approach refers to the understanding of a relational ethic that forms the basis of well-functioning relationships. "Influenced by Martin Buber, Nagy developed a relational, ethical dimension concerning families and family relationships. This is not about external or church-imposed moral and cultural norms but rather an intrinsic justice of existential relationships." According to Nagy this understanding means that "an 'invisible ledger' exists, in which all the 'balances' between the family members are recorded. If something falls out of balance in one generation, the following generation attempts to redress this imbalance."[6]

The systemic order is present, consciously or subconsciously, in all families and in each and every member. Consider the following elements:

The right to belong
Every family member has the equal right to belong. This applies even when that member is an invalid, died young, committed suicide, or ended up in a psychiatric institution. Even those who were criminals, of bad character, or addicted to drugs or suffered from depression have the right to belong.

The right to their own fates
All family members bear their own fates. Each fate belongs only to the individual. However short, difficult, or problematic somebody's life is; only that person can live it.

58

Everybody has to face up to his or her own responsibilities, including the responsibility for being irresponsible. He or she has to bear the consequences of irresponsible behavior.

Parents give—children receive

The balance of giving and taking in a family is as follows—parents give to their children what they can, and children take what is given to them. Children do not have any right to demand anything from their parents. They have to accept their parents just as they are. Children can help restore the balance of giving and taking by having children of their own to whom they give themselves as they are. If they never have children, they can do some other good deeds to restore the balance.

The hierarchy is set in time

The order of rank in a system such as a family is chronological. Whoever arrives first takes up first place. Logically the grandfather takes priority over the father and the first daughter over the second son. The first important partner has priority over the second. In a constellation representatives are set up clockwise according to their chronological ranking.

The new system takes priority over the old

The order of ranking between systems is that the newer takes precedence over the former. It follows logically, therefore, that the relationship between partners is more important than the relationship with members of the origin family. A new relationship after a divorce is more important than the previous one. Chronological order determines the priority for children from first and second relationships, which means that children from the first relationship come before the new partner and before children from a second relationship. Stepparents' own children come before their stepchildren.

Men and women are complementary and equal

The ranking between parents is defined according to the function each has. For example, the one who is most active in the world and has a more demanding career or a greater income comes first. This parent serves the parent in second place, who serves the family household. Therefore, it is the parent in second place who has the more important role because this parent tends to the children. This makes it clear how complementary men and women are. They are always worthy of each other, even if a perpetrator–victim dynamic exists.

Relationships are reciprocal

All relationships are reciprocal.* The power with which this reciprocity manifests itself is proportional to the depth of the bond and love between the partners.

(*According to my own experience, reciprocity is part of the systemic order. See my book *Heal Your Relationships* for more information.)

Respecting these principles allows love between two people in a relationship to flow. This way their children can be just that—children. Those children then have enough energy for their own developing lives.

If this order is disturbed, which often happens subconsciously or out of ignorance, painful or even catastrophic results ensue.

It is not surprising then that participating in family constellations gives one the impression that a disruption to this order goes hand in hand with any family tragedy. Whether it concerns relationship problems, accidents, suicide, illness, or addiction, whenever a family tragedy is constellated, the causing disturbance is exposed. It is, therefore, not presumptuous to say that the truth—admittedly subjective—or underlying subconscious cause can be revealed in family constellations.

Disturbances arise subconsciously and usually with the best intentions. Bert Hellinger's analysis of the conscience and an understanding of blind, childlike love make the underlying process obvious.

The Conscience

Bert Hellinger suggests everyone has an inner sense or instinct that watches over his or her interpersonal relationships—the conscience.[7] It works like the organ of equilibrium (vestibular system) in the ears. If we veer too far one way, we get impulses that seek to bring us back into balance. Usually these impulses take us too far the other way, so new countermovement's are necessary. This constant process is how balance is maintained in relationships, whether consciously or subconsciously.

This sense makes it possible for a person to instinctively and precisely perceive two states—do I or don't I continue to belong to my reference group? The most important reference group is the family, the second is the social environment, and the third is the ethnic group, religion, and culture in which one has grown up. In this context these are the only important questions: what do I have to do to belong, and what do I avoid to prevent being excluded?

> *A good conscience means nothing else than one can be sure*
> *he or she belongs, and a bad conscience means that person*
> *fears being excluded.*

The desire to belong subconsciously regulates how people behave in all relationships, both in social environments and with partners. According to Hellinger the conscience works like a subconscious reflex. He distinguishes three different dimensions of the conscience: the personal, collective, and transcendental.

Three facets, according to Hellinger, determine the personal and collective dimensions. They are bonding, balance, and order.

In one's personal conscience, the bonding facet sensitively regulates the need to bond within the family, with a partner, and in one's social life.

The second facet of one's personal conscience is the need for balance between giving and taking as well as equilibrium and compensation. When one receives something, a feeling of guilt arises. A person then has the idea he or she is indebted to the other and, therefore, has a guilty conscience. Subsequently the person wants to give something back to redress the imbalance.

The search for order is the third facet of one's personal conscience. Through order, social rules, and predictability, people know where they stand, and they feel safe. Consequently they need frameworks for their consciences.

In contrast to the personal conscience, the collective conscience or family conscience is not directly tangible or perceptible. It works in secret. People can only see and remark upon its effects. The family conscience brings unresolved family situations in subsequent generations to the surface, and this same conscience becomes visible in family constellations.

Organizations, companies, and teams also have collective or systemic consciences that can be constellated. (See chapter eight.)

The transcendental conscience is the part that wants to connect to a greater unity. This conscience demands people let go of the old and allow transformation. Through this transcendental conscience, a person surrenders to longed-for spiritual unity. It is the driving force that draws a person to a family constellation in the search for a deeper truth and meaning.

Take note, while this discusses the negative aspects, the positive effects of loyalties and the personal conscience should not be forgotten. Through them people are bestowed with great gifts such as creativity, the ability to think broadly, and all other talents.

People can feel proud and honored to be able to pass these gifts on to following generations. However, a conscious personal effort is required to separate the wheat from the chaff.

The Personal Conscience

The bonding facet of our personal consciences

The strongest need is to belong within families. When a child does something in his or her family that is considered virtuous and useful, the child feels worthy and innocent. A child feels he or she belongs and has a clear conscience. If a child does something not accepted, he or she feels bad or guilty. The child risks exclusion and has a bad conscience.

The fear of being excluded is rooted deep within us. In earlier times, living in a group was a necessary condition for survival. Those who were banished had their lives put at risk.

> *It is important to be aware that clear and guilty consciences are always related to reference groups. Under no circumstances does it refer to general principles of good and bad.*

If a person wants to belong to a family, then he or she has to conform to the accepted norms and rules. What is considered good in one family might be considered bad in another, and what is acceptable behavior in the family might be frowned upon in one's social life.

Conflicts arise when different value systems come together. A person is, therefore, constantly forced to find a new balance. If a person aims to be good in one sphere, that person might get out of balance in another. That is why the conscience is never at rest and a person is not able to stay in an innocent state. The only way to resolve this conflict of conscience is to try to please everyone, which is impossible.

To stay in an innocent state is easy to do while a person is a child because there is no need to divert from what is considered good in the family. The fear of being excluded prevents one from deviating from what is considered decent and right. So with few exceptions people play it safe and behave well. That is why it is often said childhood is an innocent phase.

The problems start in puberty when, for example, a person brings his or her first boyfriend or girlfriend home. Dad raises his eyebrows, and Mom looks disapprovingly at the new, treasured love. Mom finds her exposed midriff indecent, or he has too many tattoos for Dad's liking.

63

The bonding facet requires people to stand behind their parents and be loyal to them. This conscience simultaneously tells a person to back his or her partner in order to make the relationship work. That tattoo might be an important symbol of identification that helps the young man in question belong to his desired social group. No matter how people manage to wend their way through these situations, they are bound to lose their innocence toward one party or the other. This is a natural process and one that everyone has to go through in order to develop his or her own personality.

Exceptions for being well behaved, playing it safe, and doing whatever leaves one's conscience clear sometimes emerge in constellations. The following is an example.

John is nine years old. He has attention and concentration problems that cause an enormous amount of stress for his parents. Mom and Dad constellate their problematic child-rearing situation.

In the constellation it is revealed that John is entangled with family members on his mother's side. He is carrying the trauma of his grandmother and her brother, who spent three years as children in a Japanese concentration camp in Indochina during World War II. Traumatized by the scenes they witnessed in the camp, they carried large emotional burdens. They were unable to process these experiences to let go of the trauma. The constellation becomes especially dramatic when a little friend of the grandmother who died in the camp is brought into the constellation.

The constellation makes it very clear that John is trying to carry the unresolved pain for his traumatized family members with all the consequences that it had for his upbringing.

In all constellations where child-raising problems are present, it becomes apparent how strongly the family conscience interacts with the child's conscience. The child can only have a clear conscience if it is in line with the family conscience.

A good personal conscience demands that a man be just like his father and other males in the family. If a father is proud that he controls his feelings (just as his father did), then his sons must do the same in order to avoid being excluded. Another aspect of being the same is having the same convictions or inner statements. These could include, "You just can't trust women" or, "Women don't give you what you really want." Due to the loyalty with the men who preceded them, men take on these similar beliefs. At the same time, they copy the miseries of previous generations. Men do that with clear personal consciences.

An example is Peter, age forty-six. In his constellation there is the clear repetition of this over many generations. The relationships between his grandparents on both sides were far from harmonious. There was a closed-off (sexually frigid) attitude of the women and a sense of powerlessness of the men in his family. Both his grandfathers were unhappy; one sometimes resorted to violence, and the other was known to visit prostitutes. Peter's father was equally disillusioned and aimlessly passed away his leisure time in bars. Both Peter's mother and father were in no state to maintain a harmonious relationship. Peter experienced his wife just as frozen as his father had experienced his wife and his grandfathers had experienced their wives.

After the constellation Peter was able to let go of his loyalty toward his ancestors. He was able to give his wife more room and ensure they were on their way to having a more loving relationship.

If a daughter wants to belong and have a clear conscience, then she has to cherish the same beliefs and judgments as all the other women in her family. If all these women had difficult birth deliveries, then she would not be able to accept a nice and easy one. In her perception of reality, she risks exclusion by doing so. With a clear conscience, she then has difficult deliveries.

Another example is Lisa, age thirty-eight. She complains about regular episodes of domestic violence but cannot free herself from the relationship with her partner. In her constellation it is revealed that along with some evident entanglements with other family members, she has loyalty issues with her mother and grandmother. Both had maintained with conviction that men and aggression went hand in hand. "They are just like that [sometimes violent]. There is nothing you can do about it. You just have to put up with it," the grandmother had said. It becomes evident that Lisa, out of loyalty, has looked for and re-created a similar situation to the women in her family who came before her. At the end of the constellation, all the women are carrying their own emotional burdens. Both the *mother* and *grandmother* give Lisa permission to improve her relationship or leave if the domestic violence does not subside.

We often hear adages such as, "Life wasn't meant to be easy" or, "The apple doesn't fall far from the tree." These expressions are used to reproach us. On a subconscious level, they are really saying, "If you want to belong, then you have to live as we do. If not, we will exclude you and look down upon you with contempt." The personal conscience will not allow such a risk because that would lead to strong feelings of anxiety.

Only when people become conscious of these loyalties and let them go with respect and love will they be able to find their own ways. Only then will they have sufficient inner strength to let go of the unwritten laws of their families.

People should not lose sight of the fact that they are bound to family members through existential loyalties. That is part of their birthrights. Parents have given children the gift of life and have done a lot for them, so children do what they can in return. They allow themselves to feel, for example, just about the right amount of happiness or unhappiness that is normal in their families.

People not only develop and experience loyalties to their parents and family via personal consciences, but they also develop these toward other reference groups such as school friends, football clubs, scouts, ethnic groups, nationalities, and religions. The personal conscience gives people the same signals in these groups in the form of feelings of guilt and innocence—thus guilty or clear consciences. These feelings, however, have nothing to do with *good* and *bad*.

People belonging to a group that is damaging and scornful to another group, act with clear consciences. We have only to look at recent historical events for clear evidence of this. If people belong to a fundamentalist Muslim group, then they are permitted to be involved in terrorist attacks with clear consciences. Being American leaves people with the same clear consciences when they retaliate much more vehemently and cause the deaths of even more innocent victims. Many more innocent civilians were killed in Afghanistan and later Iraq than in the attacks on the World Trade Center towers.[8]

The fact that members of a group commit atrocities with clear consciences does not protect them, however, from the consequences of their deeds and the effects on their family consciences.

The balance facet between giving and receiving

The balance of giving and taking is also arranged through the personal conscience. It tries to seek balance by giving a person a good or bad feeling. People feel guilty and have guilty consciences whenever they receive things. By giving things back, their consciences become clear, and they feel free of guilt. That means becoming balanced again.

In societies where giving is more highly valued than receiving, becoming balanced is not so easy. Through an attitude that values giving more highly than receiving, all relationships become burdened. It is much healthier to find a balanced understanding to allow for a rich exchange. That is beneficial for everyone. The old conviction that giving is better than receiving is also questioned in contextual therapy. According to Nagy "the paradigm of continuous one-sided giving is unrealistic and potentially destructive because there is the danger of exhaustion and guilt generating control."[9]

The order facet

The personal conscience has a natural need for order, social rules, and predictability. Therefore, clear limits have to be set in raising children in order to help create frameworks for the development of their personal consciences. Children seek out these limits. It becomes more difficult when children are not given limits. They are unable to create such frameworks when an anything-goes attitude is prevalent. This includes when no consequences are given to children when they break things or are rude to their parents. Children will also be unable to find their own places in the family. If parents do not set limits, children are left in a vacuum. Naturally, when a guilty conscience is not faced, having a clear conscience will also not be experienced. A child needs structure to experience both polarities. A clear and consistent *no* at the appropriate moment gives a child his or her place in the family. This is just as necessary as all other parental expressions of love. Parents who raise their children without setting clear limits provide no reference frameworks and make it really difficult for children to develop healthy social lives.

Serious conflicts arise when following personal consciences leads to a distortion in the systemic order. This happens when a person contributes to another family member's exclusion because he or she has drifted too far from what is accepted.

If homosexuality is a taboo subject and a homosexual family member is avoided, this is an example of exclusion. This family member is not honored equally. Such a disturbance to the systemic order has consequences.

There are also consequences if people cannot grieve the premature death of a family member properly because expressing feelings is not accepted in the family. By being loyal to the family, people get caught up in serious entanglements—despite their best intentions and despite having clear consciences.

The Collective or Family Conscience

A family is not only connected by blood ties but by the family conscience as well, and this remains the case even when family members live far apart and do not know or want to know anything about each other. (See also "Genetic Sexual Attraction" in chapter nine.)

Just like the personal conscience, the collective conscience has three facets:[10]

o The need for bonding. This is reflected in the collective conscience as the equal right of every family member to belong.
o The need for balance between giving and taking. The collective conscience demands this balance in the form of compensation, equalization, and similarity.
o The need for order. This order is hierarchical in time. Those who come earlier in the family have more rights than those who come later. Everyone bears his or her own fate.

The family conscience is invisible and cannot be felt. It only comes to light in a constellation. The order of love, the systemic order, is stored in this family conscience or collective conscience. All disturbances of this order also stay present in the family memory until they are brought to the conscious level. Then the family returns to a harmonious order.

The following generations must pick up everything one generation leaves unprocessed or unresolved. Children take various aspects upon themselves to different degrees. One child might be more connected to a grandmother who had serious relationship problems, while another is connected to an uncle who ended up in a psychiatric ward. A third child might be very strongly connected to the unprocessed miscarriage that preceded him or her. These children are *entangled*. This happens totally subconsciously and out of love.

> *The motor driving all this is human evolution. The unresolved issues of previous generations confront each subsequent generation—until family members learn from them.*

It is stated in the Bible, that "children atone for the sins of their ancestors." I don't like the incriminating connotation of the words *atone* and *sin*. I believe people express their destructiveness out of ignorance and not because they are bad. What I do see is that children take on the guilt of their ancestors. For example, when someone in a previous generation created guilt and was unable to process it, a member of the following generation will take on this feeling in order to make the processing possible.

If the early death of a child has not been worked through, then one or more of the children that follow will take on this pain and not allow themselves to be happy. This goes on from generation to generation.

In the constellation of Diana, age thirty-four, the reason she had a really bad relationship with her father is revealed. He was emotionally absent. Further on in the constellation, Diana sees how strongly her father is connected to his father, Diana's grandfather, who lost comrades in the war. Through the horror of war and the pain of losing comrades, he became emotionally closed off. He also had guilty feelings toward his lost comrades because he had survived. This heavy unprocessed load prevented him from functioning properly as a father. His son (Diana's father) began a family of his own but was not able to fulfill his role adequately because he was so strongly connected to his father. In turn, his daughter, Diana, who carried the pain of her father and grandfather, was not able to allow herself a happy life. She was also only available to her children in a limited way.

There are many entanglements in this example. It begins with the grandfather. Through his intense wartime experiences, he wanted to take on the fates of his comrades. Since everyone bears his or her own fate according to systemic order, it was the fate of his comrades to die and his fate to survive. His son, Diana's father, carried over these burdens. By doing this he went too far because the heavy past was part of his father's fate. The daughter also did this for her father by taking ownership of something that did not belong in her life. All this was done out of love. It is useless to tell a person he or she doesn't have to carry it further. A solution can only be found when this love is respected, the pain is felt, and the love for ancestors is tangible and heartfelt. Once a person becomes aware of where the pain comes from, it can be given back. Only then can the pattern be stopped.

Unlike the personal conscience, the collective conscience cares for the community and not for the individual. The community or the collective conscience is above the individual and uses the individual for the fulfillment of its three facets: bonding, balance, and order.

When a disturbance arises in one or more facets, the collective conscience uses members from the following generation to restore balance.

The origin and the power of the collective conscience are archaic. Therefore, it ignores ideas, views, and fashions. Only the evolution of the collective is important. The collective conscience works most strongly in the family, followed by the social environment, then religion, and finally the nation.

The bonding facet of our collective consciences

While the personal conscience takes care of the bonding of an individual within a group, the collective conscience makes sure all members of the group have their right places and are equally valued. It strives to keep the group together. This applies to all family members, including offenders, the sick, those who died prematurely, and anyone else who was excluded, forgotten, or not honored and respected.

For example, when parents cannot work through the pain of having a stillborn child and instead try to forget and continue on in life (i.e., they do not complete the mourning process), they are in fact excluding this child. The collective conscience will react by seeking balance to compensate for the collective guilt that has arisen, and one member of the collective has to represent the person who was excluded.

The collective makes no distinction about whether this happens consciously or subconsciously or whether it's good or bad. If someone in a family was excluded because he or she was a criminal or because he or she sexually abused another, the collective conscience forces innocent members in the following generation to manifest anew the fates of the excluded family members until the excluded have received their places and due respect.

This example clarifies that the personal and collective consciences sometimes contradict each other. While the personal conscience, through the indignation over what has happened, usually requires people to help with the exclusion of the perpetrator, the collective conscience still requires this person retain the right to belong and be treated equally. In this way a clear personal conscience interferes with the laws of the collective conscience.

Some exceptions follow:
o When someone commits murder, his or her bond with the victim becomes stronger than his or her bond with the collective.
o When a parent commits serious physical or emotional abuse he or she will loose their place as mother or father.
o When someone prohibits another person's legitimate access to the family. For example, this happens when a father does not accept his future son-in-law by prohibiting marriage to his adult daughter.

In these cases the family member forfeits his or her right to belong. He or she must leave the collective in love and respect, while the collective must also release him or her.

The balance facet between giving and receiving
The need for balance between giving and taking works in a different way in the collective conscience. The balance in the personal conscience is between people, while the collective conscience attempts to find balance within the collective—the family. If a family member does not carry his or her own guilt, then somebody from a subsequent generation will do that for him or her.

The order facet
Members who have come later in the family can be compelled to take on the heavy fate (all unprocessed emotional issues that people carry) of an ancestor. This includes the previous example of someone with terrible experiences in war. Even though this descendant is innocent and grew up in peacetime, he or she abides by the collective conscience fully unaware and with a clear conscience.

A member who comes into the family later and carries with him or her some unresolved issues from an earlier generation is doomed to failure as we will see further on. Even though he or she does this with a clear conscience, he or she interferes with the third facet of the collective conscience—the need for order. This order requires that everyone bear the burden of his or her own fate. It actually comes down to arrogance when someone who comes later into the collective bears the heavy burdens of a member who lived earlier on in the family. The person who has come later places himself or herself above the member for whom he or she wants to bear the burden by basically claiming he or she can bear this burden better than his or her ancestor. This interferes with the hierarchy of time.

That is how the collective conscience forces later generations to do something in one of the facets but prohibits them in another facet and makes them pay for something that is not part of their personal fate...
—Bert Hellinger[11]

It is clear then that the collective conscience gives people no choice. Whatever people do they make themselves guilty. It indeed seems contradictory; one part of the conscience asks a person to suffer for his or her ancestors with a clear conscience, and the other part of the same conscience forbids that person to do so and makes sure this action will not succeed. It becomes clearer if you imagine that children bear some of the burden for parents. For example, they share the sadness of an event that predates their births. Of course, this is a not desirable occurrence. People find it strange that a child does this, and since it is the parents' sadness, a child can never process it adequately. It is the parents' responsibility to take care of their own sadness. Even if they suppress it, they still don't want their children enduring this sadness. This process is further explained in this chapter under the subheading "The Magical Love of a Child."

The Transcendental or Spiritual Conscience

Little can be said about the transcendental conscience. It reveals its qualities to those who want to find real understanding. I also call it the spiritual conscience because it encourages people to continue in the search to resolve dilemmas and overcome limitations that personal and collective consciences pose. The transcendental conscience includes both and simultaneously wants people to transform both.

Through this transformation process, people transcend the duality and guilt, which personal and collective consciences inevitably impose. An example will clarify the issue.

James, age thirty-three, has strong feelings of guilt and does not know why. He knows full well, however, that these feelings impact his relationships and career choices. The transcendental conscience, unbeknownst to him, has evoked a conflict situation—something must happen with these feelings of guilt.

73

In his constellation he becomes conscious that he carries the guilt of his father, who had been a Dutch citizen collaborating with the German Nazis during their occupation of the Netherlands in World War II.

This transcendental conscience makes sure people pose questions about their own lives and about the loyalties they have to their families and others. It asks people to purify themselves, to let go of the known, and to investigate who they really are. As long as people are caught up in entanglements and the consequent limitations imposed, they can never be certain whether what they do truly reflects their inner natures or whether their lives, preferences, and choices are genuinely theirs. These limitations are expressed in their thoughts and behaviors, the choices they make, their judgments, the things they avoid doing, and their actions and inactions.

The personal and collective consciences bring conflict into peoples' lives, and times come when people doubt themselves and all their achievements. A midlife crisis is such a phenomenon. If people can become aware of this process and its potential for growth and creativity, they are offered new directions, new ideas, and new insights. They return to their senses and are able to direct their attention to matters of more substance. They start to live in the present moment and come into contact with their deep inner truths. This awareness process allows people to let go of old loyalties and the burdens they have carried for others. The connection with the family and social environment is loosened. They create room for lives that feel right and proper for them.

According to Bert Hellinger, this is the biggest step of all and one that requires a determined conscious effort. In a certain way, taking this step makes people feel alone. They have to leave their families and villages, so to speak, where they know all the streets and everyone who lives there. However, if they want to *climb the mountain*, they have to leave the known behind. The route upward offers a much larger view-- one in which people can discover that the village is only a small part of the world. When people leave their villages with love and gratitude, they can open up to larger and more encompassing views of life.

The Magical Love of a Child

Through Bert Hellinger's special analysis, it is evident how children automatically earn their places in families through bonds and loyalties. Accordingly they take on the burdens of unprocessed issues. To be able to do that, children copy misery, burdens, diseases, and even death—along with all the positive aspects. People want to compensate or equalize by sharing family members' misfortunes, disorders, or deaths. People do this out of love. Hellinger calls it *bonding love*.[12]

His vision can be summarized as follows. Bonding love is active within a family and expresses itself in bonds or fate connections—in other words, entanglements. Bonding love is strongest between a person and his or her siblings and parents, and then towards the parents' siblings, and then towards grandparents, and sometimes even the great-grandparents. Anyone who has taken the place of one of the members just mentioned also forms part of this sphere of influence. For example, this includes ex-partners of parents or grandparents (married or not). Entanglements are stronger when these family members had heavy fates that might have involved suicide, early death, illness, or maternal death.

Bonding Love

Bonding love is a magical, childlike love in which the child (subconsciously) presumes that through surrogate suffering somebody can be helped or saved. The child assumes he or she is strongly connected with somebody and becomes like him or her only when he or she shares that other person's fate—be it misfortune or even death. Behind this longing to be like somebody else lies the deep desire to belong to the family and a strong thankfulness and love toward the ones who have given him or her life.

When parents have difficult lives, are very ill, or had their lives cut short for one reason or another, their children want to share the same fate out of gratitude. They feel strongly obliged to do so in order to restore the balance between give and take. Since they receive everything from their parents—their lives—children are willing to give graciously in return. This includes their health, good fortune, or even their lives.

This bonding love works through entanglements to make a child sacrifice any advantage in order to become like another family member with a disadvantage. Typically this means healthy, happy children want to be like their unlucky parents through becoming ill and unlucky themselves. In other words the ones who are advantaged want to sacrifice their luck, health, and innocence—and even their lives—for those less fortunate. They treasure the childlike hope that through their sacrifices they can save other family members, or they hope their offerings can restore health, luck, or even the life of a family member. The bonding love in a family evokes a strong and irresistible longing for similarity, compensation, and equalization. In every family the next generation tries to compensate and share the fate of the preceding generation. This means innocent children pay for the debts, mistakes, illnesses, or misfortunes of their ancestors. They do so through blind, subconscious love with the best intentions and clear consciences. In this process they formulate inner statements without being conscious of them.

Better Me Than You

The power and tragedy of this magical, blind, childlike love and the resulting inner statements leads to serious, painful consequences for the child. These are clearly revealed in constellations time after time.

Jack, age twenty-nine, has generally felt down over the last few years. In setting up his constellation, he reveals he had a brother born before him who died three days after birth. In the constellation he stands facing this *brother* and feels a very strong and loving connection toward him. Through this strong and loving connection, he formulates the inner statement, "Better me than you." (A variation of this is, "Let me do it for you.") This sentence confirms the blind, magical love of the child. The facilitator continues by asking the *brother* to voice the resolution statement, "It was my fate to die young. Honor me by leaving it with me."

In constellations it becomes clear that whenever a child with such a better-me-than-you bond becomes an adult and starts his or her own family, he or she remains strongly connected to the family member with the heavy fate. This connection pulls the person away from his or her own new family toward the person who died young, was sick, or lived an unfortunate life. The person wants to leave his or her family and carries the inner statement "I follow you" with him or her. In this dynamic one or more of his or her children will also carry the inner statement "better me than you." To prevent the parent from leaving the family system, the child becomes sick, has an accident, or commits suicide. The child sacrifices himself or herself to keep another person in the family alive. In a way the child gets in the way of the parent's connection to the unfortunate family member. He or she wants to take the place of the parent with love and so takes on illness, misfortune, or death. By doing so the child has a good conscience and feels innocent. His or her deep motivation is love and the desire to compensate.

Annie, age seventeen, has anorexia. In her constellation it comes to light that her *father* lost his older brother (*deceased brother*) in a car accident when he was ten. Annie's *father* is still strongly connected to his *deceased brother*. He wants to be with him. The inner statement of the *father* toward his *deceased brother* is, "Let me do it in your place." His daughter, *Annie,* wants to do it in his place. In the constellation she literally stands in his way. First all the entanglements between the *father* and his *deceased brother* are resolved. The *father* is able to honor the fate of his *deceased brother* and leave it with him. Then he is able to say to *Annie*, "I am here to stay. You can trust me." This relieves *Annie*. The *father* introduces her to his *deceased brother* and asks him for his blessings for his daughter. That takes even more pressure off *Annie*. Annie now enters the constellation and replaces her representative to go through the last sequence herself. The moment her *father* confirms he is staying and that he can be trusted, she bursts into tears. She is freed of a deep sadness the moment she falls into her *father*'s arms. Everybody feels it. A heavy load falls from her shoulders. The pressure to sacrifice herself for her father has been lifted.

This example clarifies that childlike, bonding love is not only magical but also blind. It is magical because the child hopes that through suffering and sacrifice, he or she can save the family member. It is blind because the child does not take into account the feelings and desires of the ones he or she wants to save. In Annie's example her father absolutely did not want his daughter to suffer in this way.

There is a variation on this theme in the constellation of Harry, age forty-two. His theme is chronic sadness. In his constellation his *mother* looks tensely toward a particular spot on the floor. The moment I ask the representative of the deceased sister of the mother to lie on the floor at that particular spot, it becomes clear that his *mother* wants to be with her *deceased sister*. In real life this means that if Harry wants to get the attention of his mother, he has to metaphorically lie down next to the young dead child. Otherwise his mother is not able to see him.

The Faith Leading to Misfortune

Both inner statements "better me than you" and "I follow you" are formulated through deep love and become manifest in life. They are also expressions related to the strongest religious convictions such as the belief that a person can carry the cross for another and by this act being convinced that he or she is doing the right thing. In connection to this, Hellinger refers to the teachings of St. John the Baptist who said, "There is no greater love than giving one's life for a friend."

Hellinger says the Christian teachings about redemption through suffering and death confirm (along with the examples of holy figures and heroes from the Bible) the belief and hope of children in taking over

78

misfortune or death from others. This is done through surrogate suffering and illness. Redeeming other people from their suffering and illnesses through their own suffering and illnesses is like paying God or fate back. More extreme is the conviction that by dying the person can redeem others from their deaths, and if that does not work, he or she wants to be reunited with the family member in the hereafter through his or her own death.[13]

This shows that some religious or spiritual principles have their roots in subconscious childlike love. This attitude is not very respectful because the person who wants to carry the cross for another puts himself or herself above the other and feels superior. Moreover he or she distorts the order of the collective conscience, so his or her action is doomed to fail.

Helpers and Love

The only way to a possible healing in situations where the above dynamic takes place is to respect the blind, childlike love at play and bring it to the conscious level. When the helpers (counselors, physicians, facilitators, and the like) are not conscious of this connection and do not take into account bonding love, there is risk of the seeker withdrawing and preventing or sabotaging a possible healing. The seeker's subconscious motivation must be seen. Otherwise his or her inner statements like "Better me than you" and "I will follow you" will continue to be manifested more strongly and secretly. In doing so his or her conscience will remain clear, and he or she will continue to treasure his or her illness or misfortune. It cannot be any other way. He or she is bound to the collective conscience, and unresolved issues will remain problems until they are identified and processed.

As long as the unresolved issues remain unidentified, it comes down to a betrayal of his or her family to be healed, to become lucky, or to withdraw suicide plans.

Only when deep love, bonding, and loyalties come to light and can really be felt will it be possible for the seeker to become aware of the impact of his or her childlike bind love, hopes, and desires.

Only then can he or she let go of problematic entanglements and make it possible to be healed. Only then can he or she say to the individual, "I honor you and your fate. Look kindly upon me when I move on in life and become happy." Bowing down in deep love for his or her fate, he or she accepts it as it is and leaves the burden where it belongs.

4

Entanglements within the Family System

The feeling of perfection arises when everyone who belongs in our system has been given a place in our hearts. If there is only one exception we continue to feel imperfect.
—Bert Hellinger[1]

Chapter three discussed how every family member has the right to his or her place as well as the right to belong. Who then belongs to the family system? What are entanglements, and what kind of events lead to these entanglements?

This chapter looks at the influence heavy, unprocessed traumas across generations have on others in the family system. These nodal events include maternal death, the premature death of a sibling, and wartime experiences. The chapter will also look at Hellinger's insight about incest, guilt, and forgiveness.

The Family System

A family system[2] is composed of all living and deceased members. In terms of constellations, it is sometimes necessary to look back at least three generations or even further.

The following people are involved:

The first level: children
The first level consists of biological children, half brothers and half sisters, children who died in their infancy, stillborn children, and mis-carried fetuses from around the fifth month of pregnancy and later. Unrecognized extramarital children are naturally also included as well as children born (anonymously) through a sperm donation.

The second level: parents

This level consists of parents and their brothers and sisters. This includes those who died prematurely, their half-sibs, and children from stillbirths and miscarriages. An abortion or miscarriage can have a strong influence on the relationship between parents and on each parent individually—especially on the woman.

The third level: grandparents

Grandparents are a part of the family system, and sometimes their brothers and sisters and half-sibs are as well—especially where there is an indication of heavy fates.

The fourth level: great-grandparents

Great-grandparents belong to the family system and still exert influence when there have been heavy fates such as maternal death, wartime experiences, serious accidents, or disease.

Less importantly but sometimes with a significant influence on the family system, are all the members who have been replaced by others from outside the family. This includes former partners of parents and grandparents and the parents of half-sibs.

Anyone who has ever had a significant positive or negative impact on the family also belongs to the family system. This could be somebody who has done a lot for a particular family member in some way or another and later on has been unjustly treated. An example would be a worker in a family business who has helped to generate a great deal of profit through hard work only to be summarily dismissed later without good reason.

Others who might have influence on the family system are people who have made huge profits from the misfortune of others or through treating others unjustly. An example is someone who has usurped possessions from a Jewish family that was deported during World War II.

Other examples are:

o A person who makes it possible for a family member to take over a business under favorable conditions due to the former owner's bad luck, such as being incapacitated after a car accident.
o A stranger who has been significantly helpful to a family member in some way, such as saving a family member's life.
o A stranger who has caused a family member serious harm or even killed a family member.
o A stranger whom a family member helped in a major way.
o A stranger whom a family member has seriously harmed or killed.

It also means perpetrators belong to the system when there are victims of one kind or another in the family—just as victims belong to the family system of the perpetrators.

What Are Entanglements?

All things are born of being.
Being is born of nonbeing.
—Lao-Tzu[3]

Entanglements or connected fates are when family members takes over feelings or attitudes from other family members and embody them in their lives. This often concerns traumatic events and the resultant conscious or subconscious feelings or attitudes that remain unprocessed as well as unresolved conflicts by those involved. Entanglements can also result from people either relinquishing their responsibilities or not being capable of accepting them. Of course influences from previous generations are often positive, and for that people can be thankful. An entanglement ensues when an influence becomes burdensome or makes life difficult. In this context it is important to understand that family members can be entangled with each other without even knowing each other. An entanglement is usually more serious with family members who were excluded, concealed, or avoided.

Entanglements can also arise when ancestors have done things they thought were right at the time but turned out to be great miscarriages of justice. This often happens in wartime, whereby actions undertaken in the name of idealism or conviction are considered inexplicably gruesome in retrospect.

What Causes Entanglements?

Entanglements always result from children taking on emotional issues from their parents or from parents making emotional appeals to their children. This is known as parentification.

An early death is the most common cause of entanglements. Examples of early deaths include:
o Brothers or sisters thirty years of age or younger
o A parent when the children are thirty years old or younger
o A miscarriage from the sixth month of pregnancy or sometimes even earlier
o Maternal death or complicated delivery

Common causes of entanglements that continue on over several generations are:
o Sexual and other serious abuse
o Death and manslaughter
o Automobile and other accidents involving death, serious injury, or permanent impairment
o Participation in all kinds of war situations, including, membership in extremist groups such as the German Nazi Party or the Khmer Rouge, or participation in resistance movements during war
o A combination of various acts of violence
o Great injustices with lasting consequences such as being unjustly ruled out from inheritance
o Ancestors involved in slavery on both sides
o Ancestors with genocide experiences, including Jews, Armenians, North and South American natives, or Australian aboriginals to name a few.

Entanglements always occur when family members bear heavy fates that usually accompany exclusion, traumatization, victimization, or not being able to process emotional problems. It is important to look back at least two generations. The most important examples of a heavy fate are:
o Suicide
o All forms of exclusion from the family
o Physical or intellectual disabilities
o Confinement (e.g., in jail or concentration or work camps)
o Homosexuality, if it leads to exclusion
o Bankruptcy, if it leads to poverty

o   Extramarital births, especially if they are concealed
o   Adoption

The most important examples of family members with a heavy fate leading other members to entanglements are:
o   Victims of crime
o   Psychiatric patients
o   Nuns, monks, or priests in the family
o   Immigrants or emigrants
o   Children who are placed in a foster family or with other family members at a young age
o   A family member who is sent away to a boarding school at a young age without valid reasons
o   Adult family members who continue to live with their parents
o   Family members who were forced to leave their places of birth
o   Family members whose parents are from different nationalities
o   Family members not able or allowed to express and live out their cultural identities

Poverty, destructive relationships, hate, or strong disrespect against women or men in the family prevails over generations and also leads to entanglements.

It is also important to become aware of the existence of any family secrets—things nobody either wants or is allowed to talk about. It is not important to uncover such secrets for a constellation to be success-ful. All the seeker has to do is give the emotional load that comes with the secret back to whom it belongs.

Parentification

Parentification or adult identification arises when children want or feel obliged to give emotionally to their parents. This happens when parents seek consolation or emotional support from their children.

A clear example of this is when a father looks for affection from his daughter to replace the affection he misses from his wife. Another ex-ample is when a mother uses her son to fill her inner emptiness or wants to make a better man out of her son than she believes his father is or was.

Parents frequently use their children as allies in their struggles during and after divorce. As a result children feel compelled to be emotionally supportive toward their parents.

Another cause of parentification is the absence or early death of one of the parents. One of the children has to replace that absent parent. If the mother dies, for example, then it is expected that the oldest daughter takes her place. If the father dies, the oldest son might become the man of the house. In these instances the balance between giving and taking is severely distorted. The child is left without any choice but to replace the absent parent and has to give instead of receive. Consequently the order of the family is disturbed. This is something that often happens in single-parent families.

It is naturally a heavy burden for the child, and the effort is bound to fail. No matter how determined the child is to succeed, he or she can never cope with the emotional burden of an adult or fill the emptiness of a lost parent. The child will end up feeling powerless, which might lead to depression later on in life, and it frequently leads to parentification of his or her own children.

In the context of family constellations, these giving and supporting attitudes are seen as destructive for the children because they distort the order that requires each person to bear his or her own fate. (See chapter three.) A child should be left unburdened. If burdens have been taken on from others, they have to be given back.

Contextual therapy has another way of looking at this. A positive outcome can take place if the child is recognized and valued for giving to the family or parent or for sharing some of the burden.[4] Nagy and Krasner see in parentification the natural potential of giving from a child. If that is acknowledged, a child develops the potential to take on responsibility that can enhance self-esteem. The ability to give is an inherent right of the child, but giving should not interfere with the child's own development as a person. Giving too much or not being recognized for giving causes destructive parentification.

The contextual vision has taught me that being recognized for giving or bearing the burden for parents can indeed be liberating.

Effectively parentification happens automatically in situations where parents carry many unresolved burdens from their families of origin with them and are thus themselves embroiled in parentification. They pass on these disturbances to the following generation. Following is an example of a classic case of parentification involving both parents.

John, age thirty-one, and his partner have a three-year-old son. Lately John has found the responsibility of being a father burdensome, and he generally feels depressed. At a particular moment in the constellation *John* stands and faces his *father*. He is angry toward his *father* and feels he is looking down upon him. His *mother* says, "I don't feel anything for my husband, but I love my son very much." In saying this she first looked at her *husband* in a denigrating way and then smiled at her *son*. I asked *John* to say to his *mother*, "Your relationship problems and anger toward Dad belong to you and in your life. I am but a child."

Upon saying this *John* feels more at ease because the statement feels right. He realizes he has been used. His *mother* confirms this and says, "Yes. I love my son much more than my husband." Then I ask the *mother* to say, "I used you. I am sorry." Instead the *mother* says, "No. I really used him to demean my husband." Then I asked her to say to *John*, "I used you. That is my responsibility. This belongs solely with me. I am sorry. You had to do so much for me." *John* nods. "That's right," he says. "I am so pleased to hear that." I then ask *John* to say to his *mother*, "Even though you used me, your problems with Dad belong to you. I leave that with you now." He is more relaxed after saying this. He looks at his *father*, and after a bit *John* says, "It's better, but I still think you are weak." His *father* agrees by saying, "Yeah. I feel weak. It's all so heavy. Really heavy." Then I ask him to say to *John*, "All these difficulties belong in my life. I can face up to them. I am the adult, and you are but a child." *John* sighs with relief and says, "Yeah. I wanted to carry some of the load for you." Then I ask him to say to his *father*, "All your heaviness belongs in your life and is part of your fate. You are an adult, and I am but a child."

John himself steps into the constellation, and I ask him to say to his *father*, "Dear Dad, you are just who you are. You are an adult; you can bear your own fate. I am but a child." Then I suggest John bow before his *father*. When John does this, both are really touched and have tears in their eyes. John wants to hug his *father*, and when he does he starts sobbing. I ask him to repeat "dear Dad" over again while breathing deeply—as if he is breathing his father in.

The following is an example of a constellation where parentification and loyalty are successfully redressed.

Mary, age thirty-nine, has a huge problem with her mother. She does not want to have anything to do with her. She tells me in the initial discussion that she has a problematic relationship with her own daughter, age fourteen, who is angry with her. She sometimes finds bringing up her daughter extremely difficult.

In her constellation she chooses representatives for her mother and her daughter, and she goes straight into the constellation herself. Her *mother* does not give her any attention but is obviously very fond of her granddaughter, Mary's *daughter*. Mary feels a lot of anger toward her *mother*. It makes her mad to see her *mother* more or less ignore her but show a keen interest in her *daughter*. A representative of Mary's grandmother is brought into the constellation. The *grandmother* looks around over all the women and shows she has a strong connection to Mary. Mary feels that as well. Mary's *mother* says, "I am angry with my mom. She can't stand me and thinks she knows it all." The *grandmother* confirms this. "Yeah. I really do know more." She smiles at Mary as she says this. Mary smiles as well. I ask the *mother* to say to Mary, "I am angry with my mother, and you might as well feel it." The *mother* confirms this. "Yes. That's right." Then I ask Mary to say to her *mother*, "I'm like you." I then advise her to speak to her *daughter*. "I am angry with my mother, and you might as well feel it. That's just the way it is in our family." The *daughter* confirms this and smiles. The *daughter* is then asked to say the following to Mary, "I know better than you—just like all the daughters here." They laugh in confirmation.

Mary says the same to her *mother*, and her *mother* in turn says this to her *mother* (Mary's *grandmother*). All the women look around at each other and break out into smiles. One says to the other, "We are really alike—out of love." At that point Mary feels like a child to her *mother*, and her *mother* says to her, "It's my responsibility that I burdened you with the anger I felt toward my *mother*. I am sorry. You had to help carry my heavy load." Mary responds, "I am but a child. That anger I leave with you." She then bows before her *mother* and falls into her arms. She breathes really deeply and is obviously deeply touched.

Premature Death

Everything that is not worked through or not given a place in the hearts of family members emerges as entanglements. That is certainly the case with painful events such as stillbirth or the death of a child at a young age. One or both parents, to protect them from the deep pain and to avoid the feeling of powerlessness, often repress the necessary grieving process.

When more siblings come into the picture, a child that died prematurely is usually not counted or remembered. This is due to repression because of the grieving process or out of ignorance. If a firstborn child dies at the age of one, for example, and two more children follow, the parents usually talk only about the two living children. They say, "We have two children." Actually, though, they have three. This comes down to exclusion. It is not necessary to talk about a deceased child with all acquaintances, but it should be a topic that is open for discussion within the family circle. The existence of the departed child should certainly be discussed with siblings and other close relatives.

The same happens with miscarriages. They generally affect the family system when they occur after five to six months of pregnancy. This is a critical stage when life for the unborn child, with the necessary help, becomes viable. It can be sometimes traumatic for parents, however, when a fetus dies earlier on in the pregnancy. Constellations enable parents to see the effects of a miscarriage, to become aware of the deep inner impact, and if necessary initiate a process of working through the grieving process.

Disremembering a lost child is tantamount to exclusion, which results in entanglements. The children that follow are not in their correct places and not in chronological order. The child considered the firstborn in the previous example is actually the second, and the one considered second is actually third.

Miscarriages, stillborn children, and children who die young still belong to the family. They are part of the family system. If adequate grieving is allowed to take place, if the child is given a place in the hearts of family members, and if the child continues to be considered a family member, nothing is amiss. No entanglements will develop.

Excluding a child who dies young will have serious consequences for the entire family system that are beyond the control of the individual. Such exclusions have the most impact on the children who are born next in line after the kinds of deaths mentioned above, and they strongly influence parents and other siblings. To varying degrees of intensity, a feeling of guilt develops subconsciously in one or more siblings because those siblings sense and will redress the injustice of the exclusion and the fact they are alive while their brother or sister has died. They feel unjustly favored over the child that lost his or her life at a young age. Considering the pain that the death of a sibling entails, they find it unfitting to lead happy lives. Subconsciously they want to share the heavy fate of the child who lost his or her life at an early age.

This is how the family conscience demands compensation from members of the system for the exclusion. That is why usually one or more siblings who follow the child who died young have difficulty finding their own places. In extreme cases they become addicted to drugs, have hidden death wishes, or are suicidal. Many also take risks by participating in dangerous sports. Hellinger calls this "expensive suicide." Many lead foots on the road flirt with death because they subconsciously want to share the burden of dead siblings. Through their behavior they want to bring unprocessed events back to the conscious level of the family system. Subconscious attitudes (or inner statements) of "Better me than you," "Let me do it for you," and "I want to be with you" underpin these behaviors. Constellations reveal that children take on these attitudes out of blind love and then give them expression in their lives. (See "Bonding Love" in chapter three.)

In her book *Broederziel Alleen*, Minke Weggemans discusses the importance of grieving and processing trauma. She suggests it is not unusual for people in their thirties and forties to still grieve for long-lost brothers or sisters. "They are often misunderstood," she says, "because the subject is taboo and almost invariably they take on the role of a rescuer upon losing a sibling."[5] The child is too busy comforting his or her parents to grieve, and as a result unprocessed trauma lingers on for years. According to Weggemans it is important to talk about the death of a sibling to surviving children in order to facilitate the grieving process. Children need assistance. Weggemans cites that in her own life she lost four brothers and one sister, and she reiterates the incredible impact that losing a sibling can have on a child's life.

It sometimes happens that a parent, usually a mother, cannot let go of a lost child. This emotional connection and dependence means she has less energy or none at all for her surviving children.

Jenny, age thirty-four, feels she cannot find her way in life and is prone to bouts of depression. She begins to constellate her family by choosing representatives for her mother, her father, her younger brother, and herself, and she placed them in the constellation space.

All representatives feel down and a little absent. They stand well apart from each other. Both *Jenny* and her *mother* stare at the same point on the floor. Upon inquiry it becomes clear the parents had a stillborn child, a girl, before Jenny was born. That child is then brought into the constellation. Jenny places a representative of this child on the spot where *Jenny* and her *mother* were staring. The *mother* begins to cry and says, "It was too painful; I don't want to think about it." *Jenny* starts to feel better and experiences a strong connection with her *stillborn sister*. I ask *Jenny* to say, "Let me die. I want to do it for you." She feels more at ease after saying this, and she spontaneously adds, "Yeah. That makes sense. I would be happy to do it for her. To give my life for hers." The *stillborn sister* feels extremely uncomfortable hearing this. Then I ask *Jenny* to look at her *stillborn sister* while repeating, "Let me die for you." *Jenny* finds it very difficult to utter this statement. She looks at her *stillborn sister* now as if an independent individual. Her *stillborn sister* finds it abhorrent that her younger sister wants to die for her. She says, "My early death was my fate and belongs in my life. You honor me if you leave it with me." That is a relief for them both. The *stillborn sister* is led to her parents, and I work with resolving statements until the child has been given a place in the hearts of her parents and has been placed in chronological order among her brothers and sisters.

Jenny's representative is relieved of her task, and Jenny takes up her own place in the constellation. She is also invited to look into the eyes of her *stillborn sister* and starts to cry. Her *stillborn sister* repeats, "My early death is my fate and belongs in my life. You honor me by leaving it with me." Jenny feels relieved, and then I ask her to say, "It was your fate to die young. It is my fate to go on living. I honor you and your fate. You now have a place in my heart forever." She feels a burden being lifted. Then her *stillborn sister* says, "You honor me by leading a happy life." The constellation ends here, and Jenny feels as though a great weight has been removed from her shoulders.

In a constellation such as this, it is important for a person with a connection to a deceased family member to stare for a period into the eyes of the representative of the dead person and repeat, "Let me do it for you" or, "I want to die instead of you." This is done so it becomes obvious that blind, magical love is the driving force, and then a person can begin to distinguish and recognize the other as an individual in order to let go of the identification with the deceased person.

This is how the dead person is given a place, and at the same time it becomes clear that this place has been taken. As the constellation develops, it becomes apparent that the deceased person also loves the living person. This person does not want another family member to take his or her place, to follow, or die for him or her. He or she wants to carry his or her own fate. When the dead and their family members deal with heavy fates in this way, it is not possible to follow family members in their fates. The subconscious inner attitudes of "Better me than you," "Let me do it for you," and "I'll follow you" can no longer be rightfully maintained.

Sometimes parents cannot accept it as an act of fate when a child dies in an accident. Instead of becoming aware of their helplessness regarding such a fateful event, they develop the belief that it might have been avoidable. By doing this they avoid experiencing the deep pain and grieving process that the death of a loved one brings. They might flee into feelings of guilt or berate themselves or their partner for the loss, which is perilous for the relationship. This makes it more difficult for the remaining siblings to lead relatively harmonious lives.

Constellations make it apparent that children who die young are carrying out their fates. The children deal with it and find peace only when their parents and siblings are able to do the same and lovingly give them places in their hearts. Constellations about children who have died young continually demonstrate that parents do not have any power over the fates of their children. If parents do not accept this, then they burden not only the surviving siblings but each child who has died as well. Children who die young cannot be free until they are honored by having their fates accepted. In such constellations the resolution statements both parents use in relation to their lost child are, "You are my dear child. You have died at a young age. I honor your fate. You continue to live in my heart." The parents say to each other, "We bear this together." By doing this the deep pain can be freed so the family can move on in life.

The Death of a Parent

The death of a parent can have a similar effect on children. Guilt and a subconscious death wish also come into play in one or more children. It is often impossible for children to lead happy lives without professional support after such a tragic event. The early death of a parent abruptly severs the natural exchange and bonding between parent and child. The pain the child experiences is so severe that he or she withdraws into the inner self and becomes closed off. Often he or she subconsciously wants to follow in the path of the dead parent in order to share the heavy fate. Suicidal tendencies, drug use, and disease sometimes become the methods chosen to achieve this aim. A person who experiences the loss of a parent also finds it difficult to build and maintain close relationships. The natural ability of a child to reach out to a loved one is interrupted. This theme is called *interrupted reaching out* and will be dealt with further at the end of this chapter.

Following is a related example from Bert Hellinger.[6] Sigrid, age twenty-four, is addicted to codeine syrup. Her mother died of cervical cancer at the age of thirty-seven when Sigrid was twelve. She chooses a representative for her mother. Hellinger asks her and the representative to lie next to each other on the floor. Then he asks Sigrid to repeat several times, "Mom, I am coming too." This makes her feel relieved but also sad. Hellinger then says, "Tell her, 'Without you I don't want to live. I am coming too.'" By uttering this she feels deep love for her mother. Then Hellinger asks her to say, "You can live a little longer in me, but I am coming with you." She feels relieved. She is no longer so sad. Hellinger asks her, "How do you think your mother feels when you say that?" Sigrid begins to sob and answers, "I think she is happy and pleased I want to be with her." Then Hellinger asks her, "Can you imagine having children yourself?" She answers in the positive. So he asks, "How would it feel if your child said that to you?" She answers, "Not good." Hellinger says, "Exactly. Tell her, 'Mom, I'm staying awhile.'" A little later he asks her to say, "You can be happy with me. There was a reason for all this happening, and I honor what has happened."

The example clarifies how Hellinger first brings the blind, childlike love to the conscious level before he turns the situation around (Sigrid takes the place of her mother, and her child wants to follow her), so the blindness of this childlike love becomes palpable for the seeker.

Hellinger comments on this. "This is a method where identification with a dead person can be resolved. When the two involved stand facing each other, love flows and the secret meaning behind their love for each other is brought to light."[7]

Children from parents who have died prematurely are often angry because they feel they have been left alone. It is difficult for them to express this anger because anger is a challenging emotion for others to deal with. People also do not associate anger with grieving. Moreover they feel guilty about their anger. They wonder how one can be angry with a parent who has died young. Of course, staying angry helps the person stop giving attention to the parent, avoid going through the whole grieving process, and avoid the feeling of powerlessness.

While this avoidance behavior in children above sixteen is not entirely subconscious, it is with younger children. They are actually traumatized. The sadness, the feelings of loss, and the pain are frozen within them, and it takes a great deal of effort to help them through the grieving process.

Veronica and Jeremy have a fifteen-year-old son and a thirteen-year-old daughter. Their son has been self-mutilating for a year. Both parents constellate the situation in the absence of their children. It becomes instantly clear their *son* is standing next to his *father (Jeremy)* and is staring at the floor. *Jeremy* looks away, and a little farther away his *wife Veronica* looks helpless. From responses to questions that I pose, I ascertain that Jeremy lost his father when Jeremy was twelve. I arrange for a representative for his dead father to lie on the floor where the *son* is staring. *Jeremy* looks away disinterestedly, and then his *son* goes to lie down next to his *grandfather* and expresses the deep bond he feels. He says toward his *father*, "I do it for you, Dad. I feel your pain. I can handle it." *Jeremy (the father)* does not want to look at first, but it becomes clear that his *son* has a problem. *Jeremy (the father)* realizes he himself is traumatized and takes a step toward his *father (the grandfather)*. I encourage him to feel what he could not feel as a twelve-year-old when his father was dying, and slowly sadness wells up inside him. He feels angry at first, and then he feels a sense of powerlessness. He realizes how closed off he became as a child.

Step by step and layer by layer, he moves through all the feelings he kept repressed as a child. His *son* creates a little distance from both his *father (Jeremy)* and *grandfather,* and he accepts the pain and sadness of his *father*. The *son* confirms he had done whatever he could to feel his father's pain and share his burden.

A week after the constellation, Veronica sent me the following e-mail:

> Hi Indra,
> You asked for permission from participants to allow their experiences to be used in your new book. You can certainly use our case, preferably anonymously. The theme of our constellation was self-mutilation of our 15-year-old son. The entanglement we could see was the unprocessed loss of his grandfather when his father was 12.
>
> After the constellation, we talked with our son and said to him that he didn't have to take on the pain of his father. Our son responded spontaneously, "How did anyone know I did that? I have to help Dad."
>
> PS: The scars have almost healed and my son has stopped self-mutilating! I think this is a rather "spectacular" result and I want to thank you once again. The least I can do is to make our case available should you wish to include it in the book.
>
> Best wishes, Veronica

Difficult Deliveries

That a complicated delivery can be traumatic is a given as a rebirther. (Rebirthing-breath work is a technique that has been successfully used for years to help people come to terms with difficult births and other problems.)

The dynamic that comes to light during constellations with this theme is that complicated births (including caesarean section deliveries) sometimes result in anxious children who are unable to participate fully and enjoy life's experiences. Apart from the trauma of the difficult births, they also carry inner guilt toward their mothers because they had to suffer. This is especially pronounced when a mother is left with serious physical and/or emotional scarring. The resolution statements for the child toward the mother are, "I take my life for the price you have paid. I'll make something beautiful from it. Then your suffering will have been worth it."

Maternal Death

The historical level of maternal deaths is probably around one in a hundred births. Mortality rates reached very high levels in maternity institutions in the 1800s—sometimes climbing to 40 percent of birth-giving women. At the beginning of the 1900s, maternal death rates were around one in one hundred for live births. (Given the fact that most families around 1900 had five or more children, at least one in twenty women died during childbirth.) Luckily this has changed. A maternal mortality rate for the United States of twenty-four per one hundred thousand was reported for 2008.[8]

Death of a mother while giving birth is so heavy that it can take generations before its effects on the whole family system begin to wane. It's not uncommon that men in affected families are left with deep feelings of guilt. There are always men willing to pay penance for this. A strange belief connected to a man's sexuality is responsible, though not entirely, for this typical male response: if a woman dies giving birth, then the man—the father of the child—feels he has murdered his wife through his passion, and he reproaches himself. Other family members also often look on judgmentally toward the father. This reproach is neither justified nor dignified toward his wife. This position negates the fact that women also have sexual desires and also want to have children. Her status is reduced to that of an object, and in the process she is made a victim. It is also an unjust position as far as the man is concerned. This state of guilt prevents feeling the deep pain and helplessness, and the mourning process is replaced by blame and accusation. This places a burden on masculine sexuality that can hamper healthy and enjoyable sexual experiences for generations.

Bert Hellinger says that sexual intercourse is the deepest human interaction and yet the one with the greatest risk.[9] Both men and women realize this. This makes the sexual act so special and deep. A woman is aware of the risk of losing her life in childbirth. That is part of being a woman.

When this theme is present in a constellation, it is usually apparent that the woman in question has not been blaming her husband. She can only find peace when she and her fate are honored and all the constructed guilt is relinquished.

Anxiety from unprocessed feelings associated with maternal death can also remain with women in the family system for generations. In constellations some women cannot allow full expression of their femininity and sexual desires due to deeply embedded anxiety. The painful feelings are frequently repressed and amount to exclusion with the described consequences. From positions of deep loyalty, these women have seriously complicated deliveries themselves. They do not allow themselves to enjoy being women by having uncomplicated births.

The resolution statement in a constellation involving a child who has survived a maternal death delivery is, "I take on my life for its full and true value and for the price you have paid. I will make something of my life so you didn't die in vain." If it concerns a woman from a previous generation, the statement is, "I leave your heavy fate with you. Look kindly upon me, give your blessings for me to be a complete woman, and allow me to enjoy my sexuality."

Death by Abortion

If a woman dies while having an (illegal) abortion, there will be a domino effect on the family system. This was more common in the past when abortions were prohibited by law and often took place in primitive circumstances. It still happens today in countries where abortion is outlawed. The following is an example from my own practice.

Patrick, age forty-six, requests a constellation because he suffers from guilt about his sexuality. In the initial interview, it was obvious his maternal grandmother had died during an abortion, which her husband, Patrick's maternal grandfather, had carried out.

It becomes clear during the constellation that neither Patrick's *maternal grandmother* nor the *aborted child* harbor feelings of blame toward the *grandfather*. Both *maternal grandmother* and *aborted child* say in the constellation that it was their fates to die in this way. According to them nobody deserves blame. They all belong together in their common fate. The *maternal grandfather* is not considered a murderer in any way at all. It was an accident. Both father and mother knew the risks involved and proceeded anyway. It was just their fates.

This constellation confirms that all conscious or subconscious blame and allegations are presumptions that are dishonorable to the people concerned.

Four weeks after the constellation, Patrick told me, "I see them lying together, deceased in love and peace. I can leave them like that now. The guilt that I harbored that caused so much havoc in my life is gone. Through the guilt and through my identification with my grandfather, the so-called villain, I also became guilty. I can now be responsible for my own actions. I feel much better."

As a practitioner of family constellations, I make no judgments about events or circumstances with which I am confronted in constellations. Life in general has no judgment. It is a human thing to judge and create a judgmental God.

The Vanishing Twin Syndrome

It is increasingly common to come across people in constellations who are sole survivors of twins or multiple fetuses, the other(s) having disappeared in the uterus during early pregnancy. According to scientific research,[10] multiple conceptions from egg cells occur in 8 to 10 percent of all pregnancies. The second egg cannot implant itself or is not viable for some reason or other. Most twin embryos die within the first two to three weeks of pregnancy. This usually goes unnoticed by the mother because any resultant minor bleeding and mucus discharge is part and parcel of a normal pregnancy anyway.

The surviving twin is subconsciously aware of his or her deceased twin, who is frequently expressed as an entanglement later on in life. This is what is known as the vanishing twin syndrome.

There are strong parallels here with people who have siblings who died prematurely. The survivors feel guilty to be alive while the siblings are not. Sometimes they prefer to be united in death with their twin brothers or sisters and are not concerned about their own lives and happiness.

People with vanishing twin syndrome very often feel profoundly left alone and subconsciously miss and seek the vanished twins all their lives.

The first time I came across this lost twin phenomenon, I knew very little about it. It was more than twenty years ago. The woman was about fifty and came for individual therapy sessions in relation to headaches. She had tried all sorts of medication without results. In one of the rebirthing sessions I conducted with her, she felt as if her headache was a small baby who wanted attention. She became aware that she felt both love and aversion for the baby at the same time. She wanted the baby to go away but was dearly attached to it. It was an unresolvable dilemma for her. I remembered that in a previous session she had told me about an operation she had. A petrified ectopic embryo was removed from her abdomen. Because I did not know any better at that moment and did not want to exclude this possibility, I asked her if it could be that this little baby was identical to the petrified ectopic embryo and suggested that what she felt was actually the soul of her twin sister. The woman burst into tears, and I knew I had hit the nail on the head.

We started an inner dialogue with the child. The baby wanted to go to her final resting place as well as be recognized. I asked the woman whom she considered the supreme spiritual authority, to which she replied Jesus. I asked her to call on Jesus to guide the soul of her twin sister to a final resting place, which she did.

It became a solemn ritual. She said good-bye, breathed deeply, and was visibly more at ease with herself. A few minutes later, she opened her eyes and felt differently—a little alone but, for the first time in memory, headache-free. The following Christmas she sent me a card with good wishes and let me know her headaches had not returned.

Two years ago, Greg, forty-two, requested a constellation. He was depressed and unhappy about his life. There seemed to be no unusual factors from his family history, but Greg was staring at the floor in front of him. As an experiment I placed a representative for a family member who had died at a young age into the constellation. Instantly Greg's representative went to lie next to the *dead family member* and wanted to embrace him lovingly. The *dead family member* was also happy and said, "Finally. Someone who recognizes and likes me."

The connection between the two seemed especially strong—stronger in fact than is normally the case between a brother and a forgotten sibling lost in miscarriage. I asked Greg if it could have been his twin brother. He immediately reacted emotionally, and his heart was touched. His representative also reacted with relief, and both were happy to be in each other's company. In the course of the constellation, the representative for the twin who had died took responsibility for his fate and wished Greg luck and success in life. He just wanted to be recognized and certainly did not want Greg to remain depressed or to continue harboring subconscious guilt.

Alfred R. and Bettina Austermann write in detail about this phenomenon of a vanishing twin. "Many clients that do not respond to other methods are presented with fundamental solutions to many of their questions and problems with the discovery of a vanishing twin."[11]

Family Members with Disabilities

This is clearly and understandably a very sensitive issue. For constellation work people have to let go of all judgments. They must also let go of political correctness as well as exclusionary or dismissive attitudes (including the idea disabilities are punishments from God) toward children and their families with these heavy fates.

It is often difficult for healthy children to lead happy lives if they have siblings with disabilities. The subconscious need for compensation, similarity, and equalization makes it difficult for healthy children to make the most of their comparatively favored positions. If they were to enjoy life, how would that make their siblings with disabilities feel? In their eyes their siblings' disabilities would become accentuated.

In this way healthy children develop guilt because of their advantageous positions. These feelings of guilt prevent them from making full use of their potential, and they avoid happy lives, or worse still they seek out difficult lives or get diseases.

Hellinger sees resolution in the healthy child saying to his disabled sibling, "You have a disability, while I am not disabled. I accept my health and wellbeing as it was given to me. I treat my health and good fortune as a gift and I share it with you. Whenever you need me I am there for you."[12] This is a way for a healthy child to accept his or her favored position and at the same time enrich the life of the disabled sibling. This also applies to disabilities that result from accidents. The plight of an older sibling who suffers an accident will have an effect on siblings around twenty-eight years of age or younger.

Nuns, Monks, Priests, or Missionaries in the Family

Until two generation ago, it was normal in many families in Western Europe for one child to go off to a monastery or seminary. Although the reason usually given by people living seminarian lives is to offer up their lives for the service of God, constellations offer an alternative understanding. There is a clear difference between family members who chose paths of religious service on their own and family members who do it out of loyalty or tradition or because they were given away.

People who chose lives of religious service are real God seekers. Through Freud, Hellinger, and other independent thinkers, we know that the search for God disguises another search—namely the search for the ideal father figure. This subconscious search develops frequently if, for example, the biological father is unknown or absent. It can also occur when the mother is dismissive toward her husband and their children subconsciously or explicitly join the derogatory behavior toward their father. In these circumstances a need for compensation can arise. This takes the form of a strong desire for an ideal father figure. Since the biological father is not or cannot be honored, an ideal replacement is longed for.

I was really shocked when I first found out about this. Over the years I was in search of God and sacrificed a lot in this quest. The surprise was even more profound when I realized that all the right ingredients for me to be a real "seeker of God" were present in my family.

After a constellation concerning my relationship with my father, my attitude toward God changed. My search for an ideal father stopped because I found him in the constellation. My biological father became the only real father from then on.

People who choose religious vocations through loyalty or tradition or because they have been given away have to do this for their families. They had no choice but to make sacrifices to God.

On the one hand, they add to the prestige of their families because everyone sees how religious they are. They are viewed as fine, upstanding families. On the other hand, it was naturally expected (subconsciously) that the children concerned would look after their families' salvation by praying and serving others selflessly. These children served, more or less consciously, as counterbalances for the sins of the families. Too often behind the sacrifices lay bartering mentalities.—"If I sacrifice something precious, I will be rewarded." The reward might be, a good harvest or having sins pardoned, for example.

Most subconscious family rationales can be reduced to this: if I offer up one of my children to God, then he somehow owes me and has to recompense me by bringing good fortune my way.

All cases involving children having to do a lot for the families or carrying loads for their families, including children who have been given to God, end in entanglements. The children are unable to lead normal lives. They live without being able to enjoy life's pleasures and do not have children of their own. It is expected they offer their lives up for others. They are incredibly disadvantaged, while other family members hope or believe (subconsciously) that God will look down upon them kindly and bestow privileges upon them. That causes entanglements. Consequently family members in following generations are loyal to such sacrificing ancestors and want to help bear the burden of their heavy fates.

Lisa, thirty-two, is unhappy with her life and wants to make sweeping changes because she feels she just cannot go on like this. She does not have a partner or an enjoyable job and generally is not comfortable in her own skin.

To begin with she constellates representatives for herself, her mother, and her father. From questioning the representatives about their positions in relation to each other, there is an indication of detachment but nothing to pinpoint an obvious entanglement. All family facts that Lisa presents to the constellation have little impact on the representatives. I ask her again if there are other significant circumstances in the family yet to be aired.

She begins to tell about her grandfather who was at one stage critically ill but eventually became well again. During his illness her grandfather promised the pastor he would send one of his daughters to the cloister if he returned to good health. Indeed that was what happened. A sister of Lisa's mother ended up in a very strict cloister, and from that moment on, she had almost no contact with the outside world.

I broadened the constellation by adding representatives for Lisa's aunt (the *nun*), her grandfather, and one for God as well. This instantly changes the dynamic of the constellation. *Lisa* begins to cry, and other representatives feel shame and pain. The *nun* is stiff and somber but glad the *grandfather* survived his serious illness. She says, "Dear Dad, I have done this for you with pleasure. I am glad you are alive." It is clear to Lisa now how loyal she has been to her vestal aunt. She prefers to stand next to her and can see she has tried to emulate her aunt's life.

I ask the representative of God if he accepts her sacrifice and if the sacrifice was necessary in God's eyes. God's representative indicates that he strictly disapproves of the sacrifice by and of children. "You cannot manipulate me through sacrifices of this sort because I don't require sacrifices. I have everything. I am God. The idea of personal sacrifice such as this is inappropriate."

Lisa's *grandfather* understands he sacrificed his daughter out of ignorance. He feels guilty, and he says to her, "You have had to do a lot for me. I have sacrificed you. I thought I had to do something in return for regaining my health. I take full responsibility for sacrificing you. It is my fault." The *nun* welcomes the recognition. She feels her niece's loyalty but does not want it and emphatically asks *Lisa* to leave all her hardships with her. A little further in the constellation, she readily gives her consent for *Lisa* to go on and lead a healthy, happy life. "If you really want to honor me, then leave me with my life of devotion to God. It is part of my fate. Your fate now is to enjoy being a woman in the prime of her life. Find a nice man, and have a wonderful relationship and kids, if that's what you want." After bowing down, Lisa feels clearly how she has denied herself a happy life—with a good conscience—out of loyalty to her aunt, the nun. An end can be put to all that now.

In this context a representative for God in family constellations represents no more than representation of the higher truth. Sometimes the representative of God shows up as a very dominant or burdened family member. As a facilitator I have learned through my work and experience to question the idea of an absolute God. It seems more of a human-devised concept.

Homosexuality

In the past, social and religious taboos about gays and bisexuals almost always guaranteed their exclusion. Thankfully things have changed for the better because contemporary society is more prepared to accept them. This form of exclusion causes entanglements, and just like with any other form of exclusion, it has far-reaching consequences for the descendants in the family concerned. One or more family members duly represent excluded brothers, uncles, aunts, and others in the following generation(s). That is one of the systemic dynamics that leads to homosexuality—an excluded gay person has to be represented once again down the line in the family system.

Another systemic dynamic behind homosexuality is opposite-sex identification. When there is a female family member with a serious and unprocessed emotional trauma or exclusion in one generation followed by a generation of only sons, then one of these boys will take on the heavy fate of his affected mother or aunt. He thus has an opposite-sex identification or gender identity disorder. Through this he has enormous difficulty accepting his own sexual identity, which can lead to homosexuality. Naturally this also applies to daughters.

A third dynamic at play is when a son is not allowed or is unable to escape the overpowering influence of his mother or even sometimes his grandmother. This means he is forced to reject his father and his own masculinity. This is serious abuse, and such a son is unable to develop his own sexual identity.

> *Hellinger sees homosexuality as a heavy fate that if accepted can give power to the person involved.[13] Being gay is not something to heal.*

A constellation can offer clarity to gays and lesbians about the ways in which they might be entangled. They usually carry feelings of exclusion with them that can have far-reaching consequences in their lives and for the stability of their relationships. It becomes easier for them to accept their fates and build up stable and loving relationships once they become aware of their entanglements and have worked through them. They no longer need to suppress their feelings just because people from previous generations had to do that.

Constellations can offer clarity to people who find it difficult to accept their genders and have as yet no strong homosexual bonds. They are mostly able to let go of their entanglements if they see they are contragender identified or bear the fates of excluded gays. That helps them to accept their own genders.

Ruth, twenty-five, is bisexual. She has had relationships with men and women. Her theme is trying to find her real place in life. She informs me she has a younger sister, and sometime before Ruth was born, her mother had a miscarriage in the eighth month of pregnancy. To begin the constellation, I get her to choose representatives for her parents, her sister, and herself. A sad picture emerges from the constellation. *Ruth* looks toward the floor between herself and her *mother*. Then I ask Ruth to choose a representative for the child who died in the womb. She chooses a man and places him between the representatives of herself and her mother. Because she chooses a man without hesitation as representative, I understand that the gender of the miscarried child is male.

Ruth's *mother* begins to cry, and *Ruth* wants to be very close to the *miscarried son*. The parents can accept the lost and forgotten child by saying the following statements, "You are our child who died early. You have a place in our hearts, and you continue to live in us." The *mother* and *father* then say to each other, "We carry our sadness and pain together." I allow them to move closer together and place the *miscarried son* in a sitting position before his *mother* and *father* with his back resting against their legs. Both lay their hands on the head of the *miscarried son*, and he visibly relaxes and says, "That feels good. Now I am finally allowed to belong."

The *parents* and the *miscarried son* are left for a while to feel and take in the new situation. Then I ask the *miscarried son* to stand in his rightful place as the oldest child. I also ask Ruth to come into the constellation herself, and I place her opposite the *miscarried son*. I ask her to look into the eyes of the *miscarried son*. She feels a lot of love for him and starts to cry. The *miscarried son* repeats after me, "It was my fate to die young. You honor me when you leave it all with me." Ruth replies, "I want to be with you." I encourage her to repeat the sentence over and over while she continues to look into the eyes of the child. "That isn't possible," answers the *miscarried son* after a while. "You belong with the living, and I belong with the dead." With this sentence Ruth takes a step back and cries even harder. By breathing deeply with an open mouth, she is able to calm down. I ask her to say, "I honor

your fate. You died young. I will live on as long as I will as a woman."
The sentence has a calming effect on the *miscarried son*, and he smiles.
Ruth also feels a great sense of relief.

The children line up in chronological order and face their parents when
I ask them to, and Ruth feels comfortable between her brother and
younger sister. She looks at them alternately and says, "Yes. This is my
real place." A moment later, after everything has been gone over and
taken in, the constellation is concluded, and the representatives step out
of their roles.

Incest

> *The indignant manner in which incest is treated makes a*
> *solution difficult and damages the victim.*
> —Hellinger[14]

Incest leads to entanglements that can work across several generations—on the one side through loyalty and on the other through the
usual exclusion of the perpetrator. In his work with incest victims,
Hellinger revealed a much deeper dynamic than people are accustomed
to. To understand this dynamic, people have to be prepared to let go of
their general understandings of the perpetrator–victim paradigm. In
people's usual conceptions, the victim is a girl or less often a boy, and
the perpetrator is a man. He is considered someone who goes way over
the boundaries because he is unable to control his sexual urges. People
look upon the perpetrator with abhorrence, and people have sympathy
for the child.

Family constellations show something else. In families where incest
occurs, sexuality and intimacy (and consequently the balance of giving
and taking between the parents) are seriously disturbed. Frequently the
wife no longer wants to be intimate with her husband. To keep the balance, one of their children, usually a daughter, steps in and gives what
is needed to restore the balance toward her father. She does this in lieu
of her mother.

There are also other reasons why the balance between giving and taking is so disrupted, causing the daughter to compensate the father or
stepfather. In the case of a stepfather, an urge to compensate can arise

when he gives or has to give excessively to his stepdaughter. This includes financing her education or giving her expensive presents. This comes about especially if the father or stepfather is not appreciated, acknowledged, or thanked for his love and what he gives to his wife, the mother of the daughter. The daughter then feels a strong subconscious urge to restore the balance and offers up herself instead of her mother.

In all these cases, the child sacrifices herself (or sometimes himself) to restore the systemic balance. The motivation is the blind and childlike love previously mentioned, so inescapable, subconscious compulsion follows. The child is, therefore, innocent and has a clear conscience.

It is clear then that a serious disturbance of the whole family system is behind incest because both parents are entangled as well, and people have to see it that way to find solutions. Hellinger describes the first step. "In the first place I see that I have to deal with the victim and that my full attention has to be with the victim. My urge as a therapist cannot be to follow up on the perpetrator because that will not help the victim. When, for example, a woman in a workshop tells me that she has been sexually abused by her father or stepfather, I ask her to visualize her mother and say to her, 'Mother, I did it gladly for you.' Suddenly, there is another connection. Then I ask her to visualize her father or stepfather and say to him, 'Dad, I did it gladly for Mom.' With this, a whole different hidden dynamic comes to light and nobody can go on like it was."[15]

A constellation with this theme is clearly illustrated by the following case from my practice.

Patricia is fifty-two. Her father sexually abused her in her youth. This had far-reaching implications in her life—principally in not being able to develop successful relationships with partners. Although she has tried, she has not been successful in working through her trauma.

During the constellation *Patricia* and her *father* stand close and face each other. Her *mother* stands well apart to the left of them. Through my prompting, *Patricia* says to her *mother*, "I did it for you." The *mother* answers ashamedly "Yes. I didn't want anything to do with your father. I was glad to be rid of him. I mean sexually." After a moment she adds, "Men are all the same. I had the same with my father. We women just have to put up with it." Then I ask *Patricia* to say the following to her *father,* "I did it for Mom." The *father* reacts with obvious guilt when he hears this and says, "I feel guilt and shame." I prompt *Patricia* to say, "You went too far, and that's your responsibility. I leave your guilt and shame with you. I am but a child." Upon saying this her *father* nods. He is racked with guilt and responds, "It was my responsibility. The guilt and shame of incest rests solely on my shoulders." To finish I ask both *mother* and *father*, one at a time, to say, "You have done so much for us. We have both abused you." *Patricia* is visibly relieved to hear this.

Following closely from the side, Patricia herself says to me with tears streaming down her face, "I've had to live with this guilt and shame my whole life, but now I see it really belongs to my father, even though I wanted to carry it for him." She enters the constellation with the departure of her representative and repeats to her *father* what she has just said to me. Her *father* once again confirms, "It was my responsibility. You were innocent. I am very sorry."

This has a profound effect on Patricia. After giving her time to repeatedly look intensely from one parent to the other, I say to her, "You wanted to save your parents, didn't you?" More sadness washes over her. Later she explains to me that at that particular moment she felt how helpless she had felt as a child. The constellation concludes with Patricia saying to her parents, "I now leave your relationship problems with you. I am but a child." Her *mother* and *father* both nod, and Patricia bows down before them. She is deeply touched and needs time and rest to process what she has been through.

Hellinger's second step is for the child to be given back dignity.[16] For this he often uses a poem by Johann Wolfgang titled "Sah ein Knab ein Röslein stehn." It is about a boy in the act of plucking a rose. In this poem the rose (symbol of the innocent child) fights back and jabs the boy with its thorns but to no avail. Even though the rose has been damaged, which is a metaphor for being raped or misused in this poem, Hellinger reveals the secret—the rose retains its wonderful scent.

The third step involves helping the child to let go of guilt, even if the abuse was not perceived as a negative experience. A child is rarely permitted or dares to acknowledge this—especially to his or her mother and potentially indignant social service agents. Apart from outside indignation and resulting guilt, a guilty conscience plagues the child. In this confused state, the child develops a negative view of his or her own sexuality. It is important that children know they are innocent irrespective of what has taken place. They only reacted as children would in those circumstances—being curious and wanting to gain experience. The responsibility of crossing boundaries always rests purely with the adult. Hellinger makes it clear to the child that sexuality is a natural and necessary experience. However, in cases such as these, the experiences come far too early in life and with inappropriate partners.

Another reason why a child becomes constricted later in development is due to the bond formed with the perpetrator through their sexual relationship. Without valuing one's first sexual relationship, it is difficult to develop healthy relationships further on in life. When the first experience is rejected and the perpetrator is excluded, it makes it even more difficult. If it was the child's first experience and the resulting bond is accepted, the child will have less trouble in developing healthy sexual relationships in the future.

No matter whether the experience was terrible or it did not feel so bad for the child, abuse is still present. The child has to leave the guilt, shame, and responsibility with the perpetrator. Only then is the child free to establish healthy boundaries and let go of the perpetrator. A child who remains angry stays bound up with the perpetrator. It sometimes happens that victims of sexual abuse become child abusers themselves as adults or (in a similar vein) become prostitutes. In this case the abused says (in a subconscious way) to his or her parents, "I am the baddie here. You don't have to worry." In this situation the child tries to carry all the guilt and shame.

Letting go of sexual abuse happens in constellations through saying the following to the *mother*, "I did it out of love for you." The abused then says to the *perpetrator*, "I did it out of love. I allowed it to happen, but you are the adult, and, therefore, you are responsible. I leave the guilt, shame, and responsibility with you. I am but a child." If these statements are said without emotional loading, anger, or resentment, the child feels innocent and can be freed from entanglements.

The following case shows something quite different. A fellow therapist and friend asked me if I could conduct a constellation about pedophilia for one of his clients. I assumed the client wanted to be helped with his disorder, so I agreed and arranged to meet up with him and his mother during one of my constellation weekends in Amsterdam. In one of the pauses in the constellation schedule before the young man was to have his own constellation, I took the opportunity to speak with him. I asked him how open he was prepared to be in his initial discussion when it came his turn to be constellated and what he expected from the constellation. In the beginning of this interaction, he was unclear, but his motive was eventually revealed. "Why can't I just practice my preferred sexual orientation just as a gay person can?" he said. I tried to make him aware that children in society are protected because they are too young to look after themselves. I emphasized that sex with an underage person is considered a serious form of abuse.

When I told him I had seen how damaging it was to children, he refused to listen. His mother came to the rescue of her son and said, "In ancient Athens it was normal practice. It doesn't harm children, so let the young man be."

In the end I refused to facilitate his constellation. I could not and would not connect with his theme. I did not want to assist him or help him in any way legitimize child abuse. Furthermore, I was sure the representatives would not or could not have participated. If his theme had been something more akin to discovering what was behind his sexual preferences, I would have facilitated his constellation without hesitation.

After the weekend I spoke to the therapist who had referred this client and his mother to me. He was shocked and declared that he was unaware of the client's intentions. He told me, however, that during a constellation with the young man's mother, it surfaced that she had also been abused as a child. Was defending her son perhaps a subconscious way of excusing her own father by saying that child abuse was not bad? Was the reason this young man wanted to abuse children actually loyalty toward his grandfather?

The reader might have seen the movie *The Celebration* (1998) by the Danish filmmaker Thomas Vinterberg in which incest in a family comes to light after one of the victims commits suicide. Everyone excludes the father. However, the "shadow perpetrator," the mother, remained not implicated. The real hidden dynamic was left unchallenged. At the end of the movie, a question was still begging to be asked. Who was going to be the following perpetrator in the family? Which one of the young family members was going to have to be loyal to the excluded perpetrator and eventually become a perpetrator himself or herself?

The difficult issue of incest presents what seems to be a contradiction. It seems obvious that the father in the movie belonged behind bars and got what he was apparently due—being totally excluded. However, he remained a father. He brought his children into this world, and this had to be valued. Suddenly, everyone hated and totally ostracized him. This subconsciously created a serious conflict in everyone involved. It real life this gets passed on to children and grandchildren because a system does not tolerate exclusion. This is made heartrendingly plain time and time again in family constellations.

Peace within the family system only arises when the contribution of the shadow perpetrator is also taken into account and when it is made clear that the child gave in the place of the mother, who would not or was not able to give. Moreover the mother's disinclination to give is naturally born of loyalty too, since she is also entangled.

Where incest is present in constellations, people see destructive relationships that go on for generations. It's like an endless war between the sexes. The ancient taboo of sexuality with its sinful connotations results in pervasive guilt. People now know that the repressive attitudes about sexuality, which are meant as moral means to keep order, only end up ensuring more damage further down the line. From this taboo it follows that intimacy is heavily loaded, which often leads to struggle and suffering in relationships that might even involve violence and rape. This burden is present to some degree in all relationships. The high incidence of divorce speaks volumes in this regard.

As a representative in a number of constellations with this theme, I have felt how a family system's dynamic can imprison a person, how frustrated and powerless family members are in blindly trying to patch up the problems, and how the many efforts to restore balance and order over generations only lead to creating more disturbances in the family system time and time again.

The same applies to both sons and daughters in this respect. When a father ceases to give love to his wife, a son becomes his mother's charmer and gives what his father could not or did not want to give.

This abuse is equally as damaging to sons as it is for daughters.

112

However, it results in physical abuse less often—usually remaining on the emotional level. Society does not consider this a real problem, but it is known that many boys abused in this way end up becoming problematic machos. Deep down they come to despise women, which can lead to maltreatment or even rape.

For the therapist who tries to work with incest victims in a systemic manner, it is important to understand he or she should not lose himself or herself in judging the perpetrator. For a start the perpetrator is entangled. Secondly, a case of exclusion is created. The therapist has to give the perpetrator a place in his or her heart. On the other hand, the perpetrator should not be excused or deprived from his or her responsibilities. The perpetrator remains responsible for his or her actions and has to bear that. In constellations the perpetrator often has to give up his or her place or right to be a parent. This is something other than exclusion. In this respect it is important that legal and therapeutic deliberations remain independent of one another.

Another consideration in all this concerns the responsibility that therapists have when family secrets such as incest are made known during family constellations. These could have serious implications for the client and his or her family and friends—particularly in situations where the client knew nothing about the abuse or the abuse was so traumatic the memory was suppressed.

The constellation I did with Bea, twenty-six, clearly shows that even a victim's feelings about incest can become carried over by another family member. The identification can be so strong that the child experiences it as his or her own fate—just like all other feelings in which people can become entangled. In her constellation it becomes obvious that incest had occurred between her and her father. It must have been at a young age, or she totally repressed the memory because Bea has no recollection of it. I get her to give all her emotional load back and go through all necessary steps in the constellation, but in the end she did not feel relieved at all. She had no feeling of being freed, as is normally the case at the end of a constellation. I ask her to just let it all sink in for a while and to contact me in a few days for an individual session. Intuitively I told her to ask her mother if she knew of any incidence of incest in the family.

She called me as arranged and eagerly told me that when she had posed that question to her mother, her mother was at first unable to answer and then burst into tears. "At that moment," Bea said to me, "I knew she was a victim, and I felt her pain in all its sharpness. Then I felt released. I had my father back."

Murder and Manslaughter

The Tao doesn't take sides;
it gives birth to both good and evil.
The Master doesn't take sides;
she welcomes both saints and sinners.
—Lao-Tzu[17]

If a person in a family has committed murder, then he or she is bound to the victim through the heavy shift in the balance between giving and taking. This connection is stronger than family bonds, and the perpetrator is obliged to follow his or her new bond and leave the family. If he or she does not do that, a serious risk arises—that family members in following generations will have to share the fate of the perpetrator. They often do so by leaving the family in acts of penitence for the perpetrator. An example would be committing suicide. The perpetrator must voluntarily undergo the same fate as the victim by going to prison or some similar manner of taking distance from normal life in order to relieve future generations.

Hellinger says, "The perpetrator must leave his or her own family; he or she has to be with the dead victims. He or she has to lie beside his victims like someone who is deserving of death so that he or she can accept his death as penitence for the deeds he or she committed. This means that a living murderer acts as someone who squandered his or her right to belong to the living and to the family. He or she has to live as though he or she belongs in the sphere of the dead. Then he or she will find freedom."[18]

Naturally this does not mean that the state has the right to decide and impose the death sentence. What Hellinger describes is an inner movement that arises in the perpetrator when he or she understands and accepts the punishment. In most cases he or she requires adequate assistance and guidance.

People often see in constellations that perpetrators are afraid of the dead. They cannot look their victims in the eyes and are afraid the victims will recognize them as murderers. Only when the perpetrators acknowledge and confess the deeds to the victims can they bow down before them. The perpetrators then understand the connection with the deceased and realize there is no escape. They can lie down next to them and withdraw from life as if dead. The victims can rest in peace only when the murderers join them and are accepted by them. They can then return to the perpetrators and give them places in the community of the dead. People who are united by such a deed can find inner peace through a constellation.

Family members of the murderer have to allow the perpetrator to leave the family and accept an emotional distance. No remnants of the perpetrator can be left behind, and nothing can be inherited from him or her. Photographs and other mementos should be disposed of. If this is not the case, there is a tremendous risk that an innocent descendant will have to restore the balance in the systemic order and take on the guilt that belongs to the murderer, which might lead to becoming suicidal.

Leaving everything with the murderer and letting him or her go is not the same as excluding or making him or her an outcast. If the family does exclude the murderer, a dynamic arises whereby someone from the following generation will again have to represent the perpetrator in the family system by doing the same thing. Even though it might seem an extremely difficult task, it is important the family accepts and honors each and every member—even if he or she is a murderer. Only then will the heavy fate remain with the perpetrator.

Not only family members in a constellation with this theme are constellated. The victim has to be included as well. Through the position and reactions his or her representative assumes, it becomes clear how strong the bond between the perpetrator and the victim is. If the perpetrator does not or cannot bear his or her responsibilities, then one or more of his or her children will feel strongly connected to the victim. The child becomes drawn to the victim. As a substitute for the perpetrator, the child does what the perpetrator should have done.

Being drawn to the victim is expressed in the descendant's life as a strong but subconscious longing to be dead through suicide, illness, or addiction.

In a constellation with this theme, the representative of the perpetrator is usually asked to leave the room and wait behind closed doors. The reactions of the remaining representatives of family members then serve as a barometer. If the mood lifts, then it is better that the perpetrator leaves the family. In constellations one sees that the representative of the perpetrator usually feels better being outside the constellation.

The entangled family members say to the perpetrator, "I let you go. I leave your guilt with you, and I honor your fate." The perpetrator is thus set free, and he or she can develop a bond with the victim. This relieves the family of its compulsive duties in following generations or penance through suicide, illness, or the like.

Guilt in cases of manslaughter can be readily seen in a constellation. If there is real guilt, then the same applies, as with a case of murder—the perpetrator must leave the family. However, if only a feeling of guilt becomes evident in a constellation, then a letting go process is embarked upon. (Refer to the section on guilt further along in this chapter.)

During a workshop in the Belgian city of Leuven, I conducted a constellation for Rose, age fifty-six. She came to realize her theme by remembering her own family story about a fight with a fatal conclusion. Her grandfather was suspected of murder and was summarily excommunicated from the family. While talking to me, she suddenly realized that everyone in her family suffered from subconscious feelings of guilt. It was obvious she was ready for her own constellation.

In the initial interview, Rose explained that she struggled with feelings of guilt and had not allowed herself much happiness in her life. According to Rose herself, her life was "a bit of a disaster area." She said it with a smile, which is typically associated with someone burdened with a heavy fate. It was as if she was actually glad about the destructive nature of her life.

I confront the perpetrator (her *grandfather*) with his *victim*, and both are able to look each other in the eye. To the amazement of all present, the *victim* says, "I got pleasure out of it. He wasn't the first. It was a case of life or death, me or him, and he won." I asked the *victim* if he considered himself a victim or a perpetrator and if so did he think the *grandfather* was only acting in self-defense? The *victim* confirmed the latter and explained this to Rose, who was now in the constellation. He considers it inappropriate for Rose or any other family member to show contrition for the fatal incident. Rose is able to feel more at ease after this. It also becomes clear for her that her grandfather's sister witnessed the tragic fight, which left her traumatized. Many family members have carried that trauma and associated feelings of guilt. Rose also realizes how much she has subconsciously done to show atonement, which has repeatedly sabotaged her own happiness in life. Her smile is naturally directed toward her banished *grandfather* with the inner statement being, "I help bear your burden." Toward the victim she says, "I repent alongside you." She is happy with the destructive events in her life because it enabled her to express her love. With these insights, Rose feels as if she has just woken from a weird dream. She bows down deeply, gives the last remnants back, and releases her guilt.

A murder within the family weighs heavily on the family system. Unresolvable loyalty conflicts arise with serious consequences for following generations. They are expressed as insanity, psychosis, and other serious psychiatric disorders. These disorders almost always connected to family secrets that sometimes can't be confined to just one person. Consciously allowing a child to die through starvation, abuse, or disease or late-term abortion can constitute murder in the family system and cause inscrutable turmoil within the family.

One therapist in family constellations, Professor Franz Ruppert, assumes that psychotic and schizophrenic syndromes are the results of confusion in familial bonding systems at the level of the soul.[19] This confusion arises through events that cause hopeless moral dilemmas for the family conscience. These events include unexplained deaths, murder, suppressed or concealed incest, and concealed child ancestry. (Chapter seven revisits this topic.)

War

Wars have a strong influence on the family conscience when family members have been caught up in the war in one way or another. According to Ulsamer the influence of World War I and II were so strong on many European family systems with traumatized members that all other entanglements fade into insignificance.[20] It is then very important to be aware of the impact of war on any family member for a constellation and to figure out what happened—if possible.

Constellations allow people to see different dynamics for soldiers who have just completed missions compared to fanatical or high-ranking military personnel. Ordinary soldiers are usually connected to their dead comrades and are often broken down and traumatized by the atrocities they have witnessed. They find it difficult to resume normal lives.

I remember to this very day how I saw prisoners of war returning home when I was four. They were empty, inwardly desolate people. Often they repress their feelings, which alone leads to serious entanglements in following generations. Most soldiers who have participated in combat suffer to some degree from post-traumatic stress disorder (PTSD) and require urgent help. Although PTSD has been well documented (if not named) in war veterans since WWI, to this day sufferers are basically left to their own devices to cope with this insidious condition.

Under the title "Suicide Epidemic among Veterans," February 11, 2009, CBS News reported that in 2005 veterans were more than twice as likely to commit suicide than the general population. "Veterans committed suicide at the rate of between 18.7 to 20.8 per 100,000, compared to other Americans, who did so at the rate of 8.9 per 100,000."[21]

A good description of what war and PTSD do to people can be found in the book *Achilles in Vietnam, Combat Trauma and the Undoing of Character*.[22] Dr. Jonathan Shay examines the psychological devastation of war by comparing the soldiers of Homer's *Iliad* with Vietnam veterans suffering from PTSD.

An ordinary soldier who carries out his or her orders is not a murderer. He or she is part of a bigger movement beyond individual control and responsibility. Fanatical soldiers and sometimes military officials often take their missions too seriously. Those who assault civilians, recklessly put the lives of subordinates at risk, or torture and kill prisoners of war go too far. These actions make them guilty. If they do not take ownership of their guilt, following generations will be made to carry the burden.

Paul, forty-seven, has been feeling down for years and suffers from an all-encompassing and inexplicable feeling of guilt. In the discussion at the commencement of his constellation, he told me, "My father was in the *Sicherheitspolizei* [Flemish security police collaborating with the German National Socialist occupation] in World War Two. He was thus a collaborator, and after the war he spent time in prison. In my family nothing was ever mentioned about this. After being released from prison, he went on to have a family with two children. Actually there were two more children because the first died only a few weeks into life, and the second was miscarried. Then my sister and I came."

119

In the constellation his *father* stands facing away from the others, and *Paul* stands behind him. The conduct of the *father* immediately suggests a serious entanglement with perhaps a focus on death. Two representatives for victims are brought into the constellation. I ask them to lie down in front of the *father*. The *father* looks at them and says upon being prompted, "Yes. There were victims. That's just part of war." In answer to my question, one of the *victims* responds, "I feel unsettled. I am dead, but I didn't die in an ordinary way. It was unspeakable." The other *victim* says, "I was tortured to death by this man." He looks at the *father* and says, "He believed he had power over me, but I knew I had control over him. He gained pleasure from his dirty deeds." The *father* responds, "I feel a bit guilty." *Paul* says, "I feel extremely guilty."

The constellation is broadened to include the sibling who died after birth and the miscarried child. Two more representatives lie down beside the representatives of the victims. They also feel unsettled in death and feel strongly connected with the *victims* beside them. I ask them to look at the *father* and say, "We did it for you." Both agree this is a fitting remark. The *father* gets angry and says, "You shouldn't. I don't want you to do that." I ask him to look at the *victims* and say to them, "I killed you. That is my responsibility. I went too far." One of the *victims* replies, "The children don't belong here. He's the one who should be lying here. Him and nobody else."

Then I also ask *Paul* to lie down beside the victims. When he does this, he feels relieved, and then his *father* comments, "That really hurts. I don't want this." I then get *Paul* to look into the eyes of the *victims*. The *victims* say, "You don't belong here. You belong with the living." I allow a moment for this to sink in, and then I invite Paul himself to enter the constellation. He begins to sob and chokes back his tears. He takes a moment to compose himself. He feels strongly connected to the *victims*. I also get him to look into the eyes of each *victim* one at a time. The *victims* repeat the sentence, "You don't belong here. You belong with the living." Paul obviously needs time to let go of these dead people. Once this happens I get him to stand, face his *father*, and say, "I let you go with your victims. I leave all your guilt with you. I am but a child." His *father* nods and says, "That's right." At the end the *father* lies down next to the *victims* upon my request. The dead people are consequently relieved and are able to find peace. It is also clear this is where the father belongs. He has to leave his family to be with his victims. Paul takes his leave from the constellation feeling touched but relieved.

120

This constellation clarifies something about guilt to all participants—victims feel respected by the recognition of guilt. Reconciliation is not possible when victims stay feeling superior and remain entrenched in their victim roles. Peace can prevail only when they can say, "It's fine now. You belong with us again."

A quote from Hellinger fittingly concludes this section. During a seminar a participant asked him, "I understand it is very important to come to terms with one's past, but what if one feels ashamed of one's ancestors? My grandparents were German National Socialists. I feel shame whenever I think about them, so I avoid looking back at my roots." Hellinger replied, "Those who feel such shame are trying to avoid their common fate. That is not possible. That feeling of shame comes from an attitude of superiority. It is the same attitude the German National Socialists had in placing themselves above Jews and other social groups they considered inferior. This attitude binds us with the perpetrators rather than with the victims. Sadness and respect are the feelings that get us in touch with the victims; these feelings are quite the opposite of shame but the appropriate feelings in respect of the victims."[23]

Guilt

Various forms of guilt are exposed in family constellations. The most prevalent is usurped guilt whereby someone carries the guilt of a family member who, consciously or subconsciously, is guilty of something but does not feel the guilt. This might be someone proud of his or her wartime excesses and glorifies them as heroic acts. Or it might be someone who brags about sizable profits procured fraudulently. Maybe it's even a father who forbids his child to marry the love of his or her life because he deems that person unworthy. Situations such as these often lead to guilt and entanglement. Guilt arises when people transgress the systemic order and go against the social ethic. Naturally every little offense is not necessarily significant. Stealing a vegetable from a field in times of need is far removed from serious misconduct such as embezzling public money, firing employees en masse without good reason, or abusing responsibilities of a high-ranking public function for self-gain.

A perpetrator who does not believe he or she is guilty for whatever reason also does not accept the appropriate or necessary consequences. The collective conscience and the rational ethic (Nagy) will see to it that the following generations will deal with the unprocessed guilt.

Hannah, thirty-nine, constellates her family situation. She has three children. The middle child is emotionally fragile and does not want to grow up. Considering the child's small stature, this even finds expression in a physical way. In the constellation it appears that Hannah's daughter carries over guilt from her grandfather. Her grandfather has accumulated millions through embezzlement and fraud. His son, Hannah's husband, is proud of his father. During the constellation the *daughter* says, "I feel strongly connected to Granddad, but he makes me frightened. Really frightened! I don't want to live." The *grandfather* has to leave the room. *Hannah* and her *daughter* feel relieved and free. The *grandfather* is brought back into the constellation and questioned. He says, "I felt better outside. Suddenly I felt really guilty, and I don't want anyone else to help me bear this burden." Then I ask him to say the following to his *grandchild*, which he does. "The guilt belongs with me and in my life. You honor me by leaving it with me." Hannah's *daughter* felt tense when her *grandfather* reenters the room but feels better hearing him say this. I ask her to say to her *grandfather*, "I leave your guilt with you. It belongs in your life and is part of your fate. I am but your grandchild." After this was said, I ask her *grandfather* to turn away from the family. Hannah's *daughter* feels relieved and unburdened.

The effect of guilt on the family system becomes clear when remaining representatives are relieved and feel a load taken off their shoulders when one particular representative is sent out of the constellation. In the example just given, the grandfather suddenly felt his responsibilities and was prepared to accept them when he was removed from the constellation. Sometimes a family member has to leave the family, but this is only necessary in cases of serious guilt such as that associated with murder. (See the example in the previous subchapter, "War.") By being turned away, the grandfather's connection to his guilt is emphasized as well as the fact that it is purely his responsibility. This frees the child of the duty to carry the guilt for him.

Another form of guilt comes about through the idea that people can determine the course of things themselves. To illustrate this, take the accidental death of a child. Parents often feel guilty, even though they were powerless to prevent the death in any way. The inner reasoning is, "If only I had done this," or to the partner, "If only we had done that." This feeling of guilt and the blame and reproach between parents are avoidance strategies that attempt to prevent the real pain of loss being felt. This naturally leads to entanglement. This form of guilt becomes tangible when someone is innocently involved in a bad car accident. The following example comes from one of my workshops.

One of the participants was involved in a car accident years earlier. He had run over a woman and had felt guilty and responsible for her death ever since. He explained, "I was driving along a multilane road, and the traffic lights turned green just as I approached, so I was able to keep going. There was a truck waiting at the lights in the right lane, and suddenly a woman on a bike came out onto the crosswalk in front of me from in front of the truck. She had not seen me coming. I braked hard, but it was too late. I wondered why she hadn't seen me. She died instantly from her injuries. It was awful."

Representatives of the victim, her three children, and the driver (the seeker) were constellated. The *victim* says, "It was my fate to die in that way." The *driver* asks for forgiveness. The *victim* refuses and says, "There's nothing to forgive. It was my choice, and your guilt deprives me of my dignity." The *three children*, however, are still angry with the *driver*. Their mother, the *victim*, says to them, "It was my fate to die in that way. You honor me when you leave my fate with me." That is difficult for the *children*. Their anger is a defense against the deep pain of their loss, which becomes obvious later in the constellation. Once the *children* appreciate that the death of their mother was unavoidable, they are able to accept their mother's fate and feel more at ease. At the end of the constellation, the *victim* says to the *driver*, "It was my fate to die, so I affirm my responsibility." The *driver* answers, "I leave with you what you were responsible for, and I accept what I was responsible for. I honor your fate. Look kindly upon me if I might live a bit longer." With these resolution statements, everyone is able to loosen up, and the session concludes.

A variation of this usurped guilt is common among people who work in helping professions such as social services, the fire department, and the police department. Sometimes people in these professions are confronted with situations and events that are difficult to process. An example would be a social worker unsuccessful in talking a client out of suicide or a train driver powerless to stop the train from hitting and killing a person on the tracks. Firefighters arriving a minute too late to save a child from a burning house experience the same thing. Situations such as these can be deeply traumatizing and often lead to PTSD. In constellations people traumatized in similar ways commonly emerge. They feel they cannot lead happy lives because of their inner reasoning. They think if they had been quicker or had done better jobs, the tragedies could have been avoided. Guilt streams from this rationale, which is embedded with the erroneous notion that people can change or determine another person's fate.

A family constellation is the ideal instrument to work through feelings of underlying guilt and blame that arise through traumatic experiences. It clarifies the necessity for everyone to accept his or her own fate. Even those, such as the accident victim above, who die early can accept their own fates. In general they do not wish the professionals involved to incorporate problems of their clients into their own lives. Victims usually find professionals who think they have the power to prevent certain events presumptuous and lacking respect for their fates.

Sometimes survivors from catastrophes such as airplane crashes or earthquakes also feel guilty. A survivor reasons, "Why was I lucky enough while so many others had to perish?" So survivors do not allow themselves to lead full, happy lives. In various constellations with themes such as depression, despair, chronic fatigue, or unfounded feelings of guilt, participants often see the pernicious effects that survivors of fatal incidents and accidents and their descendants are subjected to.

Kim, twenty-two, feels guilty without knowing why and drags herself through life continually feeling depressed. In her constellation she is made explicitly aware of how strongly connected she is to her mother, who had lost two best friends in a car accident. Her mother was seriously injured in the crash but eventually survived. It was clear to her mother she had to feel guilty. The *dead friends* are first constellated and then questioned. They say it is OK for her to be alive and that her *mother* survived. They say she certainly is allowed to be happy, and her feelings of guilt are inappropriate. Kim hears them say this many times over and still cannot internalize it.

Since Kim is not convinced and remains so hesitant in her reactions, I get her to lie down and take the place of one of her mother's *dead friends*. She is then able to really understand how the victims feel about the way she disallows herself a happy and full life. As a representative of one of the victims, she is compelled to say, "I don't want this. It isn't right that Kim makes herself feel guilty." By experiencing the other side of the coin, it all becomes so apparent to Kim that she is able to let go, and she feels an enormous sense of relief. The *dead friends* feel freed and are very relieved.

Another obvious example concerns the well-known actor Kirk Douglas and what he had to overcome in his life. In an interview he once explained, "I wanted to fly from Fillmore to Los Angeles, but shortly after the takeoff, our helicopter crashed into a sport airplane that was landing. We dropped fifteen meters to the runway below. Two passengers died of burns in the fire fueled by leaked aviation fuel. One of them was only eighteen years of age. Since that day I feel guilty that I was allowed to remain alive."[24]

An inner urge that is expressed as an unhappy life or disease stems from this feeling of guilt. In extreme cases the guilt can force a person to lose the will to live. Whether people are aware of it or not, taking on another person's guilt or feeling guilty through experiencing a grave situation can only have a negative impact on the person carrying over the guilt. The person feeling guilty will not be able to adequately tap into his or her life force and will become weak. He or she is carrying something that does not belong to him or her. A person who carries the guilt of another or who feels guilty about another person's fate has little strength to help himself or herself or others. In all Christian religions, this disposition, however, is still glorified.

Hellinger comments on this. "A person who adheres to Christian ideals has to help lighten the guilt of others or at least he *thinks* he should be doing this. Worse still, he thinks he is able to do so! Those who *carry the cross* for someone else have no strength to be of any real help. A person who carries his or her own cross and faces up to his or her own guilt becomes stronger in himself. He or she carries it with his head held high and has the necessary strength to live his life in a positive way."[25]

The latter form of guilt is one's own real guilt. Accepting guilt caused by one's own doing and facing the consequences give strength to that person. With this attitude the person is able to do good things. If he or she does not do that, the power remains out of reach, and the person stays weak. He or she remains feeling guilty. The guilt feeling ceases only when his or her responsibilities are faced up to.

Forgiving

Through Hellinger's work and my own experience with constellations as a representative and facilitator, I have had to let go of an important so-called spiritual principle. I used to be convinced of the nobility of forgiving. Family constellations have allowed me to appreciate a deeper truth. The principle of forgiving I once considered so noble has fallen away. It appears in many cases to be disrespectful toward both victims and perpetrators.

That is why no one is ever asked to forgive or be forgiven in a family constellation. When a perpetrator asks his or her victim for forgiveness, the victim is once again being asked to do something for the perpetrator—on top of all the perpetrator has done to the victim. That is too much to ask. Apart from being the victim, this person is also being asked to carry the responsibility for the forgiveness. On top of that, it makes it harder for the perpetrator to come to terms with his or her guilt. Being forgiven deprives him or her of the necessity to look at the guilt and responsibility. Moreover, the person forgiving is automatically in a superior position compared to the person being forgiven, which seriously upsets the balance of give and take. Hellinger uses an aphorism for this. "Whatever I forgive others for goes into my own emotional backpack."

The resolution statement for the perpetrator toward the victim is, "I am sorry." The difference between this and "Please accept my apology" or "Forgive me please" is obvious. The person who is asked to be pardoned or forgiven has to do something, which the soul takes on in a very different way. The statement "I am sorry" is recognition that someone has done something for which he or she is sorry. This regret makes a connection possible. The other is then seen as the rightful victim. This recognition is necessary for reconciliation.[26]

Losing One's Place in the Family

Although it rarely happens in constellations, sometimes family members lose their rights to belong and have to leave their families. As mentioned earlier this happens in cases of serious misdemeanors such as murder cases, death threats, and exclusion. This is enacted symbolically in a constellation by sending the perpetrator's representative out and closing the door behind him or her. It's a sure sign the perpetrator has squandered his or her right to belong to the family if the other representatives feel more at ease once this happens. This has to be looked at on a case-by-case basis. If it is obvious a family member has lost his or her right to belong, the family has to let that person go. The perpetrator then has a stronger connection to the victim than his or her family. There is a great risk that the family conscience will ensure some innocent descendant will have to carry over the guilt and atone in some way if the family does not let the perpetrator go. As the constellation develops, the perpetrator is asked to lie down next to the victim(s). This can be difficult for a perpetrator, but the relationship and connection with the victim is clear. Family members can then more easily leave him or her with the victim and turn away. I mostly use the former method, but sometimes when the guilt is not so heavy, it suffices to let the perpetrator connect with his or her victim while the family members symbolically turn their backs.

This theme was central to a constellation I participated in some time ago in Germany. I was chosen as a representative of the great-grandfather of the seeker, who had killed civilians as a soldier. I felt a strong bond with my victims, and it felt better to turn away from my family. I wanted my family members to move on positively in life and leave the guilt squarely with me.

Another case where someone has to turn away occurs with exclusion. A family member who excludes or denies another person or family member legitimate access to the family has also squandered his or her right to belong. In a particular constellation, it was revealed that a grandfather forbade his four daughters to marry. Even so, one of them did end up getting married but was forced to leave the country to be able to accomplish this. Her daughter was the seeker. In her constellation it was revealed she was strongly connected to her three aunts. She was afraid of her grandfather. Only when he stood at a distance and turned his back on the constellation did the daughter feel relieved.

Family Secrets

In many families there are things nobody wants or is allowed to mention. This is sometimes due to something conveniently being forgotten. Although, more often it is due to family members being anxious to keep the matter hidden. Such secrets regularly show up in constellations. The facilitator has to be alert and only set about uncovering family secrets that contribute to reaching a resolution. Interrogation, investigation, and incrimination can cause more damage than good. The purpose of a constellation is to resolve entanglements—not to expose truths behind family secrets. It is also important to respect that ancestors had their reasons for keeping secrets. A troublesome issue could be left to rest and be forgotten about for the good of the family.

> *I think it's sensible to hypothesize the good intention of ancestors. Obviously they didn't know anything about loyalties and entanglements.*

In most constellations all that is required to resolve entanglements is to honor ancestors, leave the secret, together with the emotional load, with them, and accept it as part of their fates. People are usually motivated by curiosity, pedantry, or sanctimony when endeavoring to uncover family secrets and, therefore, arrogantly place themselves above their ancestors, which can cause yet more entanglements. However, if it is necessary to find a good solution for the seeker, the secret will come to light. The following is an example.

Mary, twenty-seven, suffers from an inferiority complex. Two years of intense psychotherapy have made little difference. In the course of her constellation, the representatives of her uncle, mother, and grandmother are standing next to each other in chronological order. Her *mother* is the eldest child. Both her *mother* and *uncle* feel uncomfortable in their respective places. They respond negatively when I ask them if they are in their proper positions. When I ask them what is amiss, Mary's *mother* answers, "Something isn't right here." Then I say, "We are going to do a little experiment." Following my intuition I add another representative into the constellation. Following on from a hunch, I say to him, "You are a forgotten or concealed child. Feel what it is like." Mary's *grandmother* reacts immediately by looking away anxiously and says, "Nobody is supposed to know that." Mary's *mother* and Mary's *uncle* feel better right away, and Mary feels a deep bond with the *concealed child*. Further into the constellation, it emerges that the child was either aborted or given away. Mary's *grandmother* has been extremely ashamed about this, has felt guilty, and has never wanted to talk about it. The constellation reveals that Mary carried over this guilt, which forms the basis of her inferiority complex. After the constellation she feels emancipated and relieved.

To be respectful after a constellation such as this, people have to resist the temptation to indulge in further investigation because that can only lead to speculation.

Discovering family secrets in family constellations can be very heavy if the family secret concerns the murder of a family member such as a child or partner. Serious family secrets have enormous repercussions on the systems, and family members in following generations can be so heavily burdened that they become psychologically scarred or even develop psychiatric disorders that require institutionalization. This has been partly covered in this chapter and will be further discussed in the paragraph about mental illness in chapter seven.

Reaching Out Interrupted

Every baby has the longing to be held and cherished. A baby has an innate expectation for love and affection. Hellinger refers to this as *Hinbewegung* in German, which translates as *reaching-out movement*.[27] The baby's pull toward the mother is like a gravitational force.

In the baby and toddler stages, children are most focused on their mothers. Through pregnancy and birth, children develop symbiotic relationships with their mothers. Breast-feeding and other things reinforce this. The chance for the reaching-out movement with the mother being disrupted is high because this relationship is so intense. A baby–father relationship is less intense, so the chance of a disturbed reaching-out movement with the father is low. It can occur, however, through events such as the father dying in the first years of a child's life. Most studies show that the reaching-out movement is most commonly disrupted if the mother dies during or shortly after birth, when the baby is placed in an incubator directly after birth, or if the baby has extended periods of hospitalization in the first three years of life without the mother being in contact regularly with the child.

It is only natural that being apart from the mother (a baby's only known source of survival and love) for more than one day is disastrous for an infant. The feelings of angst, pain, and despair that well up in the baby are overwhelming. This despair turns into anger, and the child closes off. He or she formulates an inner statement such as, "Mommy doesn't want me. Hoping for love and attention is meaningless." From that moment on, the child hides behind a thick wall. Once the mother gets her baby from the hospital, the child is closed off and out of reach of the mother's showering love. As an adult this person will sooner or later be confronted with this inner wall when it comes to giving and accepting love from a partner. The memory of the pain and despair rises up from the subconscious. In his or her adult years, this person stops his or her loving movement toward the partner just as he or she did as an infant toward the mother. Instead of allowing real contact, there is a circular movement around the partner. This person orbits the partner instead of permitting closeness and intimacy. This person is unlikely to develop successful relationships.

> *"This is an exact description of neurosis. Neurosis begins at*
> *a point that a reaching-out movement toward someone,*
> *usually the mother, is interrupted and neurotic behavior is*
> *simply a repetition of this circular movement."*
> —Bert Hellinger[28]

What strikes me here is that a lot more people than I thought, including those Hellinger has written about and presented in videos, have had their reaching-out movements to people (mostly to their mothers) interrupted. It is also clear that the movement toward the mother is primarily interrupted or interfered with when the baby is unable to be with his or her mother directly after birth. This sometimes happens in hospital deliveries. For mother and baby to bond successfully, contact with the mother in the moment directly after birth is crucial. This precious moment is too often unwittingly forsaken through inflexible hospital routines, whereby the baby is checked and cleaned before being returned to the mother's arms. Heavy sedation of the mother can have a similar effect. More serious implications result from a baby being isolated in an incubator directly after a complicated delivery.

Completion of the Interrupted Reaching Out

An interrupted reaching-out movement can be recognized when a child returns home from an extended hospital stay a very different person and shows signs of being closed off. The child might not like to be cuddled anymore or initiate physical contact with his or her parents. According to Irena Precop's *festhalt* (hold on) therapy, small children can be healed if their mothers hold the children tightly and lovingly in their arms until the pain from when the moment the reaching-out movements were interrupted is felt again. This requires strength and perseverance from mothers because the obstinacy and anger that come about with the separations have to be relived until the pain, sadness, and feelings of helplessness rise up again. Once this is reexperienced, the children can relax and accept their mothers. Precop's *festhalt* therapy and her collaboration with Hellinger are extensively discussed in the book *Wenn Ihr Wüsstet Wie Ich Euch Liebe*.[29]

The process is exactly the same with adults undergoing therapy, except the facilitator replaces the mother. He or she has to wait until the client is ready and can empathize with the parent. Both are returning back to the moment when the interruption took place. All the feelings from that experience have to be relived. To do this Hellinger has his client sit on a chair, and he lays one hand on the client's neck. He asks the client to breathe deeply with his or her mouth wide open and then to yell out to his or her mother until all the feelings have been re-experienced.

I use rebirthing-breath work techniques for this. Rebirthing is a breathing technique that helps people make deep contact with repressed feelings and is, therefore, a great help to complete the reaching-out movement.[30]

Here follows a poem by Bert Hellinger.[31] You may use it as a mediation or prayer. Speak loudly enough so you can hear yourself. Open up to what it does to you.

Thanksgiving at the Dawn of Life

Dear Mommy/Mother
I take everything that comes from you,
all of it, with its full consequences.
I take it at the full price it cost you
and that it costs me.
I will make something good out of it in memory of you—
to thank and honor you.
What you did must not have been in vain.
I hold it close and in my heart,
and if I am permitted, I will pass it on
—as you have done.
I take you as my mother,
and you have me as your child (son/daughter).
You are my only mother, and I am your child.
You are big, and I am little.
You give, I take, dear Mama.
I am glad that you chose Daddy as your husband.
You both are the right parents for me.

Dear Daddy/Father
I take everything that comes from you,
all of it, with all the consequences.
I accept it at the full price it has cost you
and that it costs me.
I will make something good out of it in memory of you—
to thank and honor you.
What you did must not have been in vain.
I hold it close and in my heart,
and if I am permitted, I will pass it on
—as you have done.
I take you as my father,
and you may have me as your child (son/daughter).
You are my only father, and I am your child.
You are big, and I am little.
You give, I take, dear Daddy.
I am glad you took Mama as your wife.
You both are the right parents for me.

5
Family Constellations and Relationships

All things have their backs to the female
and stand facing the male.
When male and female combine,
all things achieve harmony.
—Lao-Tzu[1]

This chapter will look at how family constellations can help people bring back harmony into relationships and what partners can do in the long term to allow their relationships to bloom. By looking at subconscious loyalties to ancestors, it will become clear how much influence families have on the quality of relationships. Partners are always each other's mirrors in relationships, and a good balance of give and take between partners is important. This chapter will next look at the roles subconscious faith and religion play in relationships, ways in which abortion can be processed, and tools people can use to deal with adoption successfully.

A family constellation is a very good therapeutic instrument that can give clarity to relationships. It can help get love flowing again because it exposes the underlying structure of difficult relationships, making it possible to seek and find meaningful solutions to the effects of discordant entanglements.

It is also a way to improve relationships without having to engage in endless sessions with a therapist. The partner does not have to be present and indeed does not even have to be aware of the constellation. In this case the representatives look at the seeker's part in the relationship and try to find appropriate solutions for that person. Sound ethics forbid looking into the family system of the absent partner, but that is not a problem. If one partner goes through a process of change, the other partner is forced to reorient and adapt if that person wishes to remain together. From experience it is clear the efforts of one partner in addressing relationship problems impact the other. In this way they are like two cogs that fit neatly into each other. If both partners are present in a constellation, one of the partners begins by constellating the representatives. Once the representatives have "perceived" their spots, the other partner is given the chance to change the constellation until it feels right for him or her. Questioning of the representatives by the facilitator gives a clearer picture of the different versions of the relationship. The usual constellation process is followed until all entanglements are made obvious and good solutions are found. At the end of the constellation, one partner and then the other replaces his or her representative in the constellation.

A couple with relationship problems cannot expect that going to a therapist will fix their relationship like taking a faulty car to the garage. They have to be prepared to go through an awareness process. Expecting a therapist to act as a referee in relationship problems is a sign that a person is not willing to work on himself or herself. This is an attempt to get the therapist to side with him or her, to confirm his or her account of being an innocent victim, or to seek the therapist's support in helping the other partner see the error of his or her ways.[2] The therapist might also be used for his or her sympathetic nature and as a sounding board for the client's complaints. A relationship cannot be healed in this way. A therapist that allows himself or herself to be used in this manner is still entangled in his or her own system. That therapist is biased and not really able to find the necessary solutions to help others rejuvenate their relationships.

Anyone who wants to improve a relationship or be "healed" has to be prepared to look at himself or herself and come to terms with his or her entanglements. That person will discover something remarkable then. In general there is no guilt or guilty party; there are only entanglements that complicate or destroy a relationship between two people.

After years of experience with constellations (in which relationships nearly always play roles), I can say with certainty that relationships do not fail due to the reason both partners assume. That is merely the surface of the problem. Relationships are prey to subconscious loyalties and strong bonds with parents or grandparents with heavy fates. The load placed on partners means they are not fully present for each other or their children. On innumerable occasions I have heard representatives say and feel this in constellations. When the entanglement is resolved, partners look at each other as if they are seeing each other for the first time. They also literally say this. "For the first time, I see you for who you really are."

A relationship constellation helps two people look more deeply and fundamentally at their bond than is afforded by the usual superficial assessments and the blame game. Problems and solutions become explicable as a result of both partners recognizing how they are entangled in difficulties carried over from their families. Both are touched on the soul level. They are healed from something they lived out in their relationship—something that was subconsciously carried over from the collective or personal conscience. By seeing, feeling, and processing these entanglements, both partners go through a deep personal learning process that gives them the strength to rejuvenate their relationship with newfound love.

This also applies when only one partner constellates the relationship. The impact is obviously greater for the seeker, but people often see the positive influence extends to the absent partner as well. If divorce is inevitable, constellations can help partners to move apart in a mature way and be open to new experiences.

Having seen and experienced the underlying structure of truth in countless constellations where tensions were resolved and love flowed again, a number of basic rules for loving relationships have emerged. The following set of basic rules reflects the truth at this point in time and mirrors present social values and beliefs. This could be different in other circumstances and with another set of social values.

Men and Women Are Complementary

Men and women complement each other like yin and yang. There is a natural mutual attraction. A man seeks out a woman because she represents what he lacks and vice versa. In this way the genders are alike and equal.

For a relationship between a man and a woman to succeed, the man has to remain a man, and the woman has to remain a woman. If this is not the case, if one partner makes childish demands or plays the victim, the other has to take on the role of a parent or culprit, which impacts the relationship in a major way.

There is naturally much more room for interpretation in relationships between homosexuals, but basic problematic patterns of relating are also found in same-sex couples.

Hellinger declares that a relationship is the fulfillment of life.[3] A major aim of development from childhood to adulthood via puberty is learning to have successful relationships with others. The primary goal of a relationship is to procreate and add another generation to the family by becoming mother and father. Our growth occurs in steps in which we cross threshold after threshold and leave the old behind. There is no turning back. A child cannot go back to the mother's breast, an adolescent cannot return to childhood, and parents cannot return to youth.

Bonds Remain

Connectedness or bonding occurs when a man and a woman have sex, give love to each other, and accept love from one another. This is the deepest emotion people can share with each other, and it creates an enduring bond between two souls. From then on they are no longer free from each other. It is sexuality that brings about this bond—not marriage. This bond is also present through incest and rape. Sexuality is often judged negatively in many societies and religions. However, sex is the expression of our main life force and in combination with love becomes even more powerful—especially when partners are open and honest with each other.

Family constellations allow people to see that every sexual act creates a bond between partners that becomes strengthened through mutual love. If a child results from this union, then the bond is strengthened via the child, and it is no longer dissolvable. People can try all they like to reject their parents, but they will always remain their parents. People can leave their children, but those children remain demonstrably theirs.

Most people are not aware of the power of sexual bonding. People often see in constellations how this powerful bond can exert its influence and shape lives across generations. Sexual bonds, however, cannot be equated with love. Love in later relationships can very well be greater than earlier ones. Bonds in short and superficial relationships are considerably weaker. However, with one's first sexual partner a strong connection remains forever.

There is no need to fear sexual bonding because it is a natural part of life such as breathing and eating. The purpose here is not to preach a new morality. Far from it. It is more a plea for mutual respect and awareness.

All Previous Partners Must Be Honored

A person who has had multiple sexual relationships (bonds) has the chance to develop a deep, happy, and long-lasting relationship if he or she honors all previous sexual partners and feels respect, gratitude, and love for them. Then the previous relationship(s) has/have ended in peace.

Many people find this difficult to integrate into their lives. Almost as if it was a cultural duty, both partners are expected to demean previous partners or better still hate and exclude them. Respect, gratitude, and love can make people fearful at times, as if a former partner is automatically a threat to a current relationship. Sometimes this is the case, and there are people who have affairs with former partners. However, this again is a disturbance and has nothing to do with honoring and respecting a former partner.

In a constellation with this theme, the seeker's representative says to his previous partners, "I honor and thank you. This [pointing to the current partner] is my new partner. Look kindly upon us as we embark on a happy life together." When representatives of former partners nod unanimously in agreement, they do this because they really feel honored. This means that deep within his or her heart, the seeker has worked through his or her own responsibilities and entanglements that caused the relationships to end, and he or she honors and respects bonds with previous partners.

It emerges from many constellations that relationships that do not end peacefully continue to have negative influences on one or both partners. To conclude a relationship in peace does not mean a person simply gets over resentment, pain, and anger with ease. It means rather that the people involved have respect for one another, can speak courteously with each other, and look each other in the eye. Where children are involved, it means they are able to make the necessary arrangements in a respectful and fair manner.

If a former partner is not honored, then that will find expression in the new relationship—usually through the new partner feeling unsafe. Subconsciously he or she feels he or she could easily be the next casualty of the same unprocessed predicament.

Ellen, age fifty-three, struggles with a relationship problem, and in her constellation the tensions are palpable. After a short while, the representative of her former partner is brought into the constellation. When I question him, it is obvious a conflict from their former relationship remains unprocessed. I ask him to repeat the following to *Ellen*, "I carry the responsibility for my share. I leave the responsibility for your share of the conflict with you. I honor you for the love and the beauty we shared. I now let you go." Then *Ellen* is asked to say the same to her *former partner*. Both representatives visibly relax and begin to smile. Then *Ellen* focuses on her *current partner,* who has also become less tense. She says to him, "I take full responsibility for whatever there is between my ex and me. You honor me when you leave it with me." The *current partner* is happy to hear this. They look lovingly at each other. Ellen herself steps into the constellation and goes through the last steps, including expressing resolving statements. Afterward she indicates a load has been lifted from her shoulders.

At the end of the constellation for Rita, age forty-one, three representatives make up the new image: her first boyfriend, her first husband, and her current partner. I ask the *current partner* to say to her first *boyfriend*, "You were the first partner of my wife. I honor you and thank you for making room for me." Then to the *first husband* he says, "You were the second partner and the first husband of my wife. I honor you and thank you also for making room." The *former partners* relax. Next I get the *current partner* to bow down before the representatives of the former partners and say, "Look upon me kindly in our quest for happiness together." The *first boyfriend* and *first husband* smile and nod in acquiescence. They say, "We wish you both much happiness." Both *Rita* and her *current partner* feel uplifted and experience the positive, loving wishes the previous partners have sent their way.

Doubts and scorn over the new partner of an ex can indicate that the relationship with the ex has not been processed or honored. Sometimes these doubts and scorn show that people still believe they are the better match. Maybe people do not want to admit that the new partners are better matches for the exes, even though this might be obvious. In any case the new partner is an important part of an ex-partner's next stage in life and that of the children (if any). Being defensive or judgmental about an ex's new partner makes it obvious the person cannot or will not be accepting. Therefore, that person remains bound and constrained in his or her own life and in any future relationships.

The level of freedom and happiness in future relationships is dependent on the degree to which people can accept and wholeheartedly grant ex-partners long and happy relationships with others.

Children often take on unprocessed conflicts from their parents' previous relationships. They manifest these unprocessed conflicts in their parents' current relationships. This applies to all intense unprocessed relationships of parents. (The underlying dynamic will be addressed in chapter six.)

Relationships and Abortion

What has been written above regarding respect of former partners applies even more strongly to relationships in which children were conceived. The bond between partners is intensified through children, whether those children are alive or not (i.e., lost through miscarriage or abortion).

An abortion almost always serves to end a relationship. If a couple wants to continue their relationship, it is important that an aborted child is specially honored by both parents and finds a place in each heart. This significantly helps the chances of the relationship surviving and prospering. In my practice I often come across people who think they have worked through abortions, but actually they have merely pushed them to the side. A person says, "I closed that chapter of my life years ago." My automatic response is, "What happens if you look back into that chapter?" An abortion is not fully worked through if a grieving process has not taken place.

Julie, age thirty-four, constellates her current relationship. All representatives feel absent, and there is tangible tension. The moment an aborted child enters the constellation, a number of representatives show obvious signs of relief. *Julie* feels a deep pain and is barely able to look at the *aborted child*. The former partner (the *father of the child*) turns away and wants to leave. They are relieved (experience that love flow again) only when they both recognize the *aborted child* as their common child and give *him or her* a place in their hearts. *Julie* says, "You are my child. I am your mother. I have asked a lot from you. That is my responsibility. I take you now and for always in my heart as my child." I ask the *former partner* to say the same. They both feel deep pain and sadness and say to each other, "We bear this together."

In a constellation with abortion as the theme, representatives often see that partners remain connected even though the relationship has ended, which is usually the case with abortions. This can create difficulties for both people in building new long-term relationships. The difficulties disappear when both have felt the issue through, accepted it, let go of it, and understood what they have actually asked of the child.

Another dynamic that surfaces in constellations concerns women who harbor subconscious, deep longings to atone for abortions. Some women do not allow themselves to have successful relationships, and in some extreme cases, there is a chance of them developing uterine or ovarian cancers. In all constellations around this theme, it is clear the aborted child is at one with his or her fate when that child is seen and honored and lives on in the hearts of the parents. Both parents go through a learning process, and positive strength comes into being.

Apart from cases of medical emergency, this is not the case with late abortions. According to evidence from constellations, late abortions (around the fifth month of pregnancy or later) are equated with murders by the family consciences and have destructive effects on families for generations. This can also lead to psychosis. (See the constellation of Harry in chapter seven.)

> *I want to stress that constellation work is free of judgment and does not take a moral standpoint concerning abortion or any other issue for that matter. It is an instrument that enables the seeker to look at all aspects of an issue and process entanglements in a deep and thorough way. In constellations all over the world, it surfaces that abortion within three months of conception is not murder—contrary to many religious or moral belief systems.*

140

Balance of Giving and Taking in Relationships

In the contextual approach, just as in constellation work, a good balance between giving and taking is seen as the basis for a well-functioning relationship. "Ensuring relational balance is the key to keeping viable close relationships and is the cornerstone of the contextual approach. Contextual therapists work from the conviction that all family members benefit from reliable relationships that result from, firstly, giving due credit; secondly, reacting responsibly; and, thirdly, ensuring equal share of both relationship benefits and burdens."[4]

Therefore, people have to give their partners suitable recognition and allow them sufficient room to be able to receive recognition. People have the same responsibilities as their partners for the quality of the relationships and have to take equal responsibility for relationship problems. By mutual agreement all burdens and obligations that are part of relationships have to be shared.

A relationship is certainly not a static affair but rather a dynamic mutual engagement that succeeds through the continual maintenance of balance between giving and taking—united in love.

Take the following example from Hellinger. A man gives a woman something because he loves her. At the point of giving, he assumes a superior position because he is the giver and the woman is the receiver. She feels obligated because she has received. She tries to reestablish balance by giving him something in return. Because she loves him, she gives in return a little more. Now the man is in the position of obligation. He tries to find balance once more by giving to his partner (a little more again) because he loves her. In this manner a broader sharing is achieved because of the need for balance combined with love. This major exchange of giving and taking binds the couple more strongly together. Their happiness grows. This beneficial exchange is the bedrock of a good relationship.

There are, of course, relationships in which one partner causes the other pain. In these cases the partner who has been hurt feels the need to reestablish balance as well. He or she wants revenge. This partner responds by causing the other harm as well, and because this partner is convinced of his or her own virtue, he or she inflicts a little more pain. This creates the same intense exchange as described above—but now with pain. This binds the couple negatively.

Hellinger comments, "There is a simple rule to be able to step out of this vicious circle. Just like balancing whereby one partner, out of love, gives the other a little more in return, in a painful or negative balancing, people can give their partner a little less pain in return. This marks the start of a positive exchange."[5]

Other Disturbances of Balance

Every disruption to the balance of give and take nibbles away at the strength and depth of love in a relationship, which undermines the very nature of having a remarkable and exciting connection to another person. The major difference between a friendship and having a relationship is the deep bond that both partners are willing to allow. This manifests itself in intimacy and sexuality. The recognition and respect of the deeper meaning of sexual bonding are required from both partners. If one has a desire for intimacy and sexuality and the other just allows it to happen without the same longing, then the balance of give and take between them is upset. The partner who allows intimacy and sexual contact takes on a superior position because he or she only receives and does not desire. The partner who desires assumes a subordinate position because the expression of his or her longing renders him or her vulnerable. This shift of balance disrupts the love between them.

When both are willing to make a success of their relationship, they have to equally desire giving and receiving. Both have to be sure their desires are mutually respected and accepted as expressions of love. This equality in a relationship, expressed most deeply in the sexual act, carries on into other domains of life and forms the basis of a healthy and lasting relationship.

Consequently the balance in a relationship is disrupted when one of the partners cannot or does not want to be sexual with the other or if one has a negative feeling about sex and cannot allow his or her own lust and desires. A religious or moral stance that regards sex in a negative way or simply rejects it is also very disruptive. The partner taking the moral high ground becomes more superior—the *goody*. The one with natural sexual desires becomes the inferior partner—the *baddie*. The baddie is forced to leave or gets caught up in victim behavior, which can happen in a number of ways. This includes withdrawing in an inner way by escaping into alcohol, having affairs, or seeking comfort with prostitutes. This only shoves the problem to the side. When both take on their own responsibilities for an open and fulfilling sexual union, they lay the foundation for a beautiful long-term relationship.

The balance in a relationship can be disturbed in any one of the following ways:

When partners are too demanding
Love can really flow only if the partnership remains voluntary. Behind a demanding attitude, a heavy case of parentification or an attachment disorder is usually found. That means one or both parents have relied emotionally on that person as a child or there is an indication of disruption in the reaching-out movement. (See "Reaching Out Interrupted" in chapter four.)

A problematic relationship with parents or an attachment disorder is a source of many unfulfilled desires and needs in childhood, which can later on be projected onto future partners who cannot possibly set right these unsatisfied needs from childhood. The overly demanding partner risks driving away his or her partner by repeating unprocessed childhood drama.

Jealousy is a good example. A jealous husband has a subconscious fear that his wife will have an affair or leave him. Through this separation anxiety, he exercises control over his partner. His wife experiences this as a lack of trust because her partner remains ostensibly suspicious. If she eventually does what is suspected and actually subconsciously expected, the demanding (jealous) husband has his fears confirmed and plays out a dramatic victim role. He thereby repeats an unprocessed experience from his childhood—often being left alone by his mother. A childlike, demanding attitude actually underscores such *romantic* sentiments such as, "I can't live without you" or, "Stay with me forever." This demanding attitude only burdens love in a relationship.

With inner child meditation, anyone can discover and gradually fulfill needs from childhood by working with his or her inner child. More information is to be found on my website, the Systemic View.[6]

Demanding sacrifices

A relationship becomes dysfunctional when one partner demands the other give up his or her job, friends, or social life. Accordingly dysfunction is indicated when one partner goes about sabotaging these aspects of life by constant ridicule and derision. Giving up friends or a job because a partner demands it is going too far. Relationships such as this often end up dormant.

Playing the social worker

When one partner plays the helping hand role and happily gives far more than he or she receives, this partner ensures imbalance in the relationship. The partner who receives without the chance to give back will feel increasingly guilty until he or she finally wants to end the relationship.

Playing the victim

The balance is also upset when one of the partners plays the victim role and feels responsible for everything. The other partner will be made to feel bad, and sooner or later he or she will want to leave the relationship. A sentiment can camouflage victim behavior. This includes, "I was always too good and too nice."

Being overly responsible

One partner having an excessive feeling of responsibility can also disrupt a relationship. This is recognized through reasoning such as, "My partner would be happier if I could give more love." Behind this rationale is the idea that a person can exercise control over another's feelings by his or her demeanor. The person who thinks he or she has the power will become superior and make the other subordinate.

Through idealism

Another disruption happens when one of the partners fosters excessive ideals. This compels the person to strive to meet these ideals, which could include never being late and always being careful not to say or do the wrong thing. Of course, this behavior can only make the other partner feel inadequate.

Wanting to have children or not

When one partner comes to the relationship with children and does not want to have more and the other partner does not have children but would still like to have some of his or her own, the balance is upset. A relationship can only work if the partner with children specially honors

144

the partner who gives up his or her wish for children. A partner with children can never demand that the other partner remain childless. Furthermore, a relationship cannot be successful if one partner does not want children while the other strongly desires them.

Financial imbalance

A relationship can be harmed when one partner pays for a qualification or training program for his or her partner or allows the other to take time to study for a qualification or follow a training program. This disrupts the balance because the partner being offered money or time to gain qualifications feels guilty due to the extent to which he or she has received. The relationship might well break up once the qualifications have been attained. Giving time and/or money for gaining qualifications is the responsibility of parents. If one partner gives the other the opportunity to gain qualifications, the continuation of the relationship is only possible when the giver is specially honored in a fully conscious manner. The couple can then find a way to compensate together to restore balance.

The same applies when one partner gives too many or excessively expensive gifts while the other partner is unable to give sufficiently to restore relationship equilibrium.

Everyone Has His or Her Own Fate to Bear

Clichés abound regarding relationships. This includes the strong man who takes care of the weak, helpless woman or the caring woman who gets involved with an alcoholic or a criminal. Both do this out of love and from an inner longing to help and rescue. The helper/rescuer takes on a superior position through the stance taken, and the partner becomes weaker and inferior. This is a serious disruption to the balance of giving and taking.

Lisa, twenty-eight, constellates her relationship with representatives for her husband and herself. Initially they are facing away from each other. *Lisa* feels dejected, and her *husband* feels the need to keep a distance. He says, "It's all too heavy for me." As the constellation progresses, it becomes apparent that *Lisa* carries a heavy burden from her family. The *husband* says, "I leave all your heavy stuff with you." She replies, "I carry my own fate. I take responsibility for my own heavy load. I can handle it. You honor me by leaving it all with me." Her *husband* is visibly relieved on hearing this, and he brightens. He says to his wife, "I honor you. I respect your strength and your fate." Both are able to move closer to each other and look each other in the eye.

In her next constellation, Lisa constellates her family of origin. Now it is apparent she has been carrying unprocessed pain that has flowed from the premature death of her grandmother. Once she works through this, she is fully able to be with her husband and children with all her strength.

Many couples split up because the people subconsciously carry unprocessed burdens and emotional damage from their ancestors. It could be any number of unworked issues such as a grandfather's war trauma, feelings of oppression, a bad relationship with the mother, or a little brother who died prematurely.

Addiction and the emotional mess that lies behind it are also things that are taken on and can interfere in relationships. All these burdens spoil relationships with loved ones without people realizing or wanting it to happen. People will continue to follow their family consciences until they are awakened to the underlying dynamic. Everyone has to carry his or her own fate—no matter how heavy it is. According to what constellations reveal, this is the only respectful stance toward everybody involved.

You Marry the Family of Your Partner as Well

*So you thought, just like I once did, that your partner was the
only other person in your relationship? —No way!*
—Indra

When two people bond deeply and begin a relationship, two family
systems come together. The primary loyalty of each partner is toward
his or her own family system. This is an effect of the conscience. The
burdens and damage people carry from their families are the biggest
causes of relationship problems. It is not possible to work through these
as long as these loyalties remain in the subconscious realm. They interfere in relationships. People inevitably follow, subconsciously, the
pressures from their family consciences. People are unable to prevent
the burdens and damage from the past popping up time and time again
in one relationship after the other.

Gaby, thirty-nine, ended a ten-year relationship with a man because he
kept looking at other women. Her next relationship ended after two
years when her partner had an affair, and in the relationship after that,
her partner got another woman pregnant after eighteen months. In her
constellation it is clear that both her mother and grandmother (and
probably women further back in the family) had strong distrusts of
men. Out of love and loyalty, Gaby subconsciously carried over this
distrust.

Mark, thirty-six, had never had a long-term relationship. He recently
met a woman and realized he had a problem opening up to her. In his
constellation it is revealed his grandmother died giving birth to his
mother. Through his mother's trauma, he has carried over a fear that a
partner would or could die. Out of fear of this happening again, he does
not dare get close to a woman.

It is revealed again and again in constellations that people can only
begin to process carried-over burdens once they become aware of
them, leave things where they belong, and honor their ancestors.

The direct bonds people have with their parents are especially important. However, the special bonds a son has with his mother and a
daughter has with her father have to be let go of in both a positive and
negative sense. Children have to become independent of their parents
in order to develop their own relationships as adults. It is important

here that parents are honored. Otherwise unprocessed issues in the parent–child relationship are dragged into and complicate adult relationships. Men who have not detached themselves appropriately from their mothers in the process of becoming adults might be good lovers but might not be capable of developing deep, long-term relationships. Often these are men we refer to as *machos*. At the other extreme are *softies*. Both are mother's boys, and because they remain too close to their mothers, they usually have competitive relationships with their fathers (Oedipus complexes). Despite often self-assured outer appearances, these men are usually insecure. They find their real masculine strengths only when they move away from their mothers and step into the spheres of influence of their fathers.

Kevin, twenty-seven, has chosen to have an individual constellation. He formulates his theme clearly. "I am currently in my third serious relationship, and it is on the verge of collapse." I ask him to select a plastic figure from my basket for himself and for each partner and then to place them on the table just as representatives are placed in a constellation. He places the token figure for himself in the middle. The figures of the three women encircle him with a few centimeters separating him from each. Straight away I have the idea to ask him to include a figure for his mother into the constellation. He does this and positions her according to his view. He puts her next to his figure. We look together for a moment at the constellation, and it is not long before he says, "I must let my mother go. I've got to be more independent of her." I confirm this. "Yes. The position your mother holds now is actually the best place for a partner. If you can't or won't let your mother go, a successful relationship with a woman just won't happen." It was a healing shock for Kevin. It only took fifteen minutes for him to clearly realize what had gone wrong in the past.

Gerald, age thirty-three, constellates his relationship problem. He has never been in a relationship for more than two years. He has the feeling he has to do everything for women. In the beginning of a relationship, he feels happy doing this, but later on he finds this especially grating. He and his four previous partners are constellated, and the distance between all representatives is obvious. All four partners do not feel honored, and *Gerald* stands helpless in the middle. I arrange to have a representative for his mother brought in, and Gerald places her in the middle next to his representative. All *previous partners* want further distance from *Gerald*. After being asked, his *mother* says, "This is my son. He doesn't need any of these women." Further questioning makes it apparent that Gerald's mother has used him to fill up her own inner feelings of emptiness. He can leave this emptiness with his mother the moment the reason for this is revealed—one of his mother's sisters died when the mother was only ten years old. He leaves this heaviness with his mother, and he honors her fate. Only then is there space for real connection with his previous and possible future partners.

The same applies to women who are too close to their fathers. A daughters who remain *Daddy's little girl* often has difficulty building successful relationships. These women are often unsure about their own femininity and look for confirmation of this through other men who are mere stand-ins for their fathers. Women feel strong in their femininity only when they step into the spheres of influence of their mothers and let go of the special connections with their fathers.

Nancy, twenty-eight, cannot find a partner. She still lives at home with her parents, has a wonderful career, and is developing herself spiritually with the daily help of her father. In the constellation *Nancy* stands between her *mother* and *father*, and her *mother* is a little farther away. Her *father* says to *Nancy*, "You are my spiritual ideal and companion. I can't relate to your mother on this level. She is not interested in the slightest." In answer to my question about his daughter developing relationships, he responds, "That's not necessary. She belongs with me." The parentification that is clearly shown is subsequently worked through. Six months later Nancy moved into her own apartment to begin a life of her own.

Bert Hellinger has the following to say about this: "I have discovered something important about men and women—if a woman loves and respects her mother and has a bond with her mother, she is more attractive to men than a woman who has a bond with her father and rejects her mother. This is just the same the other way around. A man who gets on well with his father and is connected in heart and soul is more attractive to women than a man who has a solidary relationship with his mother and rejects his father."[7]

It is an indication of disturbance when children remain at home with their parents for too long after adulthood. Mostly practical reasons are given why children stay at home after they have graduated. Often in constellations it is seen that these people are too strongly bonded with one or both parents. They live in the grips or in the spheres of influence of one parent. This makes it impossible for the young adult in question

149

to build a life and develop relationships. A dominating parent labels all attempts by his or her child to shape a life of his or her own as useless and unnecessary. This discourages potential friendships. In such cases the underlying issues of the problems have to be seen and addressed before changes can take place.

Another reason for remaining at home too long is that the child feels his or her parents will be unable to live together peacefully once he or she leaves. He or she feels compelled to remain as a mediator.

Children must let go of their parents both inwardly and outwardly in order to build up their own family systems. They have to be aware of the adopted values and burdens they carry with them and be prepared to let them all go. If this does not happen, the patterns of their parents will continue to have strong influences over them. The chances of having happy, sustained relationships with others are slim. The same applies to cultural, political, and religious beliefs. Interfering aspects of these beliefs also have to be let go so people can find their own values.

In any event both families of origin have to be honored equally. Valuing the family of one's partner less than one's own is a poisonous ingredient in a relationship. Love can succeed only when both partners value and love their own as well as their partner's families.

Loyalty

A couple has to find and balance its own norms and values. The personal conscience *forces* a person to be loyal to his or her family and its beliefs. However, the loyalties associated with each aspect of family membership naturally vary from one child to the other. By *beliefs* I mean the whole attitude of the family to things such as money, careers, and level of contentment. People risk being excluded when they stray too far from "family norms." If a person from a wealthy family marries or gives money away to a person from a poorer family, there will be negative reactions from family members. If the family of origin is poor, family members often react with jealousy and exclusion when another family member becomes rich.

The apple never falls far from the tree. This expression is typical of the widely held belief that people limit themselves to values considered normal in their families of origin. This holds true whether it concerns a person's career, income, lifestyle, or happiness in relationships.

If people come from families where depression of one kind or another is evident, they feel pressured not to allow themselves to be happier than other family members. The subconscious inner reasoning is, "I reaffirm my family's misery and only make it more painful for them by being radiant and happy." Mostly these people don't allow themselves to be happy. To be able to belong, they hold themselves back and limit their lives by sharing in heavy family fates.

These family beliefs are usually subconscious. They only come to the surface when a member has become aware of the underlying dynamic. Family constellations allow people to become mindful of these limitations, and this enables solutions to be found. The rule that everyone has to carry his or her own fate holds for families as well. If depression is a common thread in a family, it is the family's fate. As individuals people can let go of these ties of loyalty and leave them with the appropriate family members.

Naturally loyalties play strong roles in relationships. Especially destructive are the basic subconscious assumptions that are taken as unspoken law, the prevailing emotional climate, and the way men and women in the family have related to each other over the last three or four generations. This emotional environment largely determines the extent of happiness for family members in relationships in future generations.

In the past the incidence of divorce was considerably lower than it is today. People felt enormous social pressure to stay in relationships or they were too anxious to leave. Now that divorce is more accepted, it happens a lot more. (In some countries many couples do not get married but are in relationships considered de facto marriages that have about the same legal implications.) Around half of all marriages end in divorce. From what I have seen in constellations, most relationship conflicts originate from unprocessed loyalties and subconscious basic beliefs that are usually projected subliminally between partners.

Frustratingly enough these basic beliefs operate at such a deep level of subconscious being that people normally have no way of accessing them. Accordingly they are unable to question or come to terms with them. This includes the power they exert on their lives because they are taken as reality. Constellations, however, provide platforms to view and release these entrenched basic beliefs.

Here follow a number of relevant and condensed examples from my practice.

Carol, age fifty-fife, is an incest victim, and she constellates her family system. In the course of the constellation, her *mother* says, "I know all about it. I went through the same myself. Men are just like that." Her mother, Carol's *grandmother*, says, "We just have to put up with it. It's true. Men can't help themselves." An underlying pattern of incest in the family has been clearly exposed—one that has been passed on from one generation to the next.

In another constellation one aspect of proceedings went as follows. All Karen's (age thirty-one) deliveries were difficult. Her mother also experienced complications giving birth, and she actually died from the obstructed labor of her fourth child. In the final constellation image, there is a single row of women from *mother* to *great-grandmother* and further back down the line of all the women in the family. All these women experienced difficult deliveries and remained loyal to each other. Their common mantra is, "Women have to endure pain." In the constellation Karen is able to give back the beliefs and anxiety about difficult deliveries to her ancestors. The pattern is thus finally broken.

At the end of the constellation of Ben, age twenty-seven, which concerns his relationship problems, representatives for himself, his father, his grandfather, and his great-grandfather are constellated. They convey the following deep conviction to each other: "Women can't be trusted. They never give you what you want. So, if necessary, force has to be used." These men were bound by loyalty in carrying this deep conviction. In their relationships they found reasons to repeatedly confirm these beliefs. As a result there had been all manner of problems, and that included domestic violence.

Loyalty, Subconscious Beliefs, and Religion

Loyalty strongly binds people to their families as well as to their genders. Women are connected to all other women in their families. They carry intense suppression from the past. These loyalties are sometimes expressed in deep, subconscious ways such as an aversion to men, deep vengeful feelings, and mistrust.

Men often feel guilty because they are portrayed as villains and perpetrators. They find it difficult to evade the guilt and responsibility, and their resultant helplessness tends to be expressed as aggression. In both sexes the loyalty to one's own gender is almost completely subconscious—despite the extensive consequences for relationships. This only perpetuates the war between the sexes that has been carried down through the generations.

Bert Hellinger uncovered a particular dynamic at play with his work among perpetrators and victims.[8] Reconciliation is only possible when the perpetrator can look his or her victim in the eye and acknowledge the sadness about his or her guilt. Only then can the victim take a step toward the perpetrator. It is then clear for all concerned that those people are enmeshed in a much bigger movement. This realization opens up the chance for them to resolve the victim–perpetrator interdependence.

This reconciliation can only happen through the individual. When men talk about women and vice versa, loyalty connects group members to the underlying burdens, which makes reconciliation difficult.

After a constellation (with the theme "Men are not to be trusted" and the matching belief "The less influence the father has, the better"), I became aware of an underlying aspect and the associated dynamic. I then began to present my insights to the group.

In the Christian belief system that forms the foundation of Western culture, people uphold the conviction or tenet that Mary conceived Jesus immaculately through intervention from God—not man. An ordinary man with normal sexual needs does not come into the picture. People have become accustomed to saying (and thinking) that children are *God's creations* and so also not from man. Men and their ordinary powers of procreation have been tarnished and considered bad.

If women are to remain loyal to their beliefs, which means being morally sound citizens, they have to reject the men who have tainted them—according to the (ever-present) religious and societal norms. This is a deep subconscious belief system. Since it is only the woman who is in a position to bear the godly child, she feels in a superior position to the profane man. Her husband and physical desire toward him cannot be good by definition. Otherwise she would relinquish her *Mary status*. That means she cannot acknowledge or accept her feelings of love and lust, and she has to establish distance from her husband—especially if she has children.

Women often want to make better men of their sons, and this makes sons feel manipulated by their mothers. They have to choose the *better* side and reject their fathers and their normal sexuality. As a result the young man becomes either aggressive or weak, which only serves to discredit him further in the eyes of women in his life, and that includes his future wife.

Men feel subconsciously competitive with God, and they continue to strive for recognition of their sexuality. They feel they have to prove themselves. But compared to the high ideals with which they are forced to compete, their chances are all but zero. They are, after all, ordinary men with all their human shortcomings. God in Heaven remains the eternal, unattainable ideal.

The pressure to prove something impossible makes men weak and helpless. Because they do not like feeling this vulnerability, men have tendencies to become aggressive. This generally results in men having revengeful feelings toward women, since men's sexuality and vulnerability are not acknowledged. This vengeance, I believe, is the driving force behind the oppression of women.

Through these subconscious beliefs, generations after generation of men have been made to feel guilty. It also falsely confirms for women that men are villains and not worthy of respect and recognition.

A man and a woman can only come together when both become conscious of and cast away these *romantic* and *holy* notions. They can then become aware of the godly procreation powers of men as well as the godly bearing powers of women, without which children cannot be brought into existence. This is how people can find balance.

If people keep in mind that the Christian belief is actually patriarchal (with predominantly masculine idols), it is clear how men have brought all this misery on themselves.

Freud asserted that the search for God is actually a search for a father figure. Through having to reject their own fathers, God-fearing people are looking for the benevolent father. Many fanatical believers hang on desperately to this belief. The weaker they feel towards women, the more fanatically they grasp onto their dogmas.

A Partner Is a Mirror

Beliefs play other roles in relationships as well. Namely, partners reflect subconscious beliefs. He or she is not aware of it, but he or she mirrors these beliefs and lives them out in the relationship. For example, if a person carries the subconscious belief he or she cannot trust men or women, then the partner eventually behaves in a way that gives the other person the feeling that he or she cannot trust him or her—despite the best intentions.

A relationship begins in a very different way. In the beginning being in love is like a bed of roses. As the relationship becomes stronger and long term, partners feel safe until they expose their deeper selves to each other. This is a process that can take years. These deeper aspects are actually subconscious beliefs about themselves, the opposite sex, and life in general.

Do you have a subconscious inferiority complex, a fear your loved one will eventually leave you, or are you just afraid of life? A partner will mirror whatever a person carries on from his or her family and manifest those things in the relationship. He or she does this out of love because when people are really in love, they will do anything for their partners. Out of love they want to endorse their partners in whatever way they can. That means if one partner subconsciously harbors the belief that men or women are not to be trusted, his or her partner will most likely have affairs. In this way the partner is merely confirming these beliefs.

This was the situation with Alex, thirty-four. In his constellation concerning his partner, it soon becomes apparent through questioning that he is very untrusting. He carries this over from his family of origin. Men deserted his mother twice.

A partner who confirms his or her partner's subconscious beliefs is also undergoing a learning process himself or herself. In Sigrid's (age twenty-nine) relationship constellation, it is obvious she does not trust men. In so doing she is being loyal to her mother and grandmother, both of whom had very bad relationships with men. Her partner, Joe, thirty-two, continually and compulsively eyed other women—the reason they both came to constellate their relationship. In this constellation it comes to light he is carrying an old, unprocessed feeling of guilt and exclusion. His grandfather had various affairs and a dismissive attitude toward his wife and lovers. The whole family looked down on him. Joe becomes conscious he is entangled with his condemned, excluded grandfather. Joe realizes this forced him into being loyal, and it manifested in his compulsions.

This example clarifies the vision regarding all constellations with relationship themes. People are subconsciously entangled, and it is necessary to let go of all judgments about good and evil to find positive solutions. The hidden process behind entanglements leading to relationship problems is the same process behind all entanglements—namely, the hidden, blind, and childlike love that makes people loyal and forces them to carry unprocessed issues from former generations. As soon as people recognize this subconscious, blind love, they can start healing their relationships. Then all they have to do is find the right ways to relate to their partners—without judgment and derision—since they are simply showing subconscious patterns that they carry from their families.

It is like looking in the mirror in the morning to check whether you are (or appear) well rested or deadly tired or are in a good or bad mood. Shooting the mirror is futile. The mirror never lies, and it is useless to question or condemn the messenger.

If this reciprocity or mirror function that surfaces in every relationship is acknowledged and made conscious, a much deeper and more profound love will develop. The relationship will become a rich learning and awareness process. This confirms again why it is so important to respect and come to terms with relationship problems with previous partners. Previous partners mirrored the deepest subconscious belief patterns, and in doing so they tried to help their partners become conscious of them. For a more detailed description of the way reciprocity works in relationships, see my book *Heal Your Relationship.*

The Double Shift

The double shift is a common cause of disruption in relationships that one can become aware of in a constellation. If an injustice was perpetrated between a man and a woman in a previous relationship without being compensated for, it will rise up again in another generation.

The unexpressed or unaccepted feelings are carried over by a family member in the following generation until they are expressed. This is what is referred to as the first shift—the shift in the subject. For example, this can occur from grandfather to grandson. A grandson will carry on the unprocessed spousal frustrations of his grandfather and express them toward his partner. Then comes the second shift—the shift in the object from grandmother to the current partner of the grandson. Following is a brief account of a constellation with a double shift.

Steven, age thirty-seven, is experiencing problems in his relationship. Every time he begins a new relationship, distrust soon besets him, which causes the relationship to run off the rails. In the course of his constellation, the group learns that his grandfather's wife humiliated and hurt him. He hid his suffering because he wanted to keep the peace. His grandson, the seeker, feels strongly connected to his grandfather, and it is obvious he bears the burden for his grandfather and defends him (shift in subject). He does that toward his partners and not toward his grandmother (shift in object).

The solution is for his *grandmother* and *grandfather* to say to Steven's representative, "We carry our own relationship problems. We are the adults. You are but a grandchild." *Steven* replies, "I leave it with you. I honor you and your relationship." He says to his *grandfather*, "I honor you and your relationship with your wife, my grandmother."

He follows this by bowing down deeply before his *grandfather*. His *grandfather* says, "You have wanted to do and carry a lot for me. That's special, and I feel your love. You may stop carrying it now. You

157

honor me by developing a wonderful relationship." Steven's identification with his grandfather is resolved with these statements that automatically remove the shift in object (from grandmother toward the current partners).

Sarah, age thirty-five, is divorced, but she still loves her ex-husband. Her constellation reveals how unhappy her mother was with her husband. Her mother did not dare to divorce her husband in consideration for her children among other reasons. Sarah, however, divorced her husband out of a deep sense of loyalty and love to her mother. This is a case of double shift.

The way unprocessed emotional issues are taken up by following generations out of love and expressed is demonstrated time and time again in similar constellations. It always seems as if the people who had the real problems in the first instance (the grandfather or the mother in the cases above) were not able to bear them. They absolutely did not want their children or grandchildren to step in for them or throw away their own lives. They were naturally not aware of the dynamic involved.

Ancestors feel better when they see subsequent generations prosper.

The Parental Relationship Takes Precedence over Children

It is commonly understood that raising children involves an enormous amount of energy and commitment. The idea that children take priority over one's partner in a relationship, however, is a common misconception and a common cause of disruption in relationships. Partners often lose sight of the fact that children are expressions of their love for one another. In other words love between partners can be considered nourishment for children.

Chronologically speaking the relationship comes first. Having children is dependent on the existence of the relationship. Even if the relationship is short, it was still there first.[9]

Children usually become more important than the partner when the relationship is disturbed and there are emotional deficits in the parents. Many parents try to fill in this conflict with their children, but this burdens children emotionally and can lead to parentification. This causes a

158

distortion in the balance of give and take in the relationship between parents and their children. Children pitch in to share the load when they see one or both parents are chronically unhappy. They become substitute partners, which also disturbs the balance. Children can become more important and even better "partners" when parents seek support and comfort from their children.

Consider the example of a woman who wants to make a better man out of her son than she considers her husband to be. This serves to make her son more important to her than her husband and prevents her son from building a healthy relationship with his father. Since the father is the symbol of masculinity, his son is prevented from identifying with his father as a healthy role model for masculinity.

The same applies to daughters who are adored by their fathers and favored over their wives—a situation that can lead to sexual abuse. If these disturbances are to be reduced, parents have to put their relationships first and take on the responsibility to maintain happy, liberating relationships with each other.

Children who see their parents getting on well together can relax and be free to be happy children.

Blaming Parents

Some people harbor blame and resentment toward their parents and distance themselves from them. They do not want anything to do with one or both parents, and they try (inwardly and outwardly) to live as far away as possible from them. This is a clear indication of unprocessed issues between children and parents. It comes as no surprise to see that this blame returns and manifests as trouble in future relationships.

Parents bestow upon their children all they have, and that includes their shortcomings. Because the parents have no say in the matter and are just the way they are, children have no say. That is why emotionally (and materially) deprived parents are in no state to transmit emotional wellbeing to their children. Violent parents or those with addictions cannot always prevent passing on these heavy afflictions to their children. That is just the long and short of it. Of course there are circumstances where it is very understandable that children are furious and angry. The best thing they can do is process all the emotional scars they carry and heal their inner child, as described in chapter three. This is just to make sure they do not get stuck in the emotional turmoil of their parents and pass the emotional load to their offspring.

When children do not accept their parents as they are, they place themselves above them and mess with both the hierarchical order as well as the balance of give and take. Some people find this reasoning difficult to fathom. A very common question is, "Do children place themselves above their parents if they expect more from them?" The idea that lies behind this logic is that people could have been afforded better lives if only their parents would have been more aware, more loving, richer, or whatever else. It is as if there could be alternatives for the way parents behave or who they are.

Children reason they would be happier, more successful, and just better off in general if only their parents had been this way or had that thing. Engaging in this kind of rationalizing only makes people more dependent and caught up in victim roles. This gives people the perfect excuse for their botched lives.

Experience reveals that people can only be reunited with strength and be in states of happiness with the ability to have sustained, mutually beneficial relationships once they accept their parents as they are— with all their faults and shortcomings. This implies that people have to return all the burdens they have carried over from their parents as well as honor them and their lives. Then they can thank them for the greatest gift of all—their lives.

If people do not accept their parents as they are, the family consciences will automatically ensure they will be confronted in their relationships with unprocessed aspects of their parents. Worse still children could be incapable of having sustainable relationships at all. Some people find this difficult to come to terms with, but the family conscience is uncompromising in its service of human evolution. Everything not processed comes back, just as everything that goes up must come down. Unprocessed material will continue to make people weak. Problems persist until people acknowledge and accept the situations.

Relationships and Adoption

There are often two main disturbances in constellations involving adopted children. The first one concerns the children and the fact their parents have given away or abandoned them. Even if this happens out of necessity, such children develop attachment problems. This can be equated with trauma and requires special attention. (See "Reaching Out Interrupted" in chapter four.)

Apart from attachment disorders, adopted children also inevitably carry the disturbances that led to the adoptions because they remain connected through existential loyalties to their biological parents. Whether it concerns the early death of the mother, an unwanted pregnancy, a catastrophe, or an illness, an adopted child carries the disturbance over subconsciously and is frequently in need of therapeutic help.

The second kind of disturbance comes about within the new family when the biological parents are not honored or valued. Often adoptive or foster parents regard themselves as superior to the biological parents because they have taken over the responsibility for care and upbringing of the child. This attitude disrupts the hierarchical balance. Only biological parents can be the real parents of these children, and nobody can replace them. The reasons they gave up their children are their business and beyond judgment by others.

The situation can be resolved once the biological mother and father are honored and respected and given places in the hearts of their children and adoptive or foster parents. This allows child-rearing problems to sort themselves out.

The following example is from a constellation I took part in when I was in Germany. It involved an adopted child. The adoptive mother was beset with problems from an adopted daughter of African origin. In the course of the constellation, her *adopted child* stood opposite her *biological parents* and addressed both in turn. "I thank you for the greatest gift you could have given me—my life. I honor you. The fact you gave me away is your responsibility." The *adopted child* was immediately more relaxed, and the representatives of her biological parents were relieved. The *adoptive mother* said to both the *biological mother* and *biological father*, "You are the real parents. I am the adoptive mother. I honor you and your decision to enable me to look after your child. I will do everything I can. Your child is in good hands with

161

me." Both the *biological mother* and *biological father* were obviously relieved and felt much better. Five representatives of the tribe of origin of the adopted child stood behind the *biological mother* and *biological father*. The *adopted child* said to these five representatives, "I thank and honor you as my people of origin. My special strength stems from you."

The *adopted child* relaxed visibly and felt stronger. The feeling of being cut off disappeared. The *adopted child* then addressed her *biological parents* and *tribal members*. "Look kindly upon me as I live a good life with my adoptive parents in Germany." All representatives were now considerably more relaxed. The tension present at the beginning of the constellation was now gone. Two days later the woman in question contributed to a workshop discussion. "I have seen my child only at the breakfast and dinner table," she said. "It was strange. We didn't argue."

Bert Hellinger has made an important insight via his many constellations about adoption.[10] He maintains that in most cases adoption goes too far. If parents cannot look after their children, then foster families are often better solutions than adoption. In this way parents retain a great deal of their parental responsibilities. For children it is preferable to live with family members such as aunts, uncles, or grandparents so contact with the family is ensured.

Adoption is usually only advisable when the biological parents have died, when they are really unwilling or inept, or no family members are prepared to take care of them.

When parents adopt another child and they have children of their own, the rightful place for that adopted child, despite age, is after the youngest child. According to the order of hierarchy, the children of adoptive parents take precedence over the adopted child or children, so bloodlines come first.

Relationships with Heavy Fates

A person with a heavy fate (such as being unable to have children) should not demand his or her partner share this fate. It is a personal fate, and a person cannot impose it on a partner. This partner has to be left to make up his or her own mind about whether to stay in the relationship or not. If he or she chooses to stay, then this has to be seen as a gift. The same applies, for example, to someone who becomes paralyzed through an accident or severe illness. He or she does not have the right to use this heavy fate as a way of demanding attention and love.

In Vitro Fertilization

From a systemic standpoint, artificial insemination (IVF) should be regarded with extreme caution. It is considered a heavy fate when a person cannot have children. The acceptance of this gives people the strength to use their talents positively in other spheres of life. When people resist their predicaments, they set themselves above their fates, and this can lead to severe disturbances. A woman who allows herself to be artificially inseminated has a connection to the donor, the child's biological father, whether she likes it or not. The biological father has to be honored, and the child should know about the biological father. In most cases the relationship with the donor father is usually not permissible, which causes severe disturbances for the child. The fact the woman's partner as discussed above, is not the child's father (unless he is the donor) causes a disturbance in the relationship between man and woman because she has a bond with another man, the donor, through their common child.

Donors do not realize the children they help conceive through their sperm belong to their family systems from a biological standpoint. They are half brothers and half sisters to any children the donors might have. In an extensive article in the German newspaper *Der Spiegel*,[11] the search by donor-conceived children for their real fathers is exemplified by the following case.

Rebecca (fictitious name) learned when she was four that her father was not her biological father and that the sperm came from an unknown donor from a donor bank. She had a bad relationship with her surrogate father, called him a *fake dad*, and as a teenager wanted to break off all contact with him. When she turned twenty-two, she began what turned out to be an arduous search for her real father, which uncovered her biological father's name and address. As it transpired this man was not happy with his biological daughter's desire to contact him and threatened to involve the police so he and his family could be left in peace. Despite this the young woman broke into her biological father's house and managed to see her half sister and half brother, who both resembled her in appearance. She was, however, prevented from any further contact and was left feeling totally frustrated with the painful feeling of being excluded.

This story makes it clear that a third party, apart from the mother and the surrogate father, is always invisibly present—the donor. Despite his absence he has enormous influence.

Another example is the wunderkind Doron Blake.[12] He was conceived in the private in vitro fertilization program of millionaire Robert Clark Graham for the purposes of conceiving especially intelligent children. Blake's sperm originated from an unknown Nobel Prize winner.

When Doron was six, he could recite prime numbers as well as verses from *King Lear*, and he had an IQ of 180. His mother, psychologist Afton Blake, dragged him from one talk show to another in his youth and even got him on the front page of the *Los Angeles Times*.

According to various articles on the Internet, he now refuses to participate in all the brouhaha. He does not want to study at Harvard or Yale, and he will not study the high-tech subjects for which he has a talent. He is still highly gifted, but these days he plays sitar and studies theology. Happiness is something that continues to elude him.

It is to be expected that children from unknown donors spend their lives in search of their fathers, the missing halves of their identities. According to the articles, donor-conceived children often have the feeling they have been *made*.

Divorce or the End of a Relationship

When the relationship between two people ends, the intensity of their former love toward each other is now expressed, seemingly of equal intensity, in reproach and blame. A good example is shown in the movie *The War of the Roses*, in which a man goes to a lawyer to arrange his divorce. The lawyer tells him a story of a happy couple, full of love and admiration for one another in the beginning. After getting married and settling down with children, their love soured, and they became alienated from one another. This led to arguments that continued to escalate into a full-blown war between them that culminated in death.

In family constellations it is evident that divorce is often unavoidable. According to Bert Hellinger, relationships are threatened because people are usually too entangled with unprocessed things in their own families.[13] Since partners are not aware of the entanglements, they find it difficult to understand and accept what is happening. Instead they lose themselves in the *blame game* and assume that if one or both of them would have reacted differently, everything would have been different. By reacting in this way, they push the pain of separation away. Only when this pain is really felt and when both partners are prepared to accept their powerlessness and hopelessness will they be ready to move away from each other in peace and be free to begin anew.

Experimental Relationships

These days there are many different forms of relationships—a ménage à trois being just one of many. Whenever the bond that arises through a sexual relationship is not honored, as in some alternative forms of living together, the systemic order is disturbed. Experimentation is naturally healthy and necessary. However, disturbance will ensue whenever (consciously or not) sexual relationships and bonds are not clearly defined and understood and former partners are not honored. If children are brought into the mix when underlying relationships are not clearly defined, they will carry over entanglements. The following is one such constellation in which I participated as a representative.

Helen, age forty-four, has a nineteen-year-old daughter with serious psychological problems as well as a serious drug habit. Helen lived for many years in a triangular relationship within an alternative community group, and different community members raised her daughter. In her constellation it is soon obvious Helen's daughter carried over the confusion of her mother's triangular relationship. She has no real place of her own and is entangled with the other woman in her mother's triangular relationship. It was only when this woman was honored and everyone was given a place that the daughter was able to find peace. "For the first time," says the *daughter*, "I have the feeling of having a mom and dad and know where I belong."

Can One Save a Relationship with Family Constellations?

Saving a relationship is not within the powers of a therapist and is also not his or her responsibility. A therapist who presents himself or herself in this light is presumptuous and lacks respect for the clients. In a family constellation, the role of the facilitator is to make people aware of their entanglements and work in harmony with them to seek solutions. What these might or might not be is not the facilitator's responsibility. What the seeker does with the information gained from a constellation is also not the responsibility of the facilitator.

It is only possible to continue a relationship if both partners go through a profound learning process. If they choose to break up, they still learn and become wiser, and this way they reach better states to begin new relationships. As a therapist both options have equal merit.

Control Goes against Love

If people want to control their partners or the relationships, it is usually born out of an assumption that the act of controlling is necessary. Most often this stems from unprocessed elements from the families of origin. The assumption something has to be controlled testifies to a lack of respect for a partner. This distorts the balance of give and take in a relationship.

The controlled partner will inevitably feel like the villain. In the end he or she will act just as badly as the initial assumption defined, and by doing this he or she confirms the righteousness of the controlling party. The initial assumption are confirmed subconsciously and experienced as deep loyalties with members from the family of origin. The mirroring process discussed previously is clearly manifested here.

Using the order of love as a new morality—or worse still as religious dogma—is nothing more than a form of control. It is different when people fully understand what the order of love means and reorient their lives as a result of looking at their own past experiences, loyalties, and entanglements. The motivational force originates from within instead of from an outside influence such as a moral teaching, dogma, or religion.

Forcing and manipulating a partner to adopt a particular attitude will not work for the same reasons. The systemic order has to be experienced and understood. Others cannot artificially determine it externally.

Glenda, age forty-eight, came to me about problems with her partner. Her partner had enthusiastically read all Hellinger's books and demanded she follow along because he asserted that Hellinger said, "A woman follows her man." She feels very uneasy about his demands and wants me to give her a second opinion over the matter. She wants to know if what her husband says is true—that a resolution will be found if she goes along with him. I try to make it clear that following an archaic dictum often comes up in constellations but these days has to be taken with a grain of salt. It is certainly not a position that can be forced on someone. This is equally as absurd as a wife demanding her husband be a *real man*.

In this case the full sense of Hellinger's wisdom had not been completely appreciated, for Hellinger went on to say, "The masculine serves the feminine." What Hellinger meant by saying, "A woman follows her man and the man serves the woman," or, "The feminine follows the masculine and the masculine serves the feminine," is that one partner in the relationship is more oriented to the outside world. He or she has the bigger income, for example, or is the leading partner. He or she does this to serve the partner that is more oriented to the nest. It represents an archaic inner picture all people carry with them—the hunter (man) and the collector (woman).

Fortunately society allows room for women and men to express their femininity and masculinity in a balanced way. This means neither man nor woman can be assumed to take on a subservient role. The issue here is one of attitude as a result of the inner makeup of each partner. It is not intended as a static element.

By being demanding, shifts in responsibility are brought about. A person reasons that if the partner is not able to follow, this partner is responsible when the relationship fails so the partner is guilty when things go wrong. A person might also reason that if a partner does not want the place he or she prepared for (or demanded of) him or her, that relationship cannot be harmonious, and the person won't be happy. This kind of reasoning heavily burdens a relationship and indicates entanglements in the family of origin. Once both partners let go of old entanglements, they take up their rightful places in relation to each other.

According to Hellinger every form of control works against love and a harmonious relationship.[14] Attempting to use what is written in this book as a recipe for a harmonious relationship and wanting or even pushing to implement the values described without going through a real process of constellating personal themes is a form of control. This form of control prohibits love.

6

Family Constellations and Children

Children are interwoven with the community of fate of their family. Out of love they take over a burden for one of their parents or, if one of the parents seems needy, they attempt to become a mother or father to them.
—Sieglinde Schneider[1]

This chapter looks at the possible causes of child-rearing problems and disorders such as attention deficit/hyperactivity disorder (ADHD), autism spectrum disorder (ASD), pervasive developmental disorder not otherwise specified (PDD-NOS), and other related disorders. Then it will discuss loyalty conflicts that burden children in periods of chronic tension between their parents—divorce conflict being a major one. The chapter finishes with a description of a harmonious table seating arrangement and a number of pointers for parents about what they can do for their children from a constellation perspective.

Consider children as warning lights regarding a family's state of health. When they begin to flash, parents can be sure there are serious entanglements at work. In this sense *flashing* means children showing dysfunctional behavior, diseases, learning obstacles, or other difficulties. Because family constellations bring their entanglements with the family systems into view, they often have deep and freeing results for children with all kinds of problems. They can also offer relief for parents when it becomes clear their *problem* children are not *bad* or unintelligent but entangled with people from the families. Constellations show that the mechanisms behind these problem behaviors appear to be intense, blind love.

Parents of children who are difficult to raise often blame themselves, feel guilty, or doubt their value as good parents. A constellation can show them they are entangled—just like their children. It can also help them realize that all these problems are not their fault—not in the sense of them being bad parents.

The new insights a constellation provides can help parents work through their frustration and pain. Through this awareness-raising process, they are able to take on their responsibilities in new and beneficial ways.

Sieglinde Schneider wrote in *Kindliche Not und kindliche Liebe* (*Childhood Needs and Childish Love*), "If we, as parents and teachers, look at a child only as an individual and attribute all difficulties to the child, the child will become a problem. A child's unpredictable and self-harming behavior is an attempt to come to terms with the underlying issues of a problem; however, it is not seen or appreciated. In his or her loyalty to a family member, a child cannot really be helped because each improvement will only be seen as betrayal of the person with whom the child is entangled. That is why young people often refuse therapy or sabotage help of any kind that only focuses on helping the child."[2]

Healing only takes place when the big picture is revealed and the depth of the childlike love and loyalty is appreciated and respected. (See the constellation of Veronica and Jeremy about their self-mutilating fifteen-year-old son under "The Death of a Parent" in chapter four.)

Looking at the whole family system as in contextual therapy or with family constellations is attracting more and more interest and followers worldwide. This is because, as research indicates, help is far more evident when people in all areas of a child's life are consulted.

The child's problem always exists in a certain relational context and has to be analyzed and treated within this context. This also applies to conditions such as ADHD, PDD-NOS, and obsessive compulsive disorder (OCD).

Children continually blossom when parents constellate and resolve their own problems. Once resolutions are integrated, children are given chances to be children again. They are allowed to swim freely in energy streams. They do not have to be present in constellations or even have to know anything about this process. This works best up until the early stages of puberty, but after that it is preferable for adolescents to be present in constellations. If they are well into or through puberty, they are advised to have their own constellations.

I Am but a Child

When parents get on well with each other, children prosper. This is regrettably too seldom the case. Most relationships are disturbed. According to 2007 statistics, divorce rates in Europe range from around 15 percent in Spain, 44 percent in Belgium, and nearly 55 percent in Sweden—almost the same as the rate in the United States at the time.[3]

The previous chapters have illuminated how a relationship between parents is messed up when both partners are too strongly enmeshed with unprocessed experiences from their parents and ancestors. Thus children are subject to their parents' dysfunctional behaviors and resultant relationship squabbling. When parents have problems and argue, children follow subconscious urges and step into the breaches in attempts to help their parents. This also happens when parents call upon their children for emotional support.

It goes without saying that this has dramatic consequences for the child, who has no say in the matter. He or she is bound by love and loyalty and carries a profound gratefulness toward the parents by virtue of the child receiving life from them. That is why a child is prepared to do anything for his or her parents under the influence of the systemic pressure of the family conscience. The child drags up all unprocessed burdens from his or her parents or ancestor's back into the family system. (See "The Magical Love of a Child" in chapter three.)

All examples cited in this book could also be included here because anyone who has had a problem constellated was once a child who had too much to carry as well. The resolving statements used in these constellations are, "I am but a child. I leave your problems with you. You are the adults, and you can take care of yourselves." The parents' answer is, "We are the parents. You are but a child, and you honor us by leaving our problems with us."

It becomes more complicated for a child in a situation Jay Haley calls the "perverse triangle."[4] This comes about when one of the parents feels suppressed anger or resentment toward the other and uses one of the children as an ally to vent his or her feelings and frustrations. A child is compelled to comply in such a situation. He or she takes on the emotional load of one of the parents and acts out his or her frustration and anger toward the other parent.

Children frequently take over the emotional load from the parent who seems unable to deal with the situation. Often in these circumstances, the father teams up with his daughter or the mother with her son. Such a situation creates unsolvable loyalty conflicts within the child. The balance of give and take between parents and children is seriously undermined, and later on as an adult the person will struggle with relationships. The anger and resentment he or she has taken on will be projected onto his or her partner(s). (See "The Double Shift" in chapter five.)

John, age seventeen, has severe problems with his parents and self-medicates with alcohol and other drugs. His mother accompanies him during the constellation. In his constellation *John* stands facing his *father*. *John* is angry toward his *father*. Really angry. While he expresses this to his *father*, his *mother* smiles and adopts a triumphant posture. I ask John to look back and forth between his *mother* and *father*. He takes time to do this, and gradually a change comes over him. He understands what is going on. He nods and addresses his *mother*. "It's your anger and malice." His *mother* responds, "Yeah. I hate your father."

After a few moments, I ask John to repeat the following statement to his *father*: "I'm angry with you. I do this out of love for Mom." *Father* and *son* react immediately with relief and relax. Then I ask his *mother* to say the following statements to her *son*: "I'm sorry. I have used you. Whatever is between Dad and I is our business. You are but a child."

This has a calming effect on John, who has replaced his representative and is now in the constellation himself. He slowly approaches his *father*, and after a moment his *father* takes him in his arms. They are both in tears and obviously deeply touched. A major atonement has taken place. Later on his mother resolved her entanglements in her own constellation.

It often happens that children who adopt unprocessed conflicts from their parents are plagued by this later on in their own relationships. Grant, age forty, told me the following about the end of his relationship. "I had to be normal. It was like being imprisoned. If ever I wanted to do anything special, like sleeping overnight in a forest, checking out stars on a mountaintop, or smoking a joint, she got mad. 'Be normal!' It was all I ever heard." When I inquire further, it is revealed the mother of his ex-partner was a vamp. She wore suggestive clothing, often went out dancing, and indulged in casual sex. There were frequent arguments in her family home, and her father constantly denounced his wife as abnormal. It was clear then that Grant's ex-partner carried over and projected onto Grant the recriminations of her father toward her mother (double shift).

With the rise in blended families these days, children with stepparents are common. The situation is more difficult when a stepmother or stepfather is overly giving toward children from his or her partner's first marriage. After a time it is difficult for a child to accept what the stepparent gives. The stepchild is receiving something from someone who is not actually in a position to give to him or her.

The new partner of either parent must not usurp the place of the biological parent. By being overgenerous with attention and gifts, a stepparent puts the child under pressure to return the gesture, even though it does not feel right. This leads to acting out in children or even incest. The problem disappears once the stepparent ceases to lavish gifts (course fees or living allowances) and excessive attention on the child. This is the responsibility of the biological parents.

All involved parties, especially a stepchild, will only find liberation when the stepparent says to the stepchild (as a reflection of his inner attitude), "What I give to you is actually meant for your father/mother because I love him or her so much. In fact, it has nothing to do with you." By saying this, the child is freed from all obligations to his or her stepparent.

Although it springs from love and appreciation toward his or her parents, a child can also contribute enormously to making his or her own life difficult. Let me give an example from my own life. When renovating my oldest daughter's bedroom some years back, I had an accident, which left an injury above my left eye. Two months later my daughter fell from her bike right before me and was left with a wound to her forehead just above her right eye. The same doctor who had treated me then saw her. He commented to my daughter, "Showing solidarity with Daddy?" My daughter smiled and nodded. Apparently a feeling of guilt was responsible for her accident, since I had injured my forehead while working on her room. That's how children show love to their parents.

The Origin of Child-Rearing Problems and PPDs

Problem behavior is a way for children to attract attention to disturbances in the family and in the system. Entanglements can heavily burden children and cause problematic behavior. ADHD, ASD, and other similar pervasive (developmental) disorders have become worryingly commonplace. Every time these disorders pop up in constellations, it is clear that children are overburdened. These days families have fewer children than in the past, and a lot more is expected of them. This puts them under more pressure than ever. Stress in elementary schoolchildren is taken for granted these days.

Looking at this from a systemic standpoint, burdens from the family system that were shared by many in the past are concentrated now only on a few. On top of that, never before has one generation had to deal with such a high incidence of divorce. This leaves children in constant states of emotional charge.

External influences also play their parts in the rapidly changing social sphere. Children have become the prime targets of marketing machines, creating an unprecedented consumer culture that bombards them with new sets of artificial norms and values at odds with those of their parents. Coupled with more and more gratuitous violence in computer games and on television, it is no wonder they become sick or hyperactive. Is it wise then to medicate them to allow some peace in their lives?

When ADHD is the theme of a constellation or a major factor in the problem constellated, participants regularly see the sharing of a heavy fate or an entanglement with a family member who died young. Children lose their inner balance through the burdens they carry. To deal with this, some children cannot concentrate and are lost in their own worlds. Others generate too much energy through the tension created and release this in destructive ways. ASD is often linked to exclusion in previous generations.

When Greta, age forty-two, constellated her relationship problems, her eleven-year-old son, Kevin, who had been diagnosed with ASD, was also constellated. Greta places her ex-partner, Kevin's father, on the sidelines. Her *son* wants to stand next to him. *Kevin* says, "I feel just as excluded as my dad." The *ex-partner* confirms he feels excluded, which is difficult for him to deal with, but he is happy with the loyalty he experiences from his *son*. In the constellation it's clear Greta, who wants nothing more to do with her ex, is in the grip of old loyalties with women from previous generations in her family. It seems the normal thing was for women to exclude men, which led her son to withdraw into himself and distance himself from a threatening world. Consequently he feels a destructive pressure he describes as follows: "I can't do anything right. Just like my dad and all other men. It's easier to withdraw totally." I ask him to give all burdens and the exclusion back to his mother, which immediately makes him feel so much better. When *Greta* is able to let go of and give back her loyalties to the women in previous generations, she can give her ex-partner a place. *Kevin* feels an enormous sense of relief and has a desire to get back into life.

Another kind of child-rearing problem arises when a child brings back unprocessed conflicts from relationships in the family's past. This dynamic has only been revealed through Hellinger's work.

It's evident how exclusion is created when a former partner is disgraced or repressed with anger and hatred. This also applies to all intense previous relationships of the parents and most importantly the first true love union. Previous partners belong to the community of fate, since they have made room for the subsequent partners. All former partners have to be honored. (See chapter five.)

The systemic pressure from the family conscience sees to it that previous partners of the parents who are not honored are brought back into the system through children. Strangely enough children who are entangled with former partners do not have to know anything about those former relationships. That is why parents and children do not have a clue why the children behave so oddly. A daughter can become a rival to her mother and angry toward her father because she has to represent the repressed relationship of her father, and a son constantly argues because he represents the repressed first true love of his mother.

Vivian, age twenty-five, has struggled to find balance in the relationship with her mother since puberty. In her constellation a bond between her and a former partner of her father is revealed. At the end of her constellation, she says to the *former partner*, "Your anger and pain I leave with you." The *former partner* confirms this. "It belongs with me. You can just let it all go now." Then Vivian turns to her *father* and says, "I'm staying with Mom. That's where I belong. I am but a child. I have nothing more to do with your first wife. Please see me as your daughter. I consider you my father now." To conclude she says to her *mother*, "Mom, you are my real and only mother. Daddy's former partner means nothing to me. Look upon me as your child, and I'll see you as my mom. I honor you, dear Mommy." She feels a release of tension immediately, and she feels the stream of love flow to her mother once again. She falls into her *mother*'s arms and begins to sob. After some deep breathing, she allows her mother to be the adult again so she can be the child. I ask her to say the following to her *mother*: "You're my mother, and I thank you for the most important gift you have bestowed upon me—my life." After the constellation Vivian feels so much better.

A number of issues concerning the burdening of children come to the fore in Hellinger's work. He commented about *wish children* (children who are told they are very much wanted) in a seminar once. "Do you all know that a *wish child* always has problems? *Wish children* come about for their parents' sake. Children that are just born without expectation are free." There was laughter in the group at this. "A child that is caught up being a *wish child* has a difficult fate. It is mandated in one way or another. In other words it is an enormous failure for the child if he or she cannot fulfill the parents' wishes."[5]

A woman who wants a child without wanting a relationship with the father or any other partner heavily burdens that child. In the first place, the woman wants a child—a child for herself. Therefore, the child is not free to create a life of his or her own. The child has to give or fulfill the mother's desire. Secondly, every child has the right to his or her biological father. When he is considered unnecessary or extraneous, an exclusion results, and difficult child-rearing problems are guaranteed.

This can be especially damaging for sons. As children these sons can be really nice to their mothers, but later in life they typically become machos or even develop and harbor deep grudges against women in general.

It is just as burdensome for children when parents develop and maintain friendships with their children. Children need parents who are going to be parents that lead and guide.[6] Parents cannot be buddies or mates to their children. It is important that children develop their own friendships elsewhere.

A parent should never confide in a son or daughter about adult issues such as intimate relationship details. This is no concern of the child and only serves to get him or her caught up in parental problems. This is unbearable for a child.

John, age eighteen, hates his parents. He is unhappy, does not have a partner, and has a marijuana addiction. He wants to have a family constellation but prefers to do this in an individual setting. From the initial discussion, I find out his mother often talked to her son about her husband's shortcomings in the bedroom.

He uses floor anchors as representatives. John stands on these one at a time, so he can act as each representative in turn. John begins taking up his own position and looks over at his *mother* and *father*. He then says to his *father* angrily, "You have always looked down at Mom." To his *mother* he then says, "You have always denigrated Dad and impressed upon me how much of a loser he is." To both he says, "I hate you."

I ask John to move to his father's floor anchor and become his father's representative—to feel any sensations and communicate these to me. He tells me he feels reasonably normal. Then I ask him to say to *John*, "I know how you feel." This brings a smile to his face, and he realizes he feels just the same as his father—just as powerless, angry, and disrespected. As his father I ask John to address the floor anchors of his parents (*grandmother* and *grandfather* on his father's side). I ask him, "Recognize anything here?" He looks on and nods his head somewhat in shock. "Just the same. My grandmother is just like my mother, and my grandfather is like my father." Now he is nearly in tears. He is angry and powerless feeling the immense load he has carried before this awakening. I allow him some time before asking him to say, "This is just the way we are—powerless, angry, and not respected." He feels the loyalty, love, endless repetition, and suffering. After a moment I ask him to breathe deeply, relax his muscles, and say to all representatives on his father's side, "I leave your anger for not being respected and being powerlessness with you. I am but a child." On his father's floor anchor, he feels the relief of his father to see his son let go of this hurtful attitude. He experiences the same relief on the floor anchor of the grandfather. To finish John bows down before his family members in an act of letting go. This he does calmly and with dignity in order to complete this beautiful ritual.

John looks once again to his *mother*. I ask him to stand on his mother's floor anchor and feel what it is like from her perspective. He nods. He can really feel what she has felt. I ask the *mother* to say to her *son*, "I'm sorry. I took it too far." As his *mother* John turns to me and says, "I am so ashamed. I went way too far." I ask him to step out of the role of his mother, and the first thing he says after doing this is, "If only my mother had felt what it was like for me. She would have been so ashamed." I ask him to leave the shame behind with his mother, together with her denigrating attitude toward men. He does this with a deep bow and feels the weight rise from his shoulders. (For more information about individual constellations, see "Constellations in the Individual Setting" in chapter eight.)

Loyalty Conflicts in Tense Relationships

A child really struggles if parents fight and argue—even if this is done silently with detached behavior. To love both parents in this situation, a child has to perform the splits, as it were. It becomes more damaging for a child if he or she has to choose one parent over the other. A child's love and loyalty toward his or her parents then becomes torn. A child sometimes reacts by holding in the built-up tension, which can lead to hyperactivity. Another children might close himself or herself off from the outside world.

However a child reacts, that child is not free. He or she carries and acts out (subconsciously and out of blind love) the tension between the parents. Sometimes this takes the form of being a lightning receptor or a mediator. In constellations representatives often see that one or more children from families stand between their parents. This is an untenable position for children. Parents of a hyperactive child are often heard saying their son or daughter keeps them continuously busy.[7] This is the subconscious goal of the child. In some cases this is connected with the threat that the parents might split up. The inner motivation here is, "I'm keeping you so busy you won't get the chance to think about splitting up." This is usually revealed in a constellation. One parent feels an inner urge to leave the relationship or even wants to die to be reunited with a forgotten or excommunicated family member, yet that parent is prevented from doing so by his or her hyperactive child. Hyperactivity is certainly an obvious sign of a heavy burden in the family.

178

Constellations reveal that chronic quarrelsomeness or discord among siblings serves as an expression of the underlying tension between parents. Children unveil and play out subconscious family system conflicts.

Linda, age thirty-nine, is in a desperate state. Her son and daughter are constantly bickering. These conflicts sometimes flare up and turn physical. Recently she informed me the latest skirmish between her children resulted in a broken window. On top of this, Linda has real trouble with her ex-husband, from whom she divorced four years before.

In her constellation it appears her daughter feels solidarity with her and her son with his father. Linda and her husband are caught up in angry cross-accusations. During the constellation I get both the *mother* and *father* to say the following to the *son* and *daughter*: "Our relationship problems belong with us. You honor us when you leave them with us. We are the adults, and you are the children." The representatives of the children appear much calmer.

Working around her parents in the constellation, it surfaces that Linda is strongly bound to her mother, who also had a difficult relationship with her husband, Linda's father. (This is loyalty and a double shift.) Linda's daughter is trapped in the same loyalty and has to defend her mother to her father and brother. Likewise her son is loyal to his father and defends him. This process allows entanglements that have persisted over generations to show up clearly.

Next I allow all residual feelings to be given back. I ask the *mother* to say the following to her *son* and *daughter*: "I allow you to have good relationships with your father. He is your right and proper father. My difficulties with him belong to me. I am the adult, and I will solve these problems myself." The *son* and *daughter* are now able to stand close together for the first time in the constellation and feel good about each other.

Four weeks later Linda called me to say the arguments between her children were far less frequent after the constellation. Her children were now mostly able to get along with each other in a respectful way. The communication with her ex-husband had also improved.

Children internalize distance or tension between parents. This is given shape as division or disunity between male and female—between yin and yang. Children try to resolve these imbalances later on in life and unite yin and yang in themselves. The more estranged the parents were, the more difficult it becomes to reunite (yin and yang) them.

Divorce and Loyalty Conflicts

To set up what you like against what you do not like, This is the disease of the mind... And immediately, Heaven and Earth are set far apart.
—Sosan Zenji[8]

Typically when a family breaks apart, one parent is referred to as the guilty party, and correspondingly the other is innocent. A child usually ends up with the *innocent* parent, leaving the child burdened with split loyalties. Children are used as pawns in acrimonious divorces and worse still as ammunition in parental fights.

Earlier I wrote that when family tension takes on a chronic dimension, an insoluble situation arises for the children involved. This only gets worse with divorce because the physical separation of parents causes further consternation for children. Sometimes children are required to make impossible choices—even though they love and need both parents. This leads to inner splits. It forces children to choose one parent over another, which frequently leads to problems in later relationships.

It is akin to exclusion when one parent is severely blamed and held solely responsible for the breakup. People often see in constellations that one of the children has to defend the excluded partner, which can lead to problematic behavior or even insurmountable child-rearing difficulties. Exclusion also has drastic consequences for the following generations. Children and grandchildren are forced to take up this theme to enable further processing of family trauma. The following is an example from my practice.

Helen is twenty-three. Her father is totally estranged from his ex-wife because he left her after he discovered she had had affairs during their relationship. Helen, out of loyalty, ended up with her father after the

180

divorce. She was ten years old at the time, and she has taken part in the exclusion of her *bad* mother all these years. She considers herself a better woman than her mother. After the third year in her first serious relationship, Helen also began to have affairs, even though she dearly loved her partner. She eventually lost him, and he and their mutual friends excluded her. Suddenly she felt what it must have been like for her mother, and she realized she was just as *bad* as her mother.

At the end of her constellation, Helen and her *mother* embrace. Then the *mother* asks Helen to give back problems between her and her husband (Helen's father) and to stop emulating her behavior.

According to Bert Hellinger, a child feels empty when (for whatever reason) he or she is unable or not allowed to love both parents.[9] Only being allowed to love one's mother or father is never enough.

Lynn, age thirty-five, is an example. She has had problems with her eight-year-old son, Wyatt, since divorcing his father. The constellation begins, and several family system disturbances soon become apparent. She is now aware these prevented her from happiness in her relationship with Wyatt's father. Toward the end of the constellation, *Lynn* and *Wyatt's father* stand a little distance apart. One after the other, each addresses *Wyatt*, who is standing opposite them. "Our relationship problems are our business," each says. "We are the adults. We can take care of this heavy affair." Their child is visibly more relaxed, and he replies, "I leave your relationship problems with you. You are the adults. I am just a child." He turns to his *mother* and says, "Look kindly upon me as I build a good relationship with Dad." Then he says to his father, "Look kindly upon me as I build a good relationship with Mom." Both *parents* are now able to agree. This relaxes all representatives, and it is clearly observable that love flows again.

The End of a Relationship

When children are involved in a relationship breakup, it is in everyone's best interest that parents conduct themselves like adults. A decision to stay together for the sake of the children actually just burdens them. The children then become responsible for the adults not going their own ways or opening to new things. They are used as the reason the mother and father must stay together—no matter how unhappy they

181

are in doing so. Children automatically become entangled in this process. A divorce is by nature a very difficult time for children, but parents can do a lot to make it more bearable. Most importantly children should continue to have unrestricted access to both parents as well as be allowed to love both parents equally.

It is a relief for children to be spared involvement in making important decisions, which is best done jointly by both parents. It is impossible for children to have to choose between living with their mothers or fathers. This automatically brings them into loyalty conflicts.

As it now stands, co-parenting seems the best way for both parents to continue to look after their children after a divorce. If this is not an option, children are best off, according to Bert Hellinger, with the parent who maintains a more loving and honoring attitude toward the ex-partner.[10]

Children sometimes do everything they can to preserve their parents' relationships, even when those relationships are beyond repair. By getting ill themselves or by behaving badly, they try to keep their parents together at all costs. Children themselves need attention and perhaps professional guidance when their parents are under the most strain. Parents usually forget or are too caught up in their own problems to appreciate this.

A relationship might end too easily such as when the mother or father pulls out to develop himself or herself or one leaves to flee from the relationship conflict. Even then children are not necessarily spared difficult consequences. The family conscience reacts as it would to a serious crime. This is a dynamic that surfaces by means of constellations. Children succumb to systemic pressure and pay the price instead of their parents. They express this by conspicuous or bad behavior, and sometimes they become seriously ill or in extreme cases have suicidal urges.

What Can Parents Do for Their Children?

Behaviors such as those stated above clearly show that by treating them as real children and not using or abusing them, parents can do a lot for their children. When parents fully understand their actions have direct impacts on the happiness of their children, they naturally adjust their lives accordingly.

For most people this is a new way of looking at the situation. People understandably are sometimes afraid of their responsibilities. On the other hand, constellation work shows that each step parents take to accept their responsibilities and make their relationships more loving helps their children be more relaxed. This gives them more room to be children and develop in their own ways. Parents thereby discover there is no guilty party—only people entangled with the heavy fates of ancestors.

Below are a few useful tips that can help make daily life a little easier for parents and children.

At the dinner table, children should sit to the left or opposite their parents. The hierarchy in family systems works clockwise, so the person to the right is higher up the hierarchy. It is not *healthy* for children to sit in a hierarchically superior position to their parents.

Susan, age thirty-four, is a single mother with two children—John, nine years old, and Sharon seven years old. She struggles with John. He does not always do what his mother asks or expects of him. During an introductory evening, I give Susan the option of having a table constellation.

Around their rectangular table at home, Susan sits at the head of the table with John to her right and Sharon to her left. While there is nothing to remark about *Sharon, John* is struggling. Setting the representatives in the right family order, I place Susan at the side of the rectangular table where John normally sits, and both the children are next to each other and opposite her. The position at the head of the table, on her left, remains vacant.

Everyone immediately feels better, and the atmosphere is more relaxed. Susan is surprised. She is sitting in her spot and feels rather strange. The spot to her right is vacant. It felt so good having John there. I make it clear to her this position is actually where an adult (such as a new partner) should be sitting. I explain that her son cannot be a substitute for a partner. As long as he continues to sit to her right, he will feel a bit bossy. The representative of *John* says he felt unstable and disrespectful sitting to the right of his *mother*. He felt he looked down upon her. In his new position, he is now looking at her.

By asking her to sit in various positions around the table, I allow Susan to try out various siting arrangements. Soon enough she understands the principles at work and also how important the correct order is. Out of curiosity she decides straightaway to implement the new seating arrangements at home for a week.

A few weeks later, she phoned me to thank me. "It's much more peaceful at the table now, and John is much more obedient," she told me.

It always strikes me how something that might be considered as unimportant as seating arrangements at the dinner table can influence, in a positive or negative way, the feelings of all family members.

The best (most harmonious) seating arrangements happen at a round table with consideration given to the clockwise order of hierarchy. Parents are first. Their positions are to be mutually decided upon, and the children in order of age follow. The child to the right has to be older. The same principle holds for a square or rectangular table. Parents can be next to each other or with a table corner between them. They should never sit opposite each other. Very young children are permitted to sit between their parents or between a parent and the oldest child as long as they are not able to eat independently. (See "Table Constellations" in chapter eight.)

Parents should not sit opposite each other. What in the beginning might have brought a romantic atmosphere by way of candlelight dinners becomes disruptive in a family setting in the long run. A couple should generally be facing in the same direction. This is something I had not expected, but innumerable constellations has validated this. Apparently this is just the way the system works. You can easily verify this at home by implementing a one-week modified family seating arrangement trial as described.

It is very taxing for children to sit between their parents or to sleep between their parents for an extended period of time. The child becomes a mediator or a buffer, which is too heavy for the child to handle.

It is also important that single parents do not allow their children to sleep frequently in bed with them. Children feel forced to compensate for the absence or emptiness felt by these parents. This readily leads to parentification. They will automatically and subconsciously do what they can to become replacements for real, adult partners. The worst part is that single parents sometimes lose the need for real partners because of the presence of the children, who substitute for those partners. It is best for both child and parent to keep the space next to the parent free for an adult partner rather than using a child as replacement. (Of course, if the child has a nightmare or the like and needs protection during the night, a parent must do what needs to be done.)

When parents split up, they might want to keep the following in mind:
o   It is important they continue to communicate with each other directly rather than through their children.
o   Each might want to make a gesture such as hanging up a photo of an ex-partner in the child's bedroom to let the child see that parent may also be loved.
o   They should show respect for each other, which will be a relief for the children.
o   They should avoid being reminded of the bad things about a former partner regarding the children. Instead they should see in the children reminders of the nicest moments of a former marriage.

Sometimes terminology can be confusing or even have a detrimental influence on commonly held notions. By using the term single-parent family,[11] people automatically exclude the other parent. A child has the birthright to maintain close relationships with both parents, even though he or she might live with only one.

According to scientific research at the University of Emory in Georgia, "Knowledge of family history for adolescents is a great way to prevent identity crises."[12] Researchers recommended that families should regularly talk about their pasts at the dinner table, including difficult times experienced.

In brief they recommended the following:

o   Eat together as a family as often as possible, and talk during the meal.

o   Tell as many stories as are known about the family's past, such as where grandparents grew up and how they got to know each other.

o   Talk openly about the good as well as the bad times.

o   Talk about negative occurrences in the presence of children. They happen, and children have the right to know about them as well.

o   Help children see that people have ways and means to live and cope effectively with setbacks.

7

Family Constellations and Disease

Somebody has to be re-membered.
—Albrecht Mahr[1]

The subject for the chapter is the way family constellations can be used to look at illness. A subconscious systemic dynamic is behind illnesses such as anorexia, bulimia, asthma, cancer, and chronic fatigue syndrome (CFS) as well as, suicide, physical illness, and addiction. It will become clear that constellations powerfully aid healing processes. In many cases healing is only possible with family constellations because this allows people distance from their entanglements which causes their illnesses.

Family constellations enable all kinds of physical and psychological illnesses, addictions, and even suicides to be seen in new light. Hellinger's work with illness, addiction, and people with suicidal tendencies has been documented in various books and videos. In the meantime hospitals in Germany such as the Psychiatry Center in Weinsberg have begun using his techniques.[2]

Whenever someone constellates his or her illness or addiction, an underlying entanglement surfaces. Time after time people witness the magical child love dynamic (see "Bonding Love" in chapter three), whereby a deep and subconscious desire to share in the lot of a family member with a disease, trauma, or exclusion manifests. This is how, with a good conscience, illnesses, bad luck, and death are desired and expressed. This phenomenon arises early in life and becomes entrenched by adult life. By so doing, a person sees to the needs of the family conscience and strives for compensation. This subconscious love can sometimes be apparent in the preliminary interview stage of a constellation. Consider the case of Anne, age thirty-three, who suffers from a rare form of tuberculosis. Inquiring about her disease and her prospects, she tells me her future does not look bright. Within two months she will have to undergo heavy antibiotic treatment. When I ask her if she thinks this will help, she replies with a broad smile. "Actually I don't think so."

The fact she smiles when she speaks about her *death sentence*, a subconscious act, is an obvious sign she is inviting death. However, she does this with a clear conscience and out of bonding love.

In cases where bonding love underpins these dynamics, regular medical intervention is not enough. This also applies to severe physical illnesses, psychological problems, or suicidal tendencies. Medical professionals do their best; however, they have limitations. Despite this no therapist working from a systemic, phenomenological standpoint belittles the medical input. Accordingly a therapist does not consider constellations to be substitutes for necessary medical intervention.

Just like Hellinger I consider my work supplementary to traditional medical treatments. Hellinger says, "The experienced constellation therapist works alongside the medical professional. While the doctor treats the disease in question using the battery of methods and techniques we know as modern medicine, the systemic phenomenological therapist works to bring the subconscious, blind, childlike love to the surface; he takes into account the client's past and deep-lying issues at the kernel of the problem. Subsequently, and with respect for the patient's soul, he tries to help the seeker become aware of the unfortunate entanglements."[3]

A therapist who works effectively with illness knows that only the immune system can heal an illness. He or she also knows the immune system is tied to the workings and needs of the soul. To be able to work successfully, it is essential that a therapist is at inner peace, free of worry about death, and has no compulsion to save his or her client. When dealing with consequential illness or even death, only an unconditional respect for the depth of childlike bonding love and resultant entanglements will allow a therapist to find appropriate solutions. In the end, however, it is up to the client if or how he or she applies these solutions.

Therapists who claim or are convinced they have the powers to heal put themselves under enormous pressure and are no longer at peace with themselves. Furthermore, they cannot work according to systemic phenomenological principles.[4] It is unrealistic for therapists who work according to these principles to demand wonderful results for themselves and their work. According to Hindu philosophies, people (therapists) are entitled to do the work, but they are not entitled to the fruits of action.

The special benefit of constellation work becomes clear once one participates in a constellation concerning illness, addiction, or suicide. In all constellations around these themes that I have worked with to date, family entanglements arise as the underlying causes. The basic dynamic that continues to manifest with illnesses, addiction, or suicide is the blind, childlike love discussed in chapter three. A child seeks, in blind love, to compensate or equalize by sharing a family member's misfortune, disease, or death. It makes no difference whether the illness in question arose in childhood or later in life.

The well-known therapist Albrecht Mahr, who worked together with Hellinger for twenty years and still regularly conducts constellations about illness, says, "Illness is a sign that a member of the family was either excluded or forgotten. We also often see that illness is a confirmation of loyalty to a family member with a heavy fate. The body reveals this through disease."[5]

Behind this dynamic is the blind love that finds expression as inner statements such as, "I would rather be ill or die than have you be ill or die," "Let me do it for you. Let me be ill or die in your place," or "I follow you in illness and death."

In a constellation it is essential the seeker perceive his or her subconscious and inner statements as well as feel the underlying inner blind love. The moment these statements are articulated, the seeker immediately realizes that someone actually opposes him or her. The family member to whom this inner statement is directed suddenly becomes a person who also has his or her own wishes and ideas about love.

Naturally this same family member does not want his or her descendant to repeat the suffering or disease. Through the expression of these inner statements, such as "I want to be ill or die in your place" or "I'm happy to die in your place," it is immediately clear the family member whose heavy fate or disease has been adopted does not want this to happen. The blind, childlike love of the client is unmasked, and the family member to whom the entanglement is directed is seen as a living being with his or her own unique identity. This occurs even though a representative is standing in for a dead family member in the constellation. This confrontation is somewhat disappointing, and yet it has to be this way so the blind love of the child can mature into conscious love. This is how symbiosis and identification with the family member who carries a heavy fate or disease can be broken. This process enables the seeker to step back and let this family member go. In other words a boundary is drawn between the two connected family members. It becomes clear that the seeker, standing in for and wanting to share the other's fate, cannot help or heal his or her relative. Just the opposite holds true—the ancestor actually considers the attempted assistance a burden.

Once the seeker appreciates this, he or she is able to let go of the entanglement by voicing a statement such as, "Dear Dad, although you are ill, I understand you want me to continue on and lead a healthy life." Such a statement has a relaxing and tension-releasing effect on both parties, and the entanglement in unraveled. Another statement could be, "My dear sister, even though you died young, I'm going to live on, and in the future we'll meet again. Look kindly upon me as I continue to live a healthy and happy life." A child who has died young might respond, "Dying young belongs to me and my fate. Your fate is to live on." These are just examples. Resolving statements in constellations are tailored to the dynamics that appear.

There are a variety of hidden dynamics at play in constellations about illness, addiction, and suicide. They have to be looked at on a case-by-case basis. It is unwise to work from an established pattern. According to Mahr there is no special dynamic that leads to one disease or another. Even though I will discuss different diseases and give examples, no general rules can be considered.

Anorexia

With anorexia the child, most often a girl, has an inner statement that goes something like, "I do this for you, Dad. I'll go before you do."It usually comes to the participants' attention in a constellation concerning this theme that the father is bound to and entangled with a former family member. There might be unprocessed grief, a sibling who passed away at an early age, heavy guilt, a traumatic experience in war, or the early death of a parent. The father carries this burden with him and wants to subconsciously leave the family system. In other words he wants to die. His daughter jumps into the breach and wants to die in her father's place in the vain hope her father will go on living. She begins a slow dying process by literally vanishing such as in the constellation of Annie in chapter three.

A similar dynamic is seen with tuberculosis. I mentioned that sometimes the strongest entanglements concern the father, but there are also strong entanglements with other family members, and sometimes the vanishing twin syndrome (see chapter four) can play a role.

A different dynamic was observed with fifteen-year-old Kim. She came to me under the direction of her parents to be constellated for her anorexia. It became clear early in her constellation that a child was missing in the mother's family. It turned out to be due to a miscarriage or a child who died very young—most likely her mother's sister. Kim's mother was totally unaware of this. No facts were known about this event. It was a great relief for Kim when the child was acknowledged and given her rightful place in the family. Kim saw, by means of the constellation, that out of loyalty to the *forgotten child,* she had tried to waste away by starving herself. Her subconscious self-talk or inner statement was, "If you are not acknowledged and given your rightful place, I don't want to exist either." Kim's longing to disappear ceased once the *forgotten child* was given her place in the family.

This was a constellation I will not easily forget. During the constellation Kim described a longing for an ethereal existence without corporeality to enable her to be at one with her forgotten family member. Her total love and longing went out zealously to this *forgotten child.* It was an extremely moving experience for me, and it touched me deeply to feel her inner idolization and willingness to sacrifice her own life. After the constellation I wondered if all people suffering from anorexia had similar feelings.

191

Bulimia

The bulimic patient suffers from an eating disorder that entails compulsive eating and subsequent self-induced vomiting. According to Hellinger bulimia often has roots in a family situation whereby the person's mother clearly expresses, whether consciously or not, that her child cannot receive any recognition or affection from his or her father.[6] This is considered the sole right of the mother. To be loyal and trusting to her mother, the child takes on too much from the mother, which manifests as overeating. To be trusting and loyal to the father, he or she spews it all back out again.

There is an entanglement at work behind the mother's posturing. She is almost always strongly bound with female family members from previous generations who had heavy fates with men. (For more information about oppression of women, refer to "Loyalty" and "The Double Shift" in chapter five.) In her relationship she developed the same contemptuous and disapproving attitude toward her husband as the female ancestors who had lived long before her.

The mother here is usually not aware that she pulls her children toward her. The child, usually a daughter, follows along in loyalty through her personal conscience. To be able to belong, the daughter stops identifying with her father. At the same time, however, the child loves and needs her father, which brings her into an unresolvable conflict.

A similar dynamic is found in forms of addiction with sweets, tobacco, and alcohol. That will be discussed later on in this chapter.

It needs to be stressed that I am not talking about guilt. The mother is not doing this intentionally. An entanglement is determining her behavior.

Bert Hellinger has a simple therapeutic technique to treat bulimia. He explains it as follows:
When a client feels an attack coming on, she should buy a cartload of yummy food and display it on the dining table. The client then tastes each offering while she visualizes sitting on her father's lap and saying to him, "Dad, everything tastes good in your company; I enjoy what you offer me." Subsequently, she eats with joy and with great appetite. The visualization and repeating of the statement accompany each mouthful.[7]

Despite this information each case should be looked at individually.

Karen, age twenty-nine, is an example of a different dynamic concerning extreme overeating. In her constellation it became clear that through her overeating she tried to fill the empty heart of her father. Her mother (his wife) treated her father with contempt in the same way his mother had treated him as a boy.

Asthma

In one of the presentations where I demonstrated family constellations, a young woman asked to be constellated. She had suffered from asthma since she was a child. Her mother was also present in the room. The young woman told me her grandfather had gone into hiding during World War II and was actively involved in the resistance movement against the Nazis. Other facts in the family history were that a miscarriage had taken place as well as another child dying young. There were two surviving siblings. One of these died at thirty and was the brother of the seeker's mother.

The constellation clearly showed how the seeker, a young woman (the daughter) wanted to help share the burden of her mother's heavy fate. The *mother* had also relied emotionally on her *daughter*, but it became obvious she was not aware of what was going on. The *daughter* felt this heavy burden as pressure on her chest. The mother was bonded with her father (the *grandfather*) and her *dead brother*. The *grandfather* had been involved in the resistance movement and was bonded to his *victims* he made when fighting the Nazis.

The solution was to ask the *grandfather* to lie next to his *victims* and leave his family. This enabled the representatives to feel enormous relief. Then the *mother* said good-bye to her *brother* to let him rest in peace. This also had a calming effect on the *daughter*. Toward the end of the constellation, I asked mother and daughter to replace their representatives and bow before the *grandfather*. Finally I asked the daughter to say, "Dear Mom, I am but a child. You are the adult. I leave all the sadness with you." The mother responded, "I sought your help. I relied on you for emotional support, for which I am so sorry. All my pain and sadness belong to me. You honor me when you leave it all with me."

Cancer

Constellations with seekers who have cancer show a large variation in heavy entanglements. Behind this serious life-threatening disease, deep loyalties and inner statements are at work. These include, "Let me do it for you" or, "I follow you—even in death."

Jennifer, forty-two, has cancer and is undergoing chemotherapy. In her initial interview, she tells me her mother and two aunts (her mother's sisters) have died from cancer. Early in her constellation, it appears she is strongly bonded with her mother and one of her aunts. One by one, she fixes her gaze on the representatives and says, "I want to be with you out of love." By uttering these words, sadness overcomes her, and her love for these women is palpable. She begins sobbing. Next I ask the *mother* and the *aunt* to say the following to *Jennifer*: "To die of cancer is my lot. You honor me by leaving it with me." Then the *mother* says, "You belong with the living. I, your mother, am dead. You especially honor me as you go on living." Her *aunt* repeats the sentence. This touches Jennifer deeply. She feels so much love for these dead people. I ask her to make use of this love by bowing before her *mother* and *aunt* and saying, "Look with love and kindness on me as I live on, dear Mom and Aunty." The constellation ends right there.

After a time of rest, Jennifer says, "I didn't realize how much I loved these people. I would have done anything just to be able to be with them. Now I know where my place is—here with the living."

Chronic Fatigue Syndrome

A number of short descriptions about constellations concerning CFS and their surprising results follow.

Margaret, age forty-eight, has been very tired for five years and only manages to get through each day with great difficulty. In the initial interview, she told me her maternal grandfather experienced great hardship during World War I and has never spoken about it. Apart from that she was unaware of any other heavy fate in her family. At one point in her constellation, all the representatives look in the same direction toward the floor. By their responses it is apparent they all feel pressure. I bring two new representatives into the fray as unknown dead comrades or victims, and I get them to lie down in the spot where everyone is staring.

They all react intensely to this change. The *grandfather* turns away, as it is too much for him. The *mother* stiffens, and *Margaret* wants to die. I allow her to wallow in this urge. She sits down with what appear to be the *dead comrades/victims* of the grandfather. She feels love, sadness, and a very strong bond with these people. Both representatives indicate they were previously dead comrades and friends of the grandfather and not victims. Both say emphatically that Margaret does not belong with them. I ask the *grandfather* to look at the dead soldiers. He replies, "No. I won't. It is too painful. Incredibly painful." Upon saying this he looks on, and sadness overcomes him. He breathes deeply, and tears stream down his face. He composes himself, slowly opens up to the *dead comrades*, and goes to sit down with them. He looks each in the eye. It is clear how strongly he is bound to them.

I ask both *dead comrades* to individually say to the *grandfather*, "It was my fate to die. To live on is your fate. You honor me by leaving me in the realm of the dead and going on living." That touches the *grandfather*. He seems to awaken, and he says, "It's as though I am seeing you for the first time." I ask him to say, "I accept my life as a gift. I take on my fate the way it is, and I leave you in peace in death. In my heart you live on." He appears much better and distances himself from the dead. I place him opposite his *daughter* (Margaret's mother) and get him to say to her, "I'm staying alive. I am your father. My war trauma belongs to me. You honor me by leaving it with me."

195

Margaret feels much better and less restricted as a result of the events that have taken place. It is now time for her to replace her representative in the constellation. She enters the constellation and is immediately affected. I ask the *grandfather* to take her by the hand, lead her to the *dead comrades*, and say, "These are my dead comrades. They are part of my life and my fate. Leave them in my life." She looks alternately at her *grandfather* and his *dead comrades*. She slowly relaxes. After a time she begins to nod and says, "Yes. I see it now. It belongs in your life." I ask her to bow down before her *grandfather*. She takes her time doing this. Then she grabs her *mother*, hugs her, and says to her *mother*, "I leave this heaviness and pain with you because you are the adult. I am but a child." She feels so much lighter.

Ken, twenty-two, is a student. For four years he has had insomnia and is very tired throughout the day. He failed an important examination due to his tiredness. In his constellation it appears he is bonded with a miscarriage—a pregnancy before he was born. The pregnancy was miscarried after six months.

Ken sits in the constellation and looks the *miscarried baby* in the eye. He feels enormous sadness. The *miscarried baby* is sitting in front of his *parents* with his back to their legs. Each *parent* has a hand on his head. They say to Ken, who is now himself in the constellation, "He belongs with us as well. He is the miscarried baby who came before you. The biggest part of the sadness belongs with us. We can handle that. You take care only of your small share." He slowly lets go. I ask the *miscarried baby* to say to him, "My early death belongs with me and is part of my fate." Ken responds, "I leave your early death with you. I honor you, and in my heart you live on." That gesture releases a lot of pressure, and he feels relieved.

Finally Ken stands next to the *miscarried baby*. He is close to and opposite his *parents*. He laughs and checks out the *miscarried baby* once again. "At last I have a big brother." Both laugh together.

Depression

Depression is a disease that is becoming more common. Many people depend on prescribed medication to make their lives somewhat more livable. Official statistics, however, are only the tip of the iceberg. Many more people are depressed than are diagnosed, and even more still live under veils of heaviness—states in which they are continually lethargic or despondent. They struggle to cope with day-to-day living.

Burnouts and midlife crises are part of the modern world. People en masse live in disharmony with themselves and their surroundings. They are unhappy despite living in prosperous societies. More than ever before, people are materially replete, have more apparent certainty in their lives, and have more free time on their hands than ever before. According to the World Health Organization, though, depression is the most important disease of the twenty-first century.[8] In 2000 in Flanders (in the Dutch-speaking part of Belgium where I have my practice), 1,174 people took their own lives. Depression was implicated in 60 percent of the cases. Piecing together information from a number of different studies, it appears 15 percent of men and 30 percent of women suffered from depression in 2001.[9] Similar figures apply to the Netherlands as well. In the United States, an estimated one in ten reports depression,[10] and according to the Mental Health Foundation in Great Britain, almost 9 percent meet the criteria for the diagnosis.[11]

Realistically all examples given in this book could be included in this chapter.

From a systemic viewpoint, there are two important aspects that might shed light on this problem. The first is the trend toward smaller families, and the second is due to the consequences of two world wars and other major conflicts in which vast numbers of people perished or were traumatized.

In the past families had many children instead of the one or two common today. Consequently many children shared the burden of unprocessed grief from previous generations. These days one or two children might have to bear the brunt of the whole lot. Naturally they have it much tougher.

Constellation work reveals that much suffering and insanity are carried over from the unprocessed trauma of previous generations. As such it creates an enormous burden that can last for generations. Unworked wartime trauma falls most heavily on the shoulders of grandchildren. Apparently there is a generational leap at play in the people of nations that experienced major war destruction. The general hypothesis among fellow therapists is that the next generation in line takes care of reconstruction and safe survival. This provides sufficient security to enable delving into unprocessed business, thus bringing these issues to the surface in the following generation.

Suicide

Around 4,400 people kill themselves in England each year. That's one death by suicide every two hours. At least ten times that number attempt suicide. Around 75 percent of suicide victims are men.[12]

In the Netherlands 1,600 people per year commit suicide—about double the number of road deaths. Each year 400,000 people in the Netherlands find themselves in such despair that they consider ending their own lives. Almost a quarter of these make an actual attempt. This comes down to an actual rate of just under 2 percent of all deads'.[13]

In Belgium suicide is the second most common killer in men between twenty and twenty-four. In the age group twenty-five to thirty-four, it ranks number one. Every day seven people cut their own lives short. That's twenty-five hundred people per year. From this vantage point, Belgians take their own lives more often than Dutch people. About 2 percent of all deaths in Belgium result from suicide—almost 3 percent of men and over 1 percent of women. Flanders (the Dutch-speaking part of Belgium) experiences three suicides per day, which is one of the highest figures in the European Union.[14]

The National Institute for Mental Health claims that suicide was the tenth leading cause of death in the United States in 2007, accounting for 34,598 deaths with an overall rate of 11.3 suicide deaths per 100,000 people. An estimated eleven attempted suicides occurred per every suicide death.[15]

People usually react with outrage to suicide, and it is still largely considered a taboo subject. Family members sometimes feel guilty themselves. They feel as though they have failed the suicide victims in some way. They sometimes become angry with family members who have taken their own lives or those with suicidal tendencies. In this way they often camouflage their (feelings of) powerlessness. Sometimes they feel obligated to do things to help. However, they usually have no idea at all about the underlying family dynamics. Therefore, getting angry toward the suicide victim or excluding him or her is a subconscious defense mechanism in an attempt to quell feeling unbearable guilt and powerlessness. This exclusion naturally leads to even more entanglements.

The media often portrays the suicide victim as having a troubled life, and the *last straw that broke the camel's back* is given as the reason for the suicide.

This is just a distraction. If one checked what was in the basket on the camel's back, one would discover the real reason for suicide. A look in the basket would show the heavy burdens and loyalties operating in the family system.

A systemic dynamic as the underlying cause of suicide is clearly seen in constellations. Bert Hellinger says, "When families are constellated with suicide or the suicide impulse as the theme or arising issue, it is usually directly obvious that, deep down in the soul, bonding love is the underlying power."[16] Often a child longs to be with some other member of the family and wishes to share that person's death fate. This dynamic is expressed in the statements "I follow you," "I accompany you in death," or "Let me do it instead of you." Guilt drives the child because of his or her *advantage* in life—the child is alive while a close family member has died at a young age.

If one of the parents is strongly bound with someone who died young, through seeking death the child subconsciously formulates the following inner statement: "I do it for you." He or she becomes ill or seriously addicted to hard drugs or kills himself or herself as a sacrifice for the parent. (See "Bonding Love" in chapter three.) This makes it clear that most constellation examples I have given in the previous chapters are all connected to suicide in one way or another—whether they are concerned or not with illness or accidents.

199

When Hellinger talks about "the child," he is referring to the person with the suicide urge. A life crisis such as a divorce can lead a person to commit suicide later on in life. Someone with this systemic entanglement has tried so hard to do his or her best for so long as an adult that, when a crisis comes along, disillusionment ensues and prompts an affected person to give up. Systemic therapists approach people with suicidal tendencies very differently—different to traditional methods normally employed when this dynamic surfaces.

The usual starting point (preventing suicide at all costs) can no longer be sanctioned. The therapist must respect the child's blind love and consequent wish to die, which is much more difficult.

When the underlying directives of suicide are not respected, suicidal people will secretly cherish their love and loyalties and eventually see to it that they realize their subconscious wishes. With good consciences, they kill themselves out of this powerful love and loyalty.

If a therapist has respect for the deep inner drive and the love behind the scenes, he or she is also able to respect the desire to want to die. It is only with such respect that the blind, childlike love can come to light in a constellation and enable the seeker to clearly appreciate the entanglements at play. This allows the suicidal person to distance himself or herself from the childlike manner of showing love, and the person can take an adult perspective on the matter. With this same love, the seeker can go on to lead a happy and healthy life. (Refer to Sigrid's constellation in chapter four.)

Mental Illness

According to Professor Dr. Franz Ruppert, mental illnesses develop because people are entangled with serious confusions or disturbances in the family systems. People then get confused at the soul level. Such people cannot process, bridge, or unite the disturbances in their consciousness or the underlying inner images of their families. This is traumatizing. Ruppert identifies four different types of trauma that might lead to mental illness: existential trauma, loss trauma, bonding trauma, and bonding system trauma.[17]

Existential trauma

An existential trauma arises when a person's own life has been endangered. This includes surviving a very serious car accident or an act of nature such as an earthquake in which others lost their lives. Other causes of existential trauma are:

o   Experiencing wartime atrocities
o   Being witness to death such as observing a car running down a child
o   Being a victim of a robbery or carjacking
o   Being a victim of torture during political or military imprisonment

According to Rupert the consequences of existential trauma express themselves in a variety of complaints ranging from severe anguish, phobias, and depression to obsessive compulsive behavior.[18]

Loss trauma

People experience loss trauma in the following circumstances:

o   Leaving everything behind after forced emigration
o   Losing one's job and home
o   Losing a loved one

Complaints that appear as consequences of loss trauma are feelings of futility, depression, and (sometimes) suicidal tendencies.

Bonding trauma

Bonding trauma in children emerges when bonding with one or both parents goes awry or when the bonding process is abused. This includes:

o When children are denied physical contact with their mothers for extended periods of time in the first three years of life—through serious illnesses or by the babies being confined to neonatal intensive care units
o When children are sexually abused by parents
o When severe parentification (when parents rely heavily on their children emotionally) occurs
o When parents have an addiction to alcohol, medication, or something else
o When domestic violence occurs

Children who have experienced bonding trauma often develop the following symptoms later on in life: drug addiction, psychosomatic allergies, and borderline-type disorders.

Bonding system trauma

Bonding system trauma can occur as a result of murder within the family. The family conscience finds itself in a hopeless situation because an immediate conflict of loyalty arises. According to Ruppert the bonding system of the family soul is traumatized.[19] This results if any of the following occur in the family:

o When a murder within the family is committed. An honor killing is an example whereby a son murders one of his sisters or when a father kills one of his daughters because the female refuses to abide by community rules.
o When parents or brothers and sisters kill each other.
o When a family member is not given sufficient help that leads to that member's death. Examples are leaving a child to starve to death or not assisting in saving a family member from a life-threatening situation.
o When a mother abandons, gives away, or does not recognize a child born to a relationship outside the marriage or long-term relationship.

An especially heavy disturbance comes about when a father has children with his daughter. He is father and grandfather at the same time, and his child is also his grandchild. The family system cannot cope, and there is total confusion, which leads some family members in a later generation to go insane. A bonding system trauma can give rise to major spiritual and psychological dysfunction in the following generations, including psychosis and schizophrenia.

Traumas such as these are often kept hidden, not talked about, and treated as family secrets. Making the matter a family secret exacerbates the problem for following generations through the increased compulsion to carry the load and have it manifest through severe psychiatric illness.

Harry, age twenty-nine, brings his therapist with him for his constellation. He has been deemed psychotic and is treated with medication. He does not know much about his family. "Nobody talks about the family past," he says, "but I suspect there is something going on." The constellation has to begin with scant information about Harry's family's past. Representatives for his parents and a brother of the father who died young are constellated. Harry doesn't know anything else about his family.

All representatives are depressed. Harry's *father* and *uncle* stare down toward the same spot on the floor. Since the participants do not know much about the family, I organize to have a representative of a dead relative lie on the spot where the *father* and *uncle* are looking. Both say that another belongs there, so there should be two dead people lying on the floor. Consequently I call for another representative to join the existing one on the floor. The *two dead people* feel uneasy and are really angry. "It feels as though we have been murdered," they say in unison.

I constellate the *parents* of Harry's *father*. They refuse to look at the *dead people* lying on the floor. The *two dead people* say, "We are really angry with them. They have deprived us of our lives." After more questioning it is clear the grandparents aborted both male fetuses late in pregnancy (circa five to six months). Harry comments, "I know those two. I have heard them all my life as inner voices asking for help. At the same time, I want nothing to do with them. I hate them." He understands his split loyalty. The *aborted brothers* have been given places in the family by the end of the constellation. The father's brother who died young lies next to them. Their *parents,* Harry's *grandparents* stand close by. They face away and fully accept the guilt and responsibility for what they have done.

203

Harry is able to leave everything that is theirs with them—the heavy burden of the *aborted sons*, his uncles. These uncles wish him well in life. He is so relieved, for his confusion has been transformed into clarity. "Everything has fallen into place," he says.

Split loyalties felt by people suffering from manic depression are often revealed in constellations as well. They are bound to fortune and misfortune at the same time. Ann, age forty-four, is a case in point. She went through periods of depression as well as times of extreme happiness and joy. It is revealed in her constellation that she is strongly bonded with her father. The father took over the family farm from his father and turned it into a prosperous business. He inherited the farm alone because his older brother, Ann's uncle, had died in an accident.

The constellation shows how, in her depressive states, Ann is bound up with the pain connected to the death of her uncle, her father's older brother. During these periods she metaphorically lies down next to her uncle in his grave. In her happy phases, she is happy with the prosperity of her father's business.

During the constellation she lets go of her entanglement with the *unfortunate uncle* because he says, "You don't have to feel guilty for me anymore. The fact I died is part of my fate." He says to Ann's *father*, "I wish you luck on the farm. Make it into a success. My lot belongs with me." Ann understands she has taken on the pain of her uncle to compensate for the happiness of her father.

Psychiatric patients can constellate their families, allowing them to become conscious of contradictory allegiances. The best time to do this is in periods of relative calm—even when medication is taken. This should be under the trained eye of a therapist or at least a trusted family member. A psychotic reaction after a constellation can never be ruled out, so support should always be on hand to provide the appropriate safety net.

It is also essential that constellations be seen as ideal complements—not substitutes for intensive medical treatments.

Addiction

One of the underlying dynamics that has been found in constellations concerning themes of addiction is that of a mother being contemptuous of her partner, the father of her child. This stance can be either overt or covert. The mother's inner attitude is thus: "Whatever you take from your father can't be good. Take only from me." Indeed the child takes on traits and views from his mother to excess. However, due to revenge or pain, he takes on so much that it becomes damaging. In that sense the addiction is a kind of revenge from the child toward his mother. It is an expression of pain about the exclusion of his or her father from whom the child is forbidden to assume anything.

Bert Hellinger has an immediate intervention strategy for this dynamic. "You visualize being next to your father while your mother is present, and look sternly at her and say, 'He is just as important to me as you are, so I take from him just as I take from you.' Then, using your father's surname (e.g., Johnson), say, 'I am a real Johnson!' It is also advisable to do this in reality, especially if your mother is still alive. It is a difficult task and requires a great deal of courage. This is necessary if a real connection with the underlying emotions is to be made."[20]

Another dynamic, probably the most common concerning acute alcoholism and drug abuse, is a hidden suicidal tendency. Again driving this is magical, childlike love. A child wants to help or even die for another family member who died young, was excluded, or was despised because of his or her misery. Through the sacrifice of taking over that person's pain and suffering and becoming unhappy, a child strives to help or become that person.

Following are several abridged examples of constellations from workshops I have conducted around the theme of addictions.

The theme of George, age thirty-two, is eating to excess—overeating and consuming too much candy. He constellates a representative for himself and a woman as a representative for excess. In the constellation it is soon clear that excess is connected to his mother. She relies on her son for emotional support. *George* feels abused and says, "I am but a child." His *mother* admits she has abused her son. She used him as a pawn to fill her inner emptiness. His *mother* says, "I went too far. That's my responsibility. I am sorry." *George* says, "I went along out of love. I have done too much for you. Now I leave it with you. I leave

205

your inner emptiness with you as well. That belongs to you and your fate." His *mother* replies, "The emptiness is part of my life and my fate. You honor me by leaving it all with me. Take only what you need, and leave the rest with me."

Charlotte is forty-eight. Her theme is an addiction to anything sweet. She constellates representatives for herself and for sweets. A love–hate relationship between the two representatives is soon revealed. Eating sweets is a way of protecting herself against the hostile world. Charlotte feels small and suffers from general anxiety, and the group sees clearly that she has missed out on her father's protection. A representative for her father is added to the constellation, which enables *sweets* to feel more at ease. Charlotte enters the constellation herself, and her *father* awaits his daughter with open arms. He is strong. He says, "Take strength from me as you need to. I support you." Charlotte says, "I want you to protect me, but I am frightened of your aggression." Her *father* responds, "I understand. Leave the aggression with me." Charlotte falls into her *father*'s arms. She breathes in deeply and soaks up her father's strength. While she does this, *sweets* says, "I feel superfluous." Her *father* says to Charlotte, "I am always here for you. You can take strength and certainty from me whenever you need to."

Twenty-seven-year-old Joan's theme is smoking. She chooses representatives for herself and cigarettes. *Cigarettes* feels like a monster that wants to devour her one moment and a fragile weakling the next. *Joan* feels so small and is happy that *cigarettes* is with her as her friend and rescuer.

Both representatives move slowly away from each other. This causes *cigarettes* to feel less tense but makes Joan feel abused and even vitriolic.

Representatives for Joan's mother and father are then brought into the constellation. *Joan* does not trust her *father*. He has surrendered to being powerless. Real tension is evident between her *mother* and *father*. Her *mother* does not trust her *father* in the slightest. She says to *Joan*, "Our relationship problems belong to us. My contempt of your father is also mine. You honor me by leaving it all with me." Then her *father* says, "My life and everything in it are my fate. You can rely on me, but leave the problems between your mother and me with us." At the end of the constellation, Joan ends up in the arms of her *father* and takes comfort in his caring presence.

As an example of a constellation concerning severe alcohol and drug abuse, a summary of one of Hellinger's constellations follows.[21]

Klaus is an alcoholic. His grandfather died when his father was two years of age. It soon becomes clear in the constellation that his father was strongly bonded with his dead father, whom he wanted to be reunited with in death. Klaus is entangled in the same way and wants to follow in the footsteps of both his father and grandfather. This means having a death wish. His subconscious inner statement is, "I follow you." Resolution statements from his *father* to his *grandfather* are, "Dad, look kindly upon me as I keep on living. Do likewise for my son." Statements from his *father* to Klaus's representative are, "I'm staying alive, and I'm happy you are staying as well. I love you." *Klaus* says to his *grandfather*, "I'm staying to honor you. You live on in me."

An interrupted reaching-out movement and consequently an attachment problem sometimes resonate in the dynamic operating behind a heavy addiction. (See also the constellation of Sigrid and "Reaching Out Interrupted" in chapter four.)

Eye Diseases

Both Marianne Wiendl and Uschi Ostermeier-Sitowski have years of experience with natural means to improve eyesight.[22] They take the old adage that the eyes are the mirror of the soul seriously. They use family constellations to successfully give their clients the chances to find out what is preventing their eyes from functioning optimally. It is clear from constellations regarding eye problems and eye disease that eye malfunction represents unprocessed trauma in the family system. It could be that a socially sensitive issue or conflict has to be kept obscured to protect the family name and/or to keep a very painful occurrence away. To protect against the pain associated with the issue or conflict, a haze drapes over the socially sensitive issue or conflict (hides it in mist), which acts as an emotional protection barrier. This can lead to a situation whereby one or more family members are literally unable to see clearly.

Glasses or contact lenses take over the protection so the person in question is able to see clearly. The real problem is not resolved but rather remains buried in the subconscious.

The dynamics behind this can vary. It might be unprocessed trauma connected with the early death of a parent, a miscarriage, brothers or sisters who died young, or wartime suffering. Relationship problems between parents or divorce can also be behind eye problems ranging from squinting to myopia. Wiendl and Ostermeier-Sitowski say:

Eyes are not independent living organisms. There exists a left and a right "view." Constellations indicate that each eye has a different function and that sight is the fusion of these separate interpretations. It seems that the left eye is responsible for female issues and the right eye governs male matters. This shows the schismatic nature of people and the difficulty in overcoming dualism and allowing everything to melt into one. In families with severe parental relationship problems, children often struggle with the level of discord between their parents. Children have trouble focusing their gaze so that seeing with both eyes becomes difficult and various forms of "cross-eyes" may arise.[23]

Wiendl and Ostermeier-Sitowski often constellate the client and both his or her eyes to see if there are problematic connections with one or both eyes. They are checking to see if both eyes are aligned or if one eye is fixated on a family member from the past. The authors give a number of examples of the connection between disturbances or traumas in the family system and problematic eyesight in their book, *Systemische Augentherapie (Systemic Eye Therapy)*. With pleasure I quote their noteworthy findings about how children take on disturbances from their parents. Wiendl and Ostermeier-Sitowski say:

Developing inner structures and concepts is difficult for children when parents are not good role models and do not behave according to their inner feelings. Neurobiological studies have shown that certain brain cells called mirror neurons [see "Mirror Neurons" in chapter nine] are capable of adopting feelings from other people as though they were their own. Small children are especially endowed with this gift. They are still not in a state to close themselves off from others. They are particularly good at taking on the world of feelings as well as different wounds of their parents, in all dimensions. Once they experience uncertainty, they take this on as their own uncertainty, which imprints upon their personalities. This then, is generally expressed through various sight disorders.[24]

8

Other Types of Constellation

The Tao is like a well:
used but never used up.
It is like the eternal void:
filled with infinite possibilities.
—Lao-Tzu[1]

Over the years other types of constellations have been developed alongside traditional family constellations. These include individual, organizational, and structural constellations. Examples of these will be discussed in this chapter as well as table constellations and constellations dealing with inner aspects or inner voices. Furthermore, attention will be given to constellations with multicultural backgrounds as well as political constellations. Last but not least, I will describe further developments in Hellinger's constellation work—namely Movement of the Soul and Movement of the Spirit-Mind.

Constellations in the Individual Setting

When I started as a constellation facilitator, I was convinced representatives were essential for a *good* constellation. I have since changed my mind completely. Many constellations I now give are individual sessions without representatives. There are four main ways I work in individual sessions. The first is using small dolls or figures, the second is using floor anchors, the third is working with chairs, and the fourth is working with the client's imaginary aptitude. This is using the Ursula Franke method.[2] The theme as well as the expectations and capacities of the client all influence the chosen method.

Dolls and figures are the ideal instruments for individual constellations. They are exemplary diagnostic instruments that can clearly reveal disturbances just by the way they are positioned in relation to each other. (The constellation of Kevin in chapter five is an example.)

A facilitator can continue working with the dolls or use other means throughout a constellation, as the example further on will illustrate. First, though, I will explain the other methods.

A floor anchor is an A4 sheet of paper on which the name of the family member to be represented is shown with an arrow indicating the direction this person is facing. Floor anchors are laid out on the floor in the same way representatives would be constellated. When the client stands on these places, he or she tunes in as if he or she is the representative. (A good example of this is John's constellation in chapter six.)

Using chairs with different colors is the third way. The chairs are constellated the same way representatives would be. When the client sits on the different chairs, he or she tunes in as if he or she is the representative of the person represented by the chair.

With the fourth variation, the complete constellation takes place in the imagination as visualization (the Ursula Franke method). The therapist asks the client/seeker to tune in to the perceptions of a certain family member and imagine, from that family member's perspective, how the family member feels toward him or her. For example, I tell Ron, "Imagine you could experience your mother's perception by seeing through her eyes and feeling what she feels. Once you are able to do this, please look at your son. Do you now see your son?" Ron nods, and I continue. "Please say to your son, 'You've had to do so much for me. You've had to carry so much. This may end now.'" Ron repeats this sentence aloud. Then I ask him if it sounds right and if, according to his mother, the feeling expressed is correct. He confirms this representation. As his mother, I ask him again, "Do you want your son to leave all your pain and grief with you?" From the perspective of his mother, Ron can clearly feel she means it.

I ask him to stop visualizing. After allowing him a moment to come to rest, I ask him to take a deep bow and say aloud, "I now leave all your pain and grief with you, as I am but a child. I thank you for everything in my life. I will make something special of it."

Dorothy is thirty-two. Her theme concerns her eight-year-old daughter, Jane, who cannot concentrate well and as a result has difficulties at school. I ask Dorothy to select dolls to represent her daughter, herself, and her husband, Jane's father. I tell her to constellate them. Dorothy places Jane's figure in the middle, the figure for Jane's father to the right, and her own figure to the left of the child. All are aligned. In the discussion about the placement of the dolls, Dorothy says she also felt caught between her parents and that she can remember how difficult it was for her when she was young. She understands her daughter is now in this very same difficult position and how much attention and energy it must demand from her.

We continue working with floor anchors instead of figures or dolls, and I prepare A4 sheets of paper for Dorothy. I write the names of her mother, her father, her husband, and her child. One by one she puts the sheets on the floor as if placing representatives. When this is done, I ask her to stand on each place in turn and feel what happens. By doing so she experiences how her daughter feels to be positioned between her parents. "It indeed feels just like I felt being caught between my parents and how I had to constantly act as a go-between. We treat our daughter the same way my parents treated me. My daughter is playing the go-between for me and my husband." We then focus on Dorothy's position between her parents. Ultimately Dorothy manages to return to her parents all the tension and burdens associated with having to continuously mediate between them. As a result she discovers and appreciates her real place in relation to her parents, which is as a child. She can now feel that her parents do not want her to keep mediating between them, as this only serves to interfere in their relationship. The repositioning of the floor anchors engenders a huge feeling of relief for Dorothy.

She is now able to see how she used her daughter as a go-between for her and her partner during times of tension. In these difficult times, Jane did everything to save the relationship—just as Dorothy had done with her parents. I ask her to tell Jane (represented by the A4 sheet on the floor) the following: "You have had to do a lot for us. Thank you. I feel your love. You do this in the same way I did for my parents. I know how you feel and how heavy it is for you. You may stop now. Dad and I are the adults. You are but a child. You may now leave the tensions of our relationship with us."

I also get her to feel what the new representation is like for her daughter, Jane. She can clearly feel the release of tension for her daughter as she stands on the floor anchor representing her.

I rearrange the positions of the A4 sheets, and Dorothy's parents are now at a short distance behind Dorothy. Dorothy and her husband are adjacent to each other. In front of them, at a good distance, I place Jane. This distance is appropriate for an eight-year-old girl. Dorothy tunes in one by one to all the positions of those being represented, and therein she finds clarity. She then gives the load of having to mediate and carry her parents' fate back to them. This is a big relief for her, and at the same time she is able to see her daughter much more as a child.

Two weeks later Dorothy tells me that much has since come into motion in her life and that her daughter is now a lot less tense. Dorothy and her husband also planned to constellate their own relationship.

Steven, age thirty-nine, has already done constellations surrounding family and relationship matters, and overall he is doing well—except in the employment sphere. He has completed a fine arts degree and has a proven talent for graphic design. Commenting on his talent, he says, "I don't do anything with it, and I really don't know why. I'm just too afraid perhaps. Until now I just have not thought about it." He works hard and has already done various jobs assigned to him via a job agency, but nothing long-term has eventuated.

He explains that his mother came from a family of bakers. "This dates back three generations. They are very hardworking people. They are people who just can't sit still," he says. "In my father's family, it is no different. They were farmers from the western part of Belgium who knew nothing other than hard work. During the war they lost everything in a fire. After that my grandfather had to work on a factory production line. My father did just the same. He worked his entire life in a car factory. Being able to afford education for his children was his only source of pride."

I ask him to imagine for a moment how his grandfather must have felt as his farm went up in flames and he had to work in a factory. Steven seems to do quite well feeling how his grandfather must have felt. He shares his perceptions. "It feels horrible. I feel his pain, his lack of control, and the feeling of having failed." After this I ask Steven to return to his own inner feelings and observe his grandfather from his own position while still visualizing. Upon my prompting he says, "I feel what you feel, dear Grandfather. I feel how painful it was for you." Steven can clearly feel this. Then I ask him, within his own feelings, to look straight into his *grandfather*'s eyes and say, "I also prefer to work in a factory. Just like you. I could do something different, but I want to do exactly what you have done." Halfway through the sentence, he feels a lot of sorrow and pain, which he finds difficult to express. The loyalty toward his grandfather becomes clearly tangible to Steven, and he also appreciates that his grandfather does not want him to make his life difficult by taking over his fate.

"Imagine if you could feel how your grandfather feels about your situation now. What does that do for him, and how is it for you?" I ask him. Steven visualizes and feels how it is for his grandfather to see his grandson. "It hurts to see what my grandson is doing with his life. As a grandfather I do not want my grandson to share my fate. I want him to have his own life." I ask, "Even if that means earning a comfortable living as a graphic designer?" The grandfather in Steven's imagination confirms this, and Steven clearly feels that his grandfather would be proud.

At this point I ask Steven, "What would your grandfather now tell you?" Steven answers, "Do what you enjoy doing. I support you." After this answer I ask Steven to say the following from his inner imaginary position as his grandfather toward his *grandson*: "My fate belongs to me. If you really wish to honor me, explore your talents. That hardworking element belongs to my life and me. You may leave this with me."

We repeat the sentences again but now with Steven's *father*. I ask him to voice similar sentiments in his imagination and ask him also to look at himself from his father's viewpoint. By doing this he clearly experiences that his father also prefers him to work with pleasure as a graphic designer and that he absolutely does not want his son to repeat his fate. Steven feels much better in his own skin, and he sees clearly how loyal he has been to both his grandfather and father.

We then begin to round off the constellation by looking at all other family members and asking for their blessings for Steven to work with pleasure creating beautiful works of art as well as for him to earn a decent income. When all family members are OK with this and happy for him for the first time in his life, Steven feels the positive drive to use his talents.

The biggest obstacle for individual constellation work is the client's difficulty in letting go of ideas and prejudices regarding how other family members think and feel. When *letting go* skills are developed, a person can freely tune in to the feelings and viewpoints of family members.

Sometimes it is difficult for people to feel what someone else (a mother, a father, etc.) is feeling. At times people identify with their own situations and visions so strongly that they have difficulty distancing themselves. Consequently they struggle to comprehend how their parents, for example, could think and feel differently than them. This, of course, is not a bad thing. In cases such as this, I invite them to join in group constellation seminars in order to participate as representatives. They then experience how representative perceptions operate, and they can release all difficulties they have with individual constellations.

Some clients who have already done constellations still have unanswered questions or discover that old loyalties persist in their lives. In these cases clients can easily work out unresolved issues and release them in individual constellations.

Organizational Constellations

Organizational constellations = emotional intelligence in action.

An organizational constellation is an innovative and fascinating type of constellation work. The way organizational constellations have developed, what people can achieve with them, and similarities and differences with family constellations will be explained. This section looks at the underlying order and how the systemic conscience operates in organizations.

Organizational constellations are new and highly effective methods to bring underlying causal reasons of disturbances within organizational structures to the surface in the same way family constellations do for individuals. This is faster and more efficient than time-consuming and expensive business investigations that have become the norm.

Constellating an organization provides an answer to a query in no time. People can see what is really going on, and the constellation shows the best solution. The revolutionary aspect of organizational constellations is in making unmistakably clear that every organization works like a system. It has its own order, underlying loyalties, and a systemic conscience—even sharing some traits with a family system's rational ethics (Nagy). In other words a systemic conscience exists in all group structures such as organizations, companies, institutes, teams, and associations. If the hierarchy of relational ethics has been disturbed in the past, this disturbance remains present within the system conscience. Just as in family systems, all unprocessed and unresolved disturbances from the past are carried on in organizational systems.

As a consequence subconscious and blind loyalties come into existence similar to those that surface in family constellations through the blind love of a child. These disturbances can be made apparent in the same way as in family constellations. They are brought to light through representative perceptions, which also help provide solutions.

Constellations can be applied to virtually all types of organizational issues, such as:

o Improving leadership and management
o Improving team spirit at any level, including interdepartmental cooperation
o Finding solutions to issues such as high absenteeism, low productivity, or workplace bullying
o Working through reorganization themes, complex issues during mergers by big and small companies, and removing barriers during acquisitions
o Making apparent and improving client–product relations and resolving the causes of problematic marketing issues such as customer dissatisfaction and loyalty, slow product uptake, and the defining of a customer base
o Receiving career planning and advice as an addition to the coaching process

There are myriad possibilities for organizational constellations with plenty of room for innovation still.

Ben, age fifty-two, leads a team of twenty employees in data processing. The team has a low productivity rate and a high rate of absence through illness. Ben explains that he has now been the team leader for two years, that he came from another company, and that this post became available because his predecessor was promoted to a higher management position within the company.

Together we first determine if we need to set out the whole team to get a clear picture of the problem or if it suffices to set out the most important team members. Ben chooses five team members, and I ask him to select representatives for all five members as well as for his predecessor and himself. He then sets about constellating them.

From the outset the constellation gives an overall impression of detachment because team members are not facing each other. This suggests an absence of team spirit. Further questioning reveals that the team is angry with Ben's *predecessor*, but opinions are divided. The *predecessor* does not even look at the team and is positioned some distance away. *Ben* views the whole situation with the necessary distance and feels powerless.

Ben braces himself during questioning, but he is surprised at what transpires. "Even though I recognize the angry sentiments that team members have with my predecessor, I don't understand why, and it is something I didn't expect," Ben says. When I ask again if people had been fired or if a reorganization had occurred, he first says that was not the case. However, upon thinking for a moment, he says, "There were problems three or four years ago with new software. We are still struggling with that. There is a plan to replace this software, but the team is not yet aware of the current proposal."

All team representatives vie to reply at the same time. Pointing to his *predecessor*, one of them says, "It was his responsibility, but he never involved us with the planning and implementation of the software. We knew it wasn't good." Another says, "According to him it was entirely our fault, but there were just too many bugs in the software." The predecessor looks away and says, "Indeed. It was my responsibility, but I preferred to place the blame with the team. My career was more important. I didn't get on well with the team anyway."

I ask the *predecessor* to repeat that it was his responsibility, and immediately after this I ask the team member representatives to return the blame and responsibility for the software problems back to the *predecessor*. One by one each does this and immediately feels better. The team members now feel more at ease with each other. The divisiveness within the team has somewhat dissipated.

Following my instructions Ben takes his position in the constellation and places the team members in a semicircle according to their lengths of service in the team. He does this in clockwise order from longest to shortest tenure. The *predecessor* is positioned a little behind the longest-serving team member. Everyone now feels better. At this point the feeling of division between the five representative team members has virtually disappeared.

Ben is asked to voice the following words to the team while observing the effects on himself and the team: "I see you are not to blame for the software problem. The responsibility belongs to my predecessor, and you may all leave this responsibility with him. The software will be replaced, and this time we will do things together because I need your expertise."

From the positive reaction of the five team members, it becomes clear to Ben that these words have given him and the team strength. The team members themselves also seem invigorated, and one of them says, "The fact he values our expertise makes me particularly happy." For Ben it is now clear what and how he has to communicate to get the team to work in a cooperative spirit once again.

The Origin of Organizational Constellations

Organizational constellations owe their existence and development to family constellations. In 1995 therapists and coaches saw the first requests for the application of this methodology to organizations. Michael Wingenfeld and Thomas Siefer then asked Bert Hellinger to give the first organizational constellation therapy workshop.[3] This was the start of a boom, which slowly but surely came to influence the whole business and organizational domain.

Today organizational constellations have grown to become independent instruments for advice in initiating positive changes within companies and organizations. The method appears to be an ideal complement to the conventional repertoire of organizational and business consultants.

However, the ramifications for organizational constellations go even further. The results make apparent that there is an order or principle underlying all relationships—those in private life, family life, social networks, or even the work environment. This order was not thought up or invented but surfaces in every organizational constellation. It is a systemic order, which underlies all kinds of human relationships.

When people respect this order in organizations, harmony enfolds, productivity increases, and the staff members work with pleasure. When an organization gets into trouble, a constellation shows there is a disturbance of this order and its relational ethics.

Methodology of Organizational Constellations

Just as in family constellations, organizational constellations work with the perceptions of the representatives. As a result hidden dynamics causing problems or blocking successes come to light. Typically the manager or director (seeker) constellates that component of his or her organization where a problem is apparent. In the introductory talk, the client and coach/therapist discuss only the theme and the facts. Character descriptions are avoided, just as in all constellations. The seeker chooses a representative for everyone involved. These have to be neutral people, just as in family constellations. As in family constellations, the seeker then places the representatives in the room or space according to his or her inner perceptions. He or she feels the best respective positioning.

Following this the facilitator works with representatives to find a good solution to the problem. To end the process, the seeker is placed in the improved and rearranged constellation layout. This is to allow the new organizational image to sink in and allow the manager to visually observe the implemented solutions.

In this way information found in a constellation of about forty-five minutes provides the insights that classic analysis and intervention methods would have taken much longer to achieve.

Representatives

A representative is a neutral person who represents the organization, the product, the employee, or even a problem in a constellation. The only information representatives need are the facts. By being positioned, they have access to the subconscious structure of the organization, just as in family constellations where there is access to the family system's depth structure.

Representatives work as detection instruments and reveal the entanglements. All solutions are found by working with representatives.

Differences

Apart from the many similarities, there are also major differences between family systems and organizational systems. Within a family people are all connected by existential loyalties—the loyalty concerning birth and the fact that parents have given children their lives. This is different than organizations. There a contract or agreement arranges one's place within and one's bond to the organization.

A person's birth defines his or her place in a family. The hierarchy is fixed and cannot change. In organizations this can be changed. A person can leave an organization or change his or her place in the hierarchy by being promoted or demoted. In principle a person can start as a security guard in an organization and end up as a director, so the same people who were hierarchically superior at first can become subordinates later. This is impossible in families. Parents will always be parents, and grandparents stay grandparents forever.

Another difference lies in the balance of giving and taking. In a family the hierarchy defines this balance. Parents give what they can to their children, and when their children become parents, they give their children what their parents gave them. In organizations a contract or a similar agreement determines the balance for a specific assignment or job, and a member of an organization will receive a certain reward. In volunteer work there is also a balance. Although a person does not work for monetary gain, he or she might work for recognition or to avoid boredom by using free time productively.

There is another intrinsic difference between family and organizational constellations. Constellations for organizations are typically less emotional, which generally means they are less intense and more analytical. Additionally there are more solutions possible than in family constellations. For example, an organizational constellation might show that restructuring or resignation is required. A person cannot resign from his or her family. A person's place in the family is fixed for eternity.

Systemic Order in Companies and Organizations

A team is not a team without team spirit, and every organization, no matter how big or small, needs a soul, a soul embodiment, and an inner strength or drive. This encourages productivity and helps to develop the group's full potential. Working with organizational constellations teaches people that disturbances in the systemic order strongly affect the force behind the *soul* (the size of the inner strength of an organization).

These disturbances within the underlying systemic order come to light during the constellation. Not only is the presence of the system consciousness pertaining to every organization, team, or company revealed, but how it influences all members also comes to light.

The initial image of a constellation often shows a significant divisiveness. It is typical that everyone looks askance and the representative for the goal or purpose (of the organization) feels ignored or is just not seen.

At the end of an organizational constellation, when disturbances are cleared up and the systemic order is restored, everyone shares the same vision. Trust is restored. There is clearly and observably more strength and enthusiasm, and the representative for the goal of the organization becomes the focus of this strength.

The Systemic Conscience

The systemic conscience of an organization, like that of a family, is an inner sense or instinct concerning interpersonal bonds. It operates like a sense of balance. If people shift too far in one direction, an impulse occurs that drives them back the other way toward balance. This urge or desire for balance subconsciously arranges the functioning in work relationships. It regulates and affects a person's potential for success, creativity, and communication.

It is not only the systemic order that is stored in this systemic conscience. All other disturbances within this order remain present in memory until they are made conscious and the system (the organization or company) returns to a harmonious order.

221

Just as in the family conscience, the systemic conscience has three facets or needs by which it is determined: bonding, order, and the balance of give and take.

Bonding

Bonding is the most important aspect for companies and organizations. It takes care of keeping together the team spirit and all associated loyalties. The notion of a basic right underpins the facet of bonding in the systemic order. Everyone who is a member of an organization has the right to belong equally to the organization as long as he or she satisfactorily fulfills his or her role.

The systemic conscience guards the right of all personnel to belong and have equal places in the organization. It works to keep the group or organization together. Unlike families, belonging to an organization or company is limited in time and conditional on an agreement such as a contract. Only the organization's survival surpasses the employee's right to a place within it. Therefore, the systemic conscience allows employees to be retrenched in emergency situations.

The right to belong counts equally for everyone who is or has been at any point an employee or was otherwise involved with the organization. This includes those who were, for one reason or another, excluded, forgotten, unjustly treated, not respected, or fired.

Hierarchy

The hierarchy in an organization is as follows:
o   The founder(s)—even if the founder(s) have left or passed away
o   The financier(s)/investor(s) or those who made the existence of the organization possible
o   The directors, management board, departmental heads and their departments, and employees
o   Anyone who has made contributions to the success of the organization
o   Anyone who has experienced disadvantages through the operations of the organization
o   Anyone who was ever a part of the organization or company and was unjustly treated, not respected, or unduly dismissed
o   Suppliers and customers (in some cases). They are also important. In family-run businesses, the family members and the family system also play a part.[4]

Entanglements in the bonding facet can occur when someone in an organization or company is excluded or forgotten. The conscience of the system makes sure other members of the organization represent this excluded or forgotten person. This way he or she still has his or her place.

When someone is treated unfairly, such as an employee being dismissed without good cause, this creates a very important dynamic. Unjustified dismissals tax the conscience of the system and have a strong influence on the organization's capacity for success or lack thereof. The systemic conscience safeguards the rights of all individuals, including those dismissed, and compels the remaining employees to be loyal to those dismissed. This can be expressed in a high rate of sick leave, subconscious sabotage, disunity, or bullying among employees.

John, age fifty-one, is a company manager experiencing problems in one of his departments. The department in question used to be part of a business that his employer acquired. In the first phase of the constellation, all representatives look detached and have slightly hostile attitudes toward *John* and *the management* standing behind *John*. After questioning *John* and the other representatives, it becomes clear that the founder of the acquired company was completely forgotten after the acquisition. All reminders of him were expunged. A sense of relief is apparent when the founder is given his just place within the constellation and is properly honored.

The conclusions derived from the constellation are clear to John. "I will hang a picture of the founder on the wall. It will be visible to everyone, and at the next meeting, I will speak about his legacy, about what this man did, and about his passions and talents. I will honor him," he says.

The following two examples from the IT sector demonstrate just how important company founders are.

In the eighties Commodore, founded by Jack Tramiel, was the world's most important computer company. Tramiel was ousted in 1984 because the board did not sanction his proposal to continue to invest heavily in new products. The company was insolvent within ten years due to bad management and a poorly performing PC department.

Steve Jobs, one of the founders of Apple, was forced from the board in 1985. This marked the beginning of Apple's demise, which was only turned around in 1997. That was when Jobs returned to lead Apple to become the success story it is today.

Order

The system conscience encompasses a certain order:

o Length of service: A team employee with a longer length of service has more rights and a higher place in the hierarchy than one with a shorter length of service.

o Level of risk: A person who invests more money in founding the company carries more risk and has more rights than those carrying less risk.

o Level of responsibility: A person who carries more responsibility has more rights. That means the manager has more rights than the employee. It also means that the department that does most of the work for the functioning and sustainability of a company has more rights than other departments. Accordingly the administration of a hospital comes before physicians, nurses, orderlies, and the cleaning team. This is according to Hellinger.

o Level of expertise: When a team member is particularly creative and contributes significantly more or has greater expertise than the average employee, he or she has priority over other team members.[5]

Disturbances always appear when this order is not respected. An example is when a lower-ranking member assumes the function of a higher position or when leaders cannot fulfill their leadership roles.

Disturbances will also appear when a successor does not appropriately value or honor his or her predecessor. Paying respect to the achievements of the predecessor and his or her employees (hierarchical rights according to length of service) is crucial for smooth transition in leadership.

James, age forty-one, is the human resources director of a medium-size enterprise and has an issue with one of his administration departments. Following a change of management, productivity decreased and the level of absence due to sickness rose significantly. The new manager (Peter) seemed very capable and easily met the position specifications.

Representatives are selected for Peter, the previous manager, and six other team members. James constellates them according to his inner feelings and places the team members more or less together in the constellation space. He places *Peter's predecessor* to the side with his back to the team, and Peter's representative is on the side with a view on the team. All representatives are consulted one by one. The *predecessor* says he feels good. He has new perspectives and good memories of the team. Comments reflect the *team members'* respect for him. They say things such as, "He was good," "You could ask him anything," and, "He was like a father."

The *team members* are now asked to look at the successor, *Peter*. One of them spontaneously says, "I know what he wants to achieve, but he can't communicate effectively." Another says, "There is a sad lack of communication and consultation. He tells us what to do without taking into account our experience." A third says, "I cannot work in this fashion." After being questioned *Peter* says, "I haven't been able to cut it with my new team. I don't stand a chance." He is asked to look at his *predecessor*. Everything is fine between them. There are no problems in this relationship. The *predecessor* is asked to introduce his successor to the team. He does this and even says at the end, "He has my full support. You will find him a fine leader." As a result the *team* becomes calmer as well as more curious and open toward *Peter*. I choose a new representative as a *resource* or *source of support*. I name him the *good force* and place him behind *Peter*. *Peter* responds by saying, "That's better, but I'm still somewhat anxious." I ask him to turn and look at *good force*. He seems friendly and explains his perspective. "I am ready to assist and support him." After some disbelief and hesitation, *Peter* accepts this support.

When he turns around this time to face the team, he feels unusually confident. The *team* also responds with more positive preparedness. I ask *Peter* to repeat the following to the *team*: "I am your new manager. I respect that you all have solid histories working positively for this company. I will gladly make use of your invaluable experience." This relieves *Peter* enormously. The *team members* react positively, and James realizes that the scene for more open dialogue has been set.

225

Balance

The systemic conscience demands a balance of giving and taking through compensation within the organization. This is akin to the idea that what goes around comes around. This means the contribution someone puts into an organization should be recognized and respected. Disturbances appear when particularly competent or creative employees do not get recognition or rewarded for their service or creative contributions. They will sooner or later leave the organization under pressure from the systemic conscience.

Further Application and Example

Companies and organizations can always go to professional management constellation facilitators for insights and solutions. Company advisors and coaches can invite a professional management constellation facilitator to set out management constellations for their clientele. During management constellations it is possible to test different scenarios for conflict resolution via the representatives. For example, certain questions can be posed. Is it best for a certain individual to leave the company? What is the best product selection for a specific store?

Betty, age thirty-seven, is head of the sales department of a company operating in the pharmaceutical industry. In her constellation it becomes clear she can do little to improve the performance of her team. Obstacles from her superior frequently obstruct her. He was the previous incumbent in Betty's position, but he cannot delegate well and still meddles in matters outside the scope of his current job. We test different scenarios, and all point to her resigning as the best option. Betty feels relieved with this option. The moment she enters the constellation and takes over from her representative, she fully appreciates this new awareness.

Advice and Supervision

Apart from helping to resolve company problems, organizational constellations are also ideal instruments for advising and monitoring the health or state of companies. The client does not need to be present when company consultants, advisors, and coaches use constellations as instruments for supervision. The insights and solutions that come from these can be easily taken into account and integrated into the company's current advice and coaching repertoire.

Ronald, age forty-three, is a coach who has just received an assignment to promote team building in a bank after a phase of restructuring. However, Ronald is not sure what strategy he should use. He asks to do a supervision constellation to test out various strategies. He chooses six representatives for the team, one for management, and one for himself. The initial constellation image is gloomy. By asking questions it becomes clear there is still a large worker–management divide with systemic distrust. As long as no commitments about job security are given, the situation remains restive, and the chance of him succeeding in his mission is slim. The constellation makes it apparent to him it is not just the team building that is essential, but the real issue is job security.

Marketing

Organizational constellations also lend themselves as marketing instruments. Using representatives it is possible to test how a product will perform with a target audience or to find out why a particular product is underperforming in sales.

A Dutch firm has developed a promising product. The question is how the target audience will respond. The manager sets out the following representatives: one for the firm, one for the product, and four for possible target audiences. The constellation shows that the *firm* and the *product* line up nicely. Two representatives for the target group are facing the product's representative, the third is turned partly away, and the fourth has his back facing the product. When representatives of the target groups are questioned one by one, the first, who is facing the product, says, "I think the product is good. I get a good feeling when looking at it."

The second, who is also facing the product, says, "It looks great, but I don't really know if I would use it." The third, who is turned sideways, says, "I wouldn't know what to do with it. At first glance it doesn't appeal to me." I ask him to look at the product, and now he says, "Well, it seems a somewhat good product, but I don't know if it's really something for me."

The fourth, who is completely facing away, says, "I am too old for such a thing. I'm sure there will be a complicated manual along with it." He is also asked to look at the product. He adds, "If I come home with that, my children will laugh." All these statements by various representatives of the target audience give the marketing department specialists useful hints and ways of thinking that will benefit their strategic planning.

Jill, age twenty-nine, wants to start a new boutique with various clothing brands. She wants to find out what the best mix of brands would be and which of the seven possible fashion brands she is considering would be popular and sell well. She chooses a representative for the shop, a representative for each of the seven brands, and four representatives for her target audience. On top of this, I ask her to choose a representative for the unknown or unconsidered possibilities. This is named *joker*.

Once Jill constellates all representatives, they are questioned, and we subsequently test for the best combination of brands for her target audience. They clearly respond more favorably to four of the brands. Two are disliked or barely noticed, and one is doubtful in the eyes of the audience. The response of the target group to the *joker* was mixed. Nevertheless it was received positively and was considered useful but not essential.

Jill followed up on the advice. She told me later that her shop has been doing well from the start and that she came upon an idea for the *joker* some weeks later. In a friend's secondhand shop, she spotted two unusual chairs. "These are now in the shop. They are just little things, but they give it that little bit extra," she said.

Constellations for One's Own Practice or Business

There is no reason why organizational constellations cannot also be applied to problems around one's own practice or business. These constellations sometimes start as organizational constellations but change over into family constellations. This is because the disturbances people carry from their family systems also influence the professional realm. Robert's story is typical for how loyalties subconsciously sabotage attempts at having a good life and work balance and place limitations on success.

Robert, age thirty-tree, is a visual artist who has struggled to make a living from this work. Both his parents are also artists whose success has been limited. They accept financial hardship as part of being *real* artists. The constellation confirms the dogma of his parents that a good income and being a *real* artist are mutually exclusive. Furthermore, it seems that both parents are heavily entangled. Robert's father was confronted with a brother who passed away early, and his mother has lived with unprocessed grief over her father, who died when she was only seventeen.

In a session using floor anchors, Robert revisits all these burdens, which he had taken on himself. Now, however, he goes about returning them. He understands how much these entanglements burden his luck and success. In the next session, Robert gives his parents' vision on money and art back to them. During this session the root cause of his parents' vision on poverty is revealed. Robert tells how his great-grandfather felt cheated by the financial crisis in 1921, in which he lost his entire earnings. He ended up penniless. He never recovered from this and remained bitter for the rest of his life. He died at the relatively young age of fifty-nine.

The constellation establishes that everyone in the family chose to remain poor upon his death through blind loyalty. It is a great relief for *Robert* that his *great-grandfather* wishes him lots of luck and success in his life and with his art. One thing is important for his *great-grandfather*, and *Robert* clearly senses this now. His bitterness came into existence because he saw himself as the cause of the family becoming poor. When *Robert* asks him for permission to earn a lot of money, his *great-grandfather* is enthusiastic, and the bitterness disappears. This, combined with Robert having returned his parents' beliefs about art and poverty, give him strength and make him feel relieved.

Constellations reveal that success in life is the natural state of being, and a person who is not successful is trying to avoid success with a good conscience. A person does so because the theme of *success* or *being lucky* in the family has been damaged due to events such as someone dying at an early age. There are also other kinds of trauma whereby people, out of good consciences, deny themselves happiness and success. This often happens when family members have lived in poverty for generations or a family member encounters bankruptcy with severe consequences. (See Steven's constellation at the beginning of this chapter.)

Whatever stands in the way of one's own success can be constellated so one can become conscious of the distortion and let it go. All kinds of career-related questions can also be constellated. Via representatives one can quickly judge whether a new job, retraining, or further education will be productive or not.

Conclusion

Every organization is a collective of people involving a complex interplay of relationships. All members bring their family histories with them, which has an impact on many areas of life. People tend to re-create problematic situations in all relationships, including those on the work floor. Through the use of an organizational constellation, an organization can increase the dedication and commitment of all employees. Clarity about hierarchy and leadership issues is presented, and everyone is offered the opportunity to find the appropriate place for himself or herself in the organization. Energy previously spent on personal problems is freed, which leads to working environment and productivity improvement. Whichever way organizational constellations are used, they create clarity on all levels of organizational and corporate processes. Employees become more sensitive to the meaning of the systemic laws, which then helps to create better company climates. Managers and advisors familiar with the systemic laws of organizations and companies can respond more appropriately to challenges they encounter.

With the help of constellations, managers and advisors are able to develop broader views on all jobs and interpersonal relationships. This is emotional intelligence in practice.

Structural Constellations

A structural constellation is another form of systemic constellation. Insar Sparrer and Matthias Varga von Kibéd are the pioneers in this area and have already developed over one hundred different variations of structural constellations.[6] The main differences between structural constellations and family and organizational constellations as well as descriptions of some especially meaningful types of constellations follow.

Whereas the structures in family and organizational constellations depend on the themes as well as the facts and dynamics that come to light, the setup in a structural constellation is more or less predetermined from the start. It still works with representatives and the knowing field, but this is done in a different, somewhat more abstract manner. Unlike family constellations, structural constellations do not use representatives of actual members but abstract concepts such as *life, a source of strength,* and *the goal* or functions such as *support, protection,* and *unknown resource.*

The special thing about representatives of abstract concepts is that as long as they are not burdened, they always observe the situations in impartial yet powerful ways. If these representatives sense an emotional burden, an entanglement of the client/seeker and his or her system is indicated. This could be either through loyalty or connection to the heavy fate of one or more family members.

Naturally the main point of a constellation is to expose such disturbances. The following example demonstrates an elegant way this can be achieved.

During a structural constellation, the representative for luck feels very heavy and prefers to lie on the floor rather than stand. This is clearly a sign of a connection with a heavy fate. I ask *luck* if his heavy feeling is more male or female in nature and if it is located more in front of or behind him. *Luck* answers that it is female in nature and located behind him. For a moment I place my hand at a small distance behind *luck.* I point to my hand, and I ask him if this is what he senses. The representative sees what I mean and confirms this. Then a female representative takes the place of my hand in the constellation. She directly senses that she prefers to lie on the floor, which I allow.

After she lies down behind *luck*, she says she actually feels as if she is dead. *Luck* feels relieved. The power and serenity of this purely abstract concept is now clearly perceivable. The emotional burden has been given a place. I then ask the seeker if he has any idea what the female representative on the ground could mean, and he responds directly that this must be his sister, who died at a very young age.

The constellation proceeds, and the most important thing that becomes evident is that by working with representatives standing in for abstract concepts, people can purify these energies in themselves. The example shows a constellation where the client effectively purifies his dimension of *luck*, meaning he is able to rid it of all burdens and hidden loyalties. Constellations in all domains of life such as success, serenity, lust for life, or sexuality work in the same way.

Field Constellations

One of the many types of structural constellations is the field constellation.[7] I used this type of constellation to find my house. Some years ago my wife, our children, and I wanted to find a new place to live. We identified three options: a small home with some workspace for my practice, a slightly larger home with a workspace big enough for group activities, or an even larger home with a workspace for groups and lodging rooms.

We had already been searching for a while, and it became clear we should look at the three options. However, neither I nor my wife knew with certainty which option would be best for us. Thus I was very pleased when I could use this as my theme during a specialized training session for organizational constellations I was participating in at the time.

With this type of constellation, the person must first define the fields to be able to choose the appropriate representatives for each. To receive a suitable answer to my question, I defined four different fields: comfort, workspace, accessibility for clients, and best financial option.

With the fields having been defined, I chose a representative for each field and lined them up in a row with about a yard between them. In the meantime the trainer wrote down my three options on pieces of paper plus a joker for an unknown or different option. He then placed them randomly in four different envelopes so I would not know where each option was. I then stood for a moment by each of the four representatives as each held an envelope. The representatives of the fields were asked to touch each envelope and intuitively feel and visualize a number between one and ten (with one being the lowest rating and ten the highest). They were asked to write the numbers down on the envelopes. Each envelope ended up having four numbers written on it—one from each representative.

After adding these numbers up and analyzing the results, it appeared that the first idea scored lowest. The second idea, that of a slightly bigger home with workspace and a space for group activities, had the highest score, and the option of an even bigger home with room for lodging came in second place. The score for the joker, an unknown or different option, was low.

I had clearly received my answer. With a clear focus, we found a new place within two months. We now live in a pleasant home with a nice group space.

Problem Constellations

A different type of structural constellation is the problem constellation. Here people mainly start working with representatives for abstract concepts such as *focus, resources, obstacle, hidden benefit, goal/purpose,* and *higher purpose.* According to Insa Sparrer, these are the ingredients required to find an answer to a problem.[8] The philosopher Wittgenstein influenced her reasoning. A problem needs a *focus,* or somebody with a problem. This is mostly the client/seeker. With any problem there is a goal/purpose as well as an obstacle that stands in the way of the goal/purpose.

By calling something a problem, a solution is implicated. For this people can utilize their resources. (If people do not see a solution and no resources are observable, they call the situation impossible. If there is something to be learned, they speak of a difficulty rather than a problem.)

Hidden benefit means a person has not yet solved the problem, but it has nevertheless given him or her some kind of gain or benefit. In some cases this might be love and loyalty. For example, this could include being loyal to a grandfather out of blind love and sharing his heavy fate with a good conscience. In other cases hidden gains might simply be laziness or fear of change. In these cases, by remaining in the known, problematic situations keep people in comfortable and familiar settings.

The goal/purpose is always placed within the framework of the higher purpose. This not only provides a framework but also offers more room to find solutions. Most of the time, idealists place the higher purpose before the purpose. As a result they only see the forest—not the trees.

Using conceptual representatives also enables other things to come to light. If a facilitator uses a problem constellation, he or she knows from the beginning that all obstacles are transformed into resources at the end of the constellation. Facilitators call this *intended reframing—* purposeful restructuring and redefining. In practice representatives of obstacles reveal entanglements (blind love bonding) of the seeker. The family members onto whom the blind love was earlier directed are now also brought into the constellation. It then becomes apparent that they also feel love for the descendant caught up in entanglements. However, it is undeniable that they do not want this descendant to carry their fates or remain loyal to them. They do not want their descendant to have a difficult life or copy their difficulties. This includes preventing success and contentment in life. Almost always each family member gives the seeker a thumbs-up at the end. This is like a real resource.

As an example, here is a shortened reflection of a constellation that lasted more than one hour.

James, twenty-six, is a student who has struggled for years with completing his thesis to be able to graduate. He asks, "What is stopping me? What is distracting me or getting in the way of me finishing this thesis?" He chooses representatives for *focus, resource, obstacle, hidden gains, purpose/goal,* and *higher purpose.*

Once all six have been constellated, a divided image appears. Only *purpose* and *resource* face each other. *Focus, obstacle,* and *hidden gains* are all facing different directions, and *higher purpose* is even looking out the window. I start with *focus* and question each representative. He feels insecure and is constantly compelled to look back and forth between *higher purpose* and *obstacle*. *Purpose* indicates he feels good and that he has good contact with *resource*. *Resource* feels good and says everything is present to be able to graduate. *Resource* confirms the good contact with *purpose*. *Obstacle* does not feel good at all. He senses a heavy burden, disillusionment, and pain. Responding to my questioning of whether this heavy burden is located more in front or behind him and if it is more male or female in nature, *obstacle* responds by saying it is female and located behind him.

I bring a new female representative into the constellation and place her accordingly. By questioning James and the new representative, it becomes clear this concerns James's grandmother. She was the only girl in the family and as intelligent as her two brothers. However, she was not allowed to study. This made her very angry. After raising her own children, she eventually started to study biology.

Focus is looking at her, and I ask him to say, "Dear Grandmother, I don't want to get a degree. I don't want to do what you didn't or couldn't do." He says that with a warm smile, and a moment later he feels the pain and embarrassment she felt as a young woman because she could not study and get her degree.

The loyalty of the grandson to the grandmother is clearly observable. Then the *grandmother*'s eyes open up wide, and she says, "This is not right for you, my grandson. The fact I couldn't study and didn't get my degree belongs to my fate and me. I feel your love, but you go too far. If you really wish to honor me, then finish your thesis and graduate." *Focus* leaves the heavy burden with the *grandmother* and is relieved. With this in mind, it becomes clear that *obstacle* actually symbolizes loyalty with the grandmother. This loyalty has now changed in character. At first loyalty meant not achieving a degree—just as his grandmother had not been able to do. Now it means to finish the thesis and graduate. What was an obstacle has now become a resource.

James now returns to *hidden gains*. He faces *higher purpose* and says, "All the hassle and all that compulsive behavior. I'm sick and tired of it." James identifies with this and explains that his parents always put a lot of pressure on him to keep studying. He makes the connection himself that this concerns loyalty toward his grandmother, and he returns the pressure to his parents when they have been added to the constellation. His *father* says, "He is just like me. I also preferred just hanging around. That's why I worry. Because I just scraped through. It could have been so different, but I couldn't handle the pressure my father put me under." *Father* and *son* (*focus*) smile at each other, and the *father* says, "You're really my son. I know you can do it, and now I have faith in you. It'll all work out." *Hidden gains,* therefore, concerned loyalty toward the father. It was expressed as scraping through university just as his father had done. Meanwhile, *higher purpose* looks attentively at *focus* and says he would like to become part of the constellation. I now adjust the constellation so all representatives are aligned. The *grand-mother* is at the back, and behind her is *obstacle,* which now represents *loyalty to grandmother*. Then come *mother* and *father*. *Hidden gains* is behind *father*. In front of them, I place *resource* and then James, who now takes the place of his representative for focus. In front of James is *purpose*, and behind that is *higher purpose*. James feels good being part of the constellation. He goes through the same steps with his *father* and *grandmother* that his representative went through. At the end he looks with interest toward *higher purpose* and says, "For the first time, I really want to graduate. I have never experienced this feeling. In the past I pushed away thinking about finishing my course."

Many other types of constellations have complemented organizational and structural constellations. For specific applications of constellation therapy in the field of education, I gladly refer you to the work of Marianne Franke-Grieksch.[9]

Table Constellations

Table constellations have been around for a while, and I do not know when or where I first heard of them. I actually realized the value of this type of constellation by coincidence. At the end of one of my presentations once, I wanted to let as many people as possible experience how the perception of a representative works. I thought it was a good idea to look at the way the families (and the hierarchical order) of the participants sat around their dining tables. Before this I had always given a demonstration constellation with a family theme of one of the participants. There was, however, the limitation of only some participants being needed as representatives. It was also rather lengthy.

Now I use table constellations regularly because many more people can be actively involved in experiencing what it is like to be a representative, it is less intense and serious than a family constellation, and each one only takes a few minutes. Moreover I give each participant the opportunity to set up his or her own *dinner table* to find the best seating arrangement for that family. I will provide a short recap here of the basic rules for *good table arrangements*, which I described in chapter six.

The rule of thumb is that the hierarchy flows in a clockwise manner, so a person sitting to the right of another is positioned higher up in hierarchy. A correct or harmonious order means having a seating arrangement around a round table with the parents first (whose order they must determine themselves) and then the children according to their dates of birth from oldest to youngest.

The table can also be rectangular, but parents should sit next to each other. This table order can also be applied to other domains of life such as meetings or any other situation where people communicate with each other.

Luke, fifty-six, is director of a company with sixty-eight employees, and he explains how useful knowledge of good table order can be in business. "Since my table constellation during my training, I know straightaway where to sit at the negotiating table. All negotiations have become easier, and I rarely struggle to clarify my point of view." He now sits to the far right (in a clockwise order) or at the head of the table during negotiations. If he has to discuss a problem with one of his managers, he prefers to sit next to—rather than opposite—him or her.

This reduces confrontation. When a subordinate is positioned to the left, the problem can then be more accurately identified, and solutions are more forthcoming.

Barbara, age thirty-nine, is a crisis mediator and has also greatly benefited by knowing how she can position clients to the best effect at her meeting table. This is especially useful considering she often deals with divorce cases where good seating arrangements are crucial. Before she was introduced to table constellations, she let clients choose where to sit at one of two tables positioned opposite her table, which sometimes led to the children sitting between their parents.

With the help of representatives, we tested various strategies to find appropriate seating arrangements for the parties *at war*. The tables now form a semicircle with Barbara's table to the right. There are two tables for the parents in the middle and a third to the far left for children, if they are present. A play corner for toddlers was also added. The children are no longer placed between the fighting parties, and the communication between parties runs more smoothly and is more successful.

> *It is too confronting if these fighting parties sit opposite each other. This has the tendency to increase the level of arguing, making solutions more difficult to obtain. If, on the other hand, they sit in a semicircle, the confrontation is less direct, which makes it easier to look at problems and find solutions together.*

There's another exercise I often use to demonstrate the effect of representative perception and hierarchical order. It is very simple, and you can try it for yourself. Just ask friends to practice with you. Your friend remains in the same position during the exercise and senses how it feels.

Stand for a moment to his or her right, and make note of how it feels for you. Then move around and stand opposite him or her. Observe what changes you sense. Switch again, and then stand to the left of him or her. Observe once again what changes for you. In which location do you feel better?

You can repeat the exercise with your friend as the representative for a superior and see how your feelings change in the three places. Do the exercise a third time, but this time imagine your friend is a representative for a subordinate. Observe what unfolds. Do all places feel identical? Do you observe differences? At which place do you feel more strength in relation to the other person, and in which place do you sense clearly the best way to communicate successfully?

Constellations with Inner Selves or Inner Voices

Inner selves or inner voices are aspects of personality or psyche. In this type of constellation, people work with their feelings or aspects of their characters such as the inner critic, the idealist, the dreamer, or the inner child. The famous voice dialogue therapy, originated by Hal and Sidra Stone,[10] is a way of getting to know the many selves that make people. It is closely linked to Fritz Perl's gestalt therapy[11] and the archetype theory of Carl Jung.[12] According to Jung each person has a band of inner voices or archetypes.[13] Sometimes they all talk at the same time, and people feel confused. Many know the sensation of one part wanting one thing and another part wanting something totally opposite. These inner conflicts can also be put into a constellation.

Donald, thirty-four, gets sweaty hands from being nervous when he has to buy something expensive such as a new computer to replace an old computer. To relieve anxiety he has the tendency to indefinitely postpone taking action.

In the introductory discussion, we decide to choose representatives for Donald's inner critic, his inner technician, and his inner wisdom. Donald gives them places in the constellation. It quickly becomes apparent that the *inner critic* and the *inner technician* are at war. The *inner technician* wants quality, whereas the *inner critic* focuses on reducing cost. Donald immediately laughs and says, "Just like my parents. There were endless discussions during the renovation of our home when I was seven or eight years of age. It was terrible, and now I do the same thing." I ask Donald to choose representatives for his parents and include them in the constellation. Then I ask the *inner critic* and the *inner technician* to give their conflict back to the *parents*.

Both representatives appear to have awakened from dreams. They look at each other, and the *inner critic* says to the *inner technician*, "Isn't it logical? The best computer at the right price. I trust you."

People can also set out feelings, optimism, creativity, and a lot more. Amy, age twenty-seven, has difficulty with sex. She cannot allow herself to explore her sexual feelings and does not dare let go of control. "It's really frustrating," she says. "I love my partner, but I don't have any pleasure in bed."

We work with floor anchors and set out one for her, one for control, one for her sexual desires, and one for her feelings. She places the anchor for herself to one side of the available space and the anchor for her sexual desire on the other side. It faces the wall. Somewhere in the middle of these and close together, she places the floor anchors representing control and feeling.

Then she stands on each anchor and opens up to perceptions. She knows very well how it feels being in her own spot. On the anchor of sexual desire, she really feels up against the wall. I ask her to turn to look at the other representatives. After looking for a moment, she says, "Control is in the way. It blocks everything."

On the anchor for feeling, she says, "I feel guilty. I sit in front of control as if it is a kind of army sergeant, and I feel guilty even about the fact that I feel. I am not allowed to be happy." Amy is shocked at the strength of this observation in this spot. "But," she says, "I know that feeling of not allowing myself pleasure. I find it stupid and childish."

Now she stands on the spot for *control* and says, "I am very cold and feel stiff. Very stiff." Her whole posture changes with these words, and she then seems bitter. Drastic changes in posture happen frequently in these types of sessions. For me this is most probably a sign there is a strong connection or entanglement with a family member from a previous generation.

I test this by asking Amy if *cold* really belongs to that spot. She feels for a moment and replies in the negative. I ask her if the *cold and stiff* is more male or female in nature and if it is positioned behind or in front of her. She says it is female and located behind her.

I create a new floor anchor and put it behind *control*. "Yes. That's it," Amy says. She is still standing at the *control* spot. "I feel really relieved now, and for the first time, I can see there are others involved. It's much better like this." When I get her to stand on *cold and stiff* and ask her to tune in, she says, "I belong farther back. Farther away from them." She points to *control* and *feeling*. When we shift the anchor a few meters back and to the left, she says, "That's better. I feel as if I am a woman. I am frozen inside and closed off." On request she partially turns around and visualizes her ancestors. Almost immediately she starts crying, and all the heavy feelings that come up are difficult for her to deal with.

I take her away from the floor anchor to take a little pressure off and remind her she probably felt the life and fate of her ancestors. She confirms this and tells me what she experienced. "This must have been a great-great-grandmother. She apparently had a very difficult life and had to shut off all emotion in order to survive. Her pelvis and the surrounding area are like a block of ice." Amy does not know anything about her great-great-grandmother, but it appears this woman had to carry a heavy fate a long time ago. From the floor anchor positions for *control, feeling,* and *sexual desire,* I now get her to make a deep bow and repeat resolution statements to enable her to pass back this heavy fate to her cold and stiff ancestor. All three of her inner parts/voices now feel much better. At the position for *feeling,* Amy says, "I can now start feeling for the first time. It's so good. What a change!" At the floor anchor for *sexual desire,* she feels real relief as well. "It feels as if for the first time I'm allowed to be part of and really connected to feeling. Control doesn't seem so threatening and heavy anymore."

Amy now feels enormous relief. After this constellation she did few individual sessions on rebirthing-breath work. I gave her bodily exercises to further dissolve the physical blockages. Step by step she has begun to actually enjoy her sexuality.

Constellations with a Multicultural Background

If you don't realize the source,
you stumble in confusion and sorrow.
When you realize where you come from,
you naturally become tolerant,
disinterested, amused,
kindhearted as a grandmother,
dignified as a king.
—Lao-Tzu[14]

It is an illusion to think that society exists as a homogenous entity. There have always been mixtures and movements between different nationalities, ethnic populations, cultures, and religions. In the past this was often whole population migrations due to wars and invasions as well as the natural movement of people most evident on trade routes and around harbor cities. Through industrialization this movement of people grew enormously and peaked with the mass migration of foreign workforces in the sixties and seventies.

The United States, typical of melting pot countries, has 13 percent foreign-born residents. It also has a higher share of immigrants among its residents than most European countries.[15] In almost all countries, this intermingling has come about through occupation and colonization.

This fact is also naturally reflected in constellations. The systemic conscience operates in two different domains in this regard—the personal and the collective.

The personal domain encompasses all relationships between people, organizations, or companies wherein differences in nationalities, cultures, and religions are a given.

The collective domain embodies all intercultural, international, and interreligious themes or conflicts—everything that interacts between communities.

In both these areas, the systemic conscience for different communities has an interrelational impact or effect, meaning that just as a family has a systemic conscience and systemic order, so do cultures, religions, and nations. Loyalty holds these communities together.

The Personal Domain

With intimate relationships between people of different nationalities, cultures, or religions, both partners are connected with the religions or nationalities of their own civilizations and cultural groups as well as their families of origin. These aspects can become part of the dynamic of the relationship.

Children who come from such relationships have to resonate with both cultures, nationalities, or religions. It is not always easy—especially if the communities or religions are poles apart. However, it is a step toward a common future if it does work.

Not all people are prepared to realize that humans are already more mixed than some care to acknowledge. However, people can narrow the gap between different races, cultures, and religions, so people can achieve lasting peace, as this will mean mutual recognition, feelings of equality, and respect among the collective.

Belgian and British people have similar cultures, yet both are different nations with different religions. Both these nations and religions live in peace and in mutual recognition and respect, so there is little tension between these collectives. There are few difficulties in the relationship between Belgian and British people. This also means people largely accept mixed Belgian and British relationships.

This is different when there is tension between the collective—for example, through the unresolved history of the world wars. People see these collective tensions return in the relationships of members of different collectives. Sometimes this has a larger impact on one relationship than on another, but it always plays a role. Imagine a relationship between a German and an Israeli, an American and a Japanese person, or an Australian and an Aboriginal person. One can immediately sense the tensions that might burden such relationships, even though this might only happen subconsciously.

From my own experiences with constellations, I know people from other European nations who still feel sensitive to events from Germany's recent past. German invasions drew direct ancestors face-to-face in armed combat, and many elderly people alive today still have vivid memories of such experiences. It still exists fresh in the collective conscience.

Even events that occurred more than a hundred years ago have an influence today.

Robert, age thirty-eight, comes from Suriname. His relationship problems with his Dutch wife are the reasons for his constellation. He is not sure if he should end the marriage. One of the most important facts he mentioned in the introductory talk is that his ancestors were slaves forced to work on Dutch plantations.

Laws that forced family members to be separated intentionally severed family ties among slaves. If a child was born, the father was transferred or sold and sent to another plantation far away from his wife and child. The pain of this cruelty is clearly visible in the constellation. His *ancestors* are positioned far apart and do not dare look at each other for fear of painful repercussions. *Robert* carries this pain, and it is so difficult for him to leave this burden with his *ancestors*. He feels a strong urge to share their fate and thus not cultivate his own family ties.

The representatives for his ancestors do not want him to carry their *forced separation* fate, which he repeats in his relationship by leaving his wife. The real solution comes via the representative for the Dutch slave keepers. They take responsibility for having torn apart the family.

Roberts's *ancestors* further clarify that in their eyes, his Dutch *wife* is not guilty. They point to the representative for the Dutch slave keepers and say the blame belongs with them. The representative for the Dutch slave keepers confirms this and shows regret for the slave keepers' deeds. He adds that in their time equality between Dutch people and slaves was unthinkable, but now slavery had long been abolished, so this idea no longer had relevance.

Robert frees himself by bowing deeply and allowing the responsibility and blame to remain with the *Dutch slave keepers*. His *ancestors* can now truly sanction the continuation of his marriage. They wish him a stable and happy family life.

Nora, age thirty-seven, is an Antillean woman, and she poses her constellation theme. "I want to speak out and feel free as a black person without fears and barriers." She says all her jobs end in conflictual situations, typically culminating in arguments with her boss. She does not feel at home and wonders where her real *home* or *soul country* is.

244

Nora's ancestors were deported for slavery from Africa, and her mother's father was a Native American. She chooses seven representatives. There is one for each of the following: herself, the Netherlands (the rulers), Africa (her country of origin), Native Americans, her current boss, daring to express, and being heard. She places them according to her perceptions. The representatives take their places and tune in. *Africa* and *Nora* both look toward a spot on the floor. The others stand around and surround them. They are divided and at a distance. In questioning the two representatives, it becomes clear that both are fixated on this particular spot. *The Netherlands* feels powerful. *Native Americans* feels rigid and immovable, and *daring to express* wants to kneel. *Being heard* feels under great pressure. "A lot needs to be expressed," he says while looking at the same location where *Africa* and *Nora* are staring and where *daring to express* is now kneeling. *Africa* looks away from that spot as well as away from *the Netherlands*. *Current boss* explains there needs to be more communication.

I place a representative for the victims of slavery into the constellation and ask him to lie on the spot where *Africa* and *Nora* are focusing. This affects everyone in the constellation. Nora says from the outside, "Nobody wants to look at the victims. We look down on them and consider them weaklings. What we really don't want to appreciate is that we were once weak ourselves." *Victims of slavery* also feels ignored and says, "No one has ever mourned for us, but everyone uses us." *Nora* says, "I use you as victims and as a means to power. I want retribution because it is a part of my identity."

To allow the real Nora to experience how the victims feel, I ask her to lie down on the *victims of slavery* spot. Here she feels something different. It becomes clear to her *the victims* do not want retribution but want to be seen. I ask her to repeat the following statement, "We were slaves, but we also had our feelings of honor and worthiness. If you really wish to honor us, then mourn for us and stop abusing us as a means of power or retribution." The real Nora confirms the sentiment as tears stream down her face. "There is so much suffering here. It's terrible," she says. A moment later I ask her to get up so *victims of slavery* can resume his position.

The real Nora sits next to *victims of slavery* and looks deeply into his eyes. Slowly a very deep pain stirs up inside her. She now knows how it feels for the victims, and for the first time, she can surrender herself to her grief. This has a clear effect on all the representatives. *The Neth-*

erlands loses his power and becomes aware of his responsibilities. I also ask him to look at and acknowledge the victims. The real Nora looks back and forth between *current boss* and *the Netherlands*. She tells *current boss*, "I confused you with the master. The slave driver. I see now you are innocent." That relaxes *current boss*. *Daring to express* and *being heard* are more relaxed. They want to position themselves behind *Nora* to support her and help her feel the loss so that healing can begin.

Native Americans now also feels seen and honored and says, "We feel seen by her, and we hold hope for her that she remembers us as her strong ancestors." *Africa* is direct. "We are proud people." Nora realizes that until now she had always looked down on her enslaved ancestors and looked up to the rulers—the masters. That may stop now. She bows down before *victims of slavery, Africa,* and *Native Americans,* and her desire for retribution dissolves.

She now sees that the heavy fates of her ancestors belong with them. They were strong enough to survive slavery. As a result her view of her ancestors has changed. Before the constellation she had always found them to be weak. Now she appreciates how strong they were. Nora bows one last time and says, "I'll make sure we keep you in good memory. Now I'll start the mourning process that till now has been avoided."

The magnificent thing about constellations is they show people paths to harmony and reconciliation. If a wrongdoer can acknowledge his or her mistakes and look his or her victim in the eye, he or she can allow regret to take place by bowing down to his or her victim. If victims can accept this, reconciliation is possible. The use of victims to take revenge or to keep in place a generations-long victim attitude is seen by the victims as burdening and degrading.

Reconciliation usually only takes place if the following generations of both the wrongdoer and the victim mourn the deceased together and rise up to accept their own responsibilities. The suffering for both can then have their places, and the dead will find their peace.

Commenting on this, Hellinger says, "As long as the past is not permitted to be over, there is no future. If the descendants of victims want to take revenge, what happens to the victims? How must they feel? Can they then really rest in peace?"[16]

People often find subconscious loyalties in mixed relationships as sources of disturbance between partners. Both must let go of loyalties toward their native cultures for harmony in the relationship to be established. They must both be prepared to unite on cultural and religious domains. While the members of most communities would rather not see a mingling with *foreigners*, it becomes clear in constellations that the *home* (the country of origin) actually has nothing against this arrangement. Under the condition that the two nations and/or cultures trying to come together are equally honored, both partners will be enriched.

Fatima, age twenty-nine, is a woman of Moroccan descent who lives in Belgium and has a relationship with a Belgian man. She cites relationship problems as the reason for her constellation. When Fatima was young, her mother divorced. The Moroccan community in the Netherlands consequently shunned her because divorce was socially unacceptable. As a consequence Fatima and her siblings were also shunned. The pressure became so intense they were forced to move to Belgium.

In the constellation the power that the *Moroccan community* (in the Netherlands) has over the situation becomes very clear. *Fatima* experiences this as a feeling of division. She feels anger about her exclusion. On the other hand, she feels a bond with the *Moroccan community*. "They are my roots," she says. The constellation image changes the moment I bring a representative for Morocco (the nation) into the constellation and place him to the right of *Moroccan community*. *Morocco* looks at *Moroccan community* and says spontaneously, "You make yourself larger than you really are, but in reality you are scared." *Moroccan community* clearly feels weaker and becomes aware of his lack of strength. "We are fearful. That's right. We hope to do what we can to preserve our way of life. We feel insecure." *Morocco* says to *Fatima*, "You remain Moroccan, even if you live together with a Belgian person and even if your mother is divorced. Your connection with me is greater than the fear, the religion, or the preferences of the Moroccan community." *Moroccan community* does not like to hear this but has to confirm that he feels even smaller but is less fearful.

Fatima is deeply touched and sees she has always viewed Morocco and the Moroccan community as one in the past. That she can now differentiate between them feels liberating. She still wonders if Morocco is bigger or older than Islam. *Morocco* says, "I existed before Islam, and I shall continue to exist even if another religious code replaces the current one. I exist beyond religion."

She can now look at her partner in a much more open and relaxed manner—one in which the attitude of the *Moroccan community* has less relevance. She says to *Morocco*, "You have an important place in my heart. You live on in me and my family." Addressing *Moroccan community* she says, "What belongs with you, I now leave with you." To end the constellation she takes a deep bow.

Bert Hellinger states:

> *Morality:*
> *Now so many people shall say "I am better" or "I am good and the other is bad." What does this mean in practice? The one saying he is better is saying "I have more rights than you to belong here. You have fewer rights to belong here" or even "You have no right to belong." This is what one calls morality. All major conflicts find their roots in this moralistic point of view*[17]

The Collective Domain

After an experience of enlightenment
the Zen master Bodhisattva was asked by a student
what he had observed.
"A vast emptiness, nothing holy therein," was his answer.
—Zen-Tradition

Alongside the personal domain where differences of nationality, cultures, and religions play a role in interpersonal relationships, there is also a collective domain. This is where people search for solutions to problems that exist when different populations and cultural groups or religions live together and impact upon each other. Old and new conflicts can be investigated through constellations. In this way people can find appropriate solutions via representative observations. Facilitators of constellations then speak of intercultural or political constellations.

In all these constellations, it becomes clear that nations, civilizations, cultures, and religions are also systems with order and systemic consciences. In constellations they respond as (complex) personalities with their own idiosyncrasies, limitations, fears, complexes, and (of course) histories.

As with all systems, systems theory applies here. All aspects are connected and have influences on each other. The dimension of the relational ethic, as formulated by Buber and Nagy,[18] and which people know from family relationships, has just as strong an influence here as it does in families or organizations. An *invisible ledger*, therefore, exists between civilizations, cultures, minorities, and religions as well as within nations, whereby balance sheets are kept.

Later generations try to bring back into balance what was put out of balance between communities in earlier generations. If the relational ethics between or within these groups is then disturbed, what Nagy calls a feeling of *destructive justice* is evident. This means that communities and their members feel justified in being destructive toward another group. As a collective they feel victimized and as a result feel justified to retaliate.

People do things to members of another group—the enemy—that they could or would never do to their own collective members. They go about these atrocities with clear consciences. They feel justified doing

249

what they do. While the inhumanity of these deeds is sometimes difficult to understand as an outsider, members delude themselves about their rights to redress what they consider unjust events from the past.

The memory of lost, cherished members is used as the reason for the present revenge. Despots, dictators, and even politicians who seem to mean well have always been able to exploit this dynamic for their own (sometimes sinister) purposes. They might look sinister from the outside, but the purposes are just personifications of the collective consciences (unresolved trauma and blind love) of their communities.

At the foundation of conflicts and disturbances between and in communities, people find blind love and loyalties to the systemic consciences—the collective conscience in this case. This is just as in families.

If followed blindly this impairment leads to problems. Inherent in systems is the need to be distinguishable from other systems. To strengthen community spirit, there must be a clear boundary between one community and another comparable community. Although this differentiation is necessary, it can lead to competition between different communities. If the sense of demarcation and competition go too far, an attitude of superiority takes hold in the community. This feeling of superiority will then lead to conflicts with other competitive communities.

The best examples of this are religions based on the Old Testament, which have more in common than their followers care to consider. Religions offer people space for spiritual experiences and their longings to be in contact with some higher source of truth. Every religion sets itself up as superior or more sacred. It is the only *real* religion. Each religion also has its own holy book that is holier and more transcendent than any other, and each religion discounts the validity of other religions. Being so similar in this regard, religions need to clearly stress their differences to create group identities.

As long as the members of nations, civilizations, cultures, or religions foster senses of superiority and focus more on differences than similarities, the us-against-them attitude remains embedded and promotes conflict. History is, therefore, written in blood. In countless constellations Hellinger and other systemic therapists have clearly observed how peace between civilizations traditionally antagonistic to each other is possible. "Peace can only be achieved between civilizations when both accept that despite their differences they are alike."[19] This also applies to cultures and religions.

Bert Hellinger says:
I want to point out something very important. Something that gets in the way of peace. Many of those who have suffered, or who belong to a group that has suffered much, are angry with the perpetrators. They reproach them. They don't want to forgive in any way. What happens? Those who reject the perpetrators become in their souls like them. Suddenly, they have perpetrator's energy and they continue the conflict just the other way around. Like a wheel that turns, but is always the same, without any solution. Furthermore, those who are reproached have their aggression reinforced. So all the accusations and all the blaming by the survivors of ethnic conflict against the perpetrators just achieves the opposite of what is intended. They stand in the way of reconciliation.[20]

Commenting on the conflict between Israelis and Palestinians, Hellinger says, "This would be the reconciliation in the end—both parties see the suffering that takes place again and again on both sides. They both suffer together. Rather than looking back, they look forward to when they can help one another in the future. On this foundation, they can start something new, which is beneficial to both sides. Reconciliation is only possible if both parties can grieve about what was lost."[21]

Movements of the Soul

In the last few years, Hellinger has continued to develop his ideas. One particular development is constellations without speaking, which he calls *Movements of the Soul*. Later he established constellations that he called *Movements of the Spirit-Mind*.

After a period of experimentation, he officially introduced Movements of the Soul to a large group of people in 2000. This was a form of constellation executed without questioning, without talking, and without Hellinger's intervention. In one of these demonstrations, he got representatives for Holocaust victims from a Jewish family to stand opposite representatives of their murderers, and he asked them to allow any spontaneous urges to move that might come up.

This delivered a particularly intense experience because the force of the knowing field guided the representatives. All movements stem from this source—just like the perceptions representatives have in the traditional constellations. While representatives in traditional constellations share their findings by being questioned, in this style of constellation, they might transform these findings into movement and changes in posture. These constellations take place without talking. The beauty of these constellations is that representatives can clearly feel the impulse to move and/or change body posture while guided and carried along by the knowing field. This is the same process seen in traditional constellations.

For some time Hellinger continued to use Movements of the Soul in his workshops—many of which have been recorded. The issue with Movements of the Soul usually concerns reconciliation between offenders and victims, and it often involves questions that cannot so easily be answered using common sense, as they exist beyond the normal understanding of what is *good* or *bad*.

These constellations reveal a special kind of power and beauty, and in my own experience, they require special frameworks. Hellinger has done these constellations with hundreds of participants using a group of very experienced representatives. The field that comes into existence during these gatherings is more strongly perceived by most participants than during, for example, a weekend workshop family constellation with about thirty participants.

These gatherings operate on an entirely different level. A very intense collective field comes into existence during these large-scale constellations. Such constellations can be interpreted as historical records. They initiate collective awareness processes.[22]

In my workshops I sometimes work in this manner, but I refer to them as *constellations without words*, and I integrate each into a traditional constellation to facilitate communication of the seeker's (subconscious) inner movement. If I get the feeling the representative of the client is being strongly pulled toward a family member who died at a young age, I will ask the representative to flow with these urges to move. Very often the representative moves toward a family member who passed away at a young age and sometimes even wants to lie next to the dead family member. I seldom conduct an entire constellation without words because this type of constellation has to really fit in with the seeker's situation and needs.

Like traditional constellations this type of constellation often brings me into a deep connection with the seeker. It enables him or her to gain powerful insights—on a nonverbal level—into his or her situation.

The difference is best revealed through the following example. Imagine a group of people all absorbed in an interesting conversation and another group that is connected via deep meditation. The first group is connected through overt communication—an obvious exchange. The other group is connected through a silent communication that is directed inside and toward a more inner consciousness. Something happens in both groups. Both groups are connected, but the ways they are connected are different.

Working with constellations without words feels different to me than traditional constellations. There is the feeling that I *hold and support* the constellation in my own meditative space.

Forty-four-year-old Anne's constellation is a good example. In the introductory talk, it was revealed she had already done various types of constellations, and she still struggled with a heavy issue unresolved by previous constellations. The theme was her anger and self-hatred as well as hatred toward her brother. Her brother had sexually abused her when they were both teens. From the very beginning, I sensed this constellation needed a different approach than the classic type. This is why I asked her to choose experienced representatives for herself and her brother and constellate them. I asked the representatives to open up to perceptions and in a relaxed way follow urges to move. Throughout the constellation I felt strong connections with both representatives—more intense connections than would have been the case in a classic constellation.

The *brother* only moved slightly, but from his body language, it was apparent he was slowly collapsing on the inside. At the end of the constellation, he slumped defeated to the floor. *Anne* moved repeatedly toward him and then away. She was just like a marionette, but she finally settled with standing with her back toward him.

I asked the representatives to succinctly verbalize their observations. The *brother* at first said he was not aware of the seriousness of his actions, but then he became more and more aware of what had happened. Then came a feeling of guilt and shame, which changed into self-hate and anger toward his sister. The representative for Anne oscillated between feeling powerless and feeling attracted to her brother. It was as if she had to help him. This changed gradually into feeling anger and shame.

Months later Anne told me she felt freer and more open after the constellation. She realized she and her brother had actually repeated the abuse situation that existed between her mother and her mother's father. She appreciated that she had done this out of love and loyalty toward her mother, who had suffered terribly from the abuse, and her brother was motivated by love and loyalty toward his mother's father (Anne's grandfather), who was excluded from the family by being labeled as a *sex maniac*. Loyalty toward the grandfather meant Anne's brother also became an offender and carried over his grandfather's guilt and self-hatred.

Movements of the Spirit-Mind

Bert Hellinger's latest development is called Movements of the Spirit-Mind.[23] This involves a single person and no constellated representatives for family members. It is, therefore, not important where he or she stands. In these constellations a movement suddenly takes hold of the person, which, according to Hellinger, comes from the Spirit-Mind. These movements are always born out of love, which unites what was previously divided. All movements during these constellations happen peacefully. Sometimes Hellinger brings another representative into the constellation. Sometimes he or she voices a meaningful sentence, which arises in him or her. These are minimalistic, condensed constellations. They reveal very deep inner movements, which is why he calls this method of working new family constellations or constellations of the Spirit-Mind.

Prominent constellation therapists are divided about this method. For some therapists such as Margreet Mossel, it is clearly a natural progression, and she enthusiastically embraces it. She compares it to Mozart's development and says, "His genius compositions as an adult were of a more brilliant quality than what he composed as a child."[24]

However, other constellation therapists do not see a worthy difference or progression with the Movements of the Soul, and some are even critical. Wilfried Nelles formulates his criticism sharply:
"It seems to me that with his latest constellation method, the Movement of the Spirit-Mind, Hellinger only follows his own inner movement of the soul and no longer confirms these via representatives or through an explanation for the client and seminar participants. The constellations then become more like some kind of magical ritual that hits the participants with amazement. The spectators follow the therapist like a magician but they do not really understand what is happening. This creates a fascination as long as the magician performs well, but I have my doubts as to how understandable, professional, and practically oriented this method is."[25]

Many constellation facilitators do clearly see that the different methods of constellations complement each other and that it is about selecting the right type at the right time. The work on constellations is still continuously developing. For me there is no conflict. I work with the method that best fits the moment and the needs of the client/seeker. I have no preference for working with traditional family constellations or the newer styles. I do find working with concepts of soul or spirit confusing, as most people have divergent definitions of these things. Moreover, it carries with it the risk that people value these concepts differently and start to put one above the other.

In this context I prefer to use the term *awareness*. This puts me in a state where the concept of awareness describes the entire path—from a first limited awareness of people who feel separated and very burdened and traumatized to the completely liberated cosmic awareness wherein we are all one. This includes oneness with all that surrounds us. In this oneness all differences become meaningless.

Three Zen students stand on a bridge.
The first one says,
"Look at the way water flows under the bridge."
The second one says,
"Look at how the bridge moves over the water."
The third one says,
"I only see minds moving."
—Classic Zen story

9

Science and Constellations

Scientific theories come about through experimentation and observations via empirical methods of testing. When the results of these observations are adequately reproducible, they can be referred to as scientific proof upon which the scientific community explains its notions and concepts.[1]
—Wikipedia

From a scientific point of view, there are two types of research questions that recur in family and organization constellations. The first one is of a practical nature. How efficient are constellations? The second question is tougher to answer. How can the knowing field, present during all constellations, be explained? This phenomenon, whereby representatives can feel emotions and inner attitudes so clearly, serves as the basis of constellation therapy.

The previous chapter has even shown that representatives can clearly sense the emotional context of abstract notions and their meanings. I remember vividly an organization constellation in which the head of a school had the teachers, parents, and students represented as well as the school building. In the middle of the constellation, the school building representative burst into tears. Micky Masset, the facilitator, asked the representative of the building what was the matter. The representative replied, "It's terrible. I feel so neglected. No attention is ever given to me, and I feel miserable and dirty." He had difficulty speaking through his tears as he continued crying.

The school head was deeply moved by this and admitted, "Indeed. We have had insufficient financial means to keep the building tidy and properly cleaned." The straightforward part is that the perception of the representative was spot-on, but that a school building can be considered a sentient entity is not an easy concept for the average scientist to accept.

How Efficient Are Constellations?

The market is always right.
—Stock market maxim

In my opinion only efficient therapies and treatment provided by competent and well-qualified professionals are therapeutically beneficial. The market—and, therefore, the general population—decide if it's useful or not. In the long run, the market always prevails.

What about constellations then? How efficient are they? If constellations were ineffectual and participants concluded that no benefit was gained, then no one would spend their time, effort, and money on constellations. In reality the opposite is true. Constellations are becoming more popular and have secured an important place in the therapeutic landscape. Precisely because constellation therapy has been found effective, a lot of research has recently been taking place into this form of treatment. I will now provide an overview of this research. There is a lot more information available on the website of the *Deutsche Gesellschaft für Systemaufstellungen* (International Systemic Constellations Association) and *The Knowing Field Journal*.[2]

Gerd Höpper, a Professor at the Ludwig-Maximilian University in Munich who wrote his dissertation under guidance of clinical psychologist Professor W. Butollo, spent five months studying the inner workings and intricacies of family constellations. This was done together with Insa Sparrer and Professor Matthias Varga von Kibéd. His research was documented in the book *Heilt Demut Wo Schiksal Wirkt*? (*Does Humility Heal When Faith Acts?*).[3]

Eighty-five clients performed family constellations and were scientifically observed. There was a control group without constellations, and four evaluation studies were done. The results were clear. Clinically significant therapeutic improvement was noted in four out of five of the most significant variables being observed. This was not the case in the control group.

In another empirical study, Peter Schlötter studied the fields of perception of representatives in constellations.[4] His research serves as one of the most important studies on constellation therapy. He managed to examine and verify the existence of a representative's perceptions with 240 test subjects and more than four thousand independent tests.

Realistic constellations were set up multiple times in which different representatives were used interchangeably. Different people were placed consecutively on a specific position within the constellation and asked to record their feelings. The results indicated there was a high probability that different representatives, without consulting each other, had the same sensations on the same location in the same constellation. Schlötter's study is particularly interesting because he was able to show that the similarities of representatives' perceptions are not coincidental but reproducible and measurable.

Another relevant study still in progress is Dr. Robert Langlotz's concerning the efficacy of constellations in reducing the symptoms of illnesses such as anxiety, depressive disorders, suicidal tendencies, and psychotic behaviors in borderline individuals.[5] This study is recording significant improvements on all levels in individuals with these symptoms. He uses standardized questionnaires from the field of psychiatry (VEI and MMPI) and has introduced and included additional questionnaires into his research study.

Adding to my own experiences and those of many colleagues with constellation therapy experience, it is clear that a growing number of scientific studies are showing family constellations are an efficient and effective method of treatment.

Science and the Perceptions of Representatives

A good traveler has no fixed plans
and is not intent upon arriving.
A good artist lets his intuition
lead him wherever it wants.
A good scientist has freed himself of concepts
and keeps his mind open to what is.
—Lao-Tzu[6]

My aim for this book has been to describe the effects of family and organization constellations as clearly as possible. Allow me then to take a closer look at a specific component of this form of treatment deserving more attention—namely, the perceptions of the representatives and the fact that representatives have access to the feelings and sensations of complete strangers during a constellation.

For a long time, Hellinger called this strange phenomenon *a secret*. Albrecht Mahr gave it the name the *knowing field*, by which he meant that a type of field comes into existence during a constellation whereby information is available and in which the conscience and knowing of the system is present. For many practitioners a direct comparison is made here with Rupert Sheldrake's theory on morphogenetic fields and morphic resonance.

Morphogenetic Fields and Morphic Resonance

How do birds find their way over thousands of kilometers? How is it homing pigeons find their way back without having maps or navigation systems? Where do bacteria such as the influenza virus and other living organisms get the information they use to adapt themselves continuously to altered environments?

According to Sheldrake, these animals—like people—have access to information fields, which he calls *morphogenetic* (shape-forming) *fields*.[7] (See also "The Knowing Field" in chapter one.) He calls the transfer of information from these fields *morphic resonance*. The basis of this theory goes back to Aristotle's theories about the soul. According to Aristotle, the soul that exists in the seed of every plant is what creates the plant. Over the years the concept of the *soul* has changed to *field*, and in the last century, the biologist Paul Weiss developed the concept of *morphogenesis*. This concept concerns the regeneration process that enables some reptiles to entirely regrow limbs. This is one of the processes in living cell division that the DNA theory alone cannot explain. Sheldrake's work is notable in that he fused different theories and fragmented studies on this topic, transforming them into a usable hypothesis. To Sheldrake the morphologic fields are just as real and evident as gravitational or magnetic fields. People also cannot see these with their eyes, but they do not doubt their existence for one moment.

To illustrate the operation of morphic resonance, we will now take a look at a famous short story titled "The Hundredth Monkey."[8] The biologist Lyall Watson published this book in 1979 about a Japanese monkey colony. He writes about a particular monkey on the island of Koshima. In 1952 this monkey took to washing sweet potatoes left by researchers before eating them. Slowly, after he learned this skill, other monkeys began to mimic this behavior. On a particular day in 1958, when a certain number of monkeys had learned this trick, something special unfolded. Just before sunset all the monkeys on Koshima were suddenly able to wash sweet potatoes. Indeed, even monkeys on islands kilometers away were washing sweet potatoes without an obvious information transfer system. Apparently a critical mass was reached in the evolution of these monkeys that influenced the morphologic field of the species. The number of monkeys that had to first learn how to wash potatoes in order to reach critical mass is not known. The unknown number is now referred to symbolically as one hundred. Thus it is the hundredth monkey.

According to Sheldrake this true story illustrates the point that morphogenetic fields help humans and mammals to develop. These fields can instantly relay information via morphogenetic resonance without the passing of time and apparently without tools of communication. This is comparable with what is seen every day in constellations when the representatives express the feelings of total strangers.

When Rupert Sheldrake first witnessed a constellation, he commented that he had seen a morphogenetic field in action for the first time.[9]

For Sheldrake it is a foregone conclusion that morphogenetic fields are present in everything around us. These fields are responsible for the formation of crystals in their typical shapes and the reason why all cells in the creation of an embryo know where they belong. Morphogenetic fields play key roles in the survival of animals and other organisms. According to Sheldrake these fields operate throughout nature, and each organism or inorganic structure in the universe has its own morphogenetic field. These fields are all connected with each other and influence each other.

Sheldrake's research is impressive, but to explain his theory fully goes beyond the scope of this book. For further information and explanation, I refer readers to his books. However interesting his hypothesis on morphogenetic fields is for constellation practice, it remains controversial and is not widely accepted in the general scientific community.

Epigenetics

The BBC documentary *The Ghost in Your Genes*[10] details an investigation into periods of famine conducted in an isolated part of Sweden by British professor Marcus Pembrey and Swedish professor Lars Olov Bygen. With the help of accurate and complete Swedish population records, significant rises in the number of cases of diabetes in certain generations throughout history were shown to follow three generations after periods of relative famine that had occurred in the area. In other words, famine at critical times in the lives of the grandparents could affect the life expectancy of their grandchildren.

According to Marcus Pembrey, this *information* is passed on (genomically imprinted) via *epigenetic* instructions. (The prefix *epi* means here *on top of*.[11])

As a family constellation therapist, this phenomenon is easily recognizable. Nevertheless, it is remarkable that even in genetics research, connections between generations are now being found. When I investigated this further, I came across more notable scientific data. I had always thought that all genetic information passed on from parents was stored in the DNA. According to an article in the *New Scientist*,[12] there is evidence that as well as DNA, we also have *instruction manuals* that pass on necessary information to the genes. This is not only for them to know when they should be active, but it's also to direct which cells should build which tissue in the development of the different organs and in the creation of the embryo. This is called *cellular differentiation.*

> *Without this epigenetic instruction manual, multicellular organisms could not exist because every cell that functions currently as a liver cell or a skin cell carries the same genes. It is the epigenetic manual that tells the cells which tissues to construct or develop.*[13]

Marcus Pembrey, a geneticist at the Institute of Child Health in London, provides other examples of epigenetic information transfer in the same article in the *New Scientist*. He gives the example of a Dutch woman who conceived a child smaller than what was considered normal during the famine of World War II. This in itself was not so special. However, the fact this child bore children who were also smaller than normal is special. This is particularly special because these children had healthy diets, and none of her genes were found to be defective. Marcus Pembrey commented, "Bizarre things are going on that we are just beginning to get a handle on."

Is it possible that the collective conscience and memory have their places in this epigenetic instruction manual? I see clear connections with Sheldrake's morphological fields, but I am no geneticist. Sheldrake is viewed as a kind of new age guru among geneticists, but Marcus Pembrey is a recognized geneticist whose findings are published in reputable journals.

What is important here is that there is scientific evidence of information transfer across generations.

Genetic Sexual Attraction

A newspaper article alerted me to yet another scientifically confirmed fact. In an article headlined "British Couple Discovers that They Are Twins,"[14] two people discovered after their marriage that they were twin brother and sister. They were immediately adopted after birth and knew nothing of each other's existence. Their story even became the subject of debate in the British Parliament.

When the two first met as adults, they felt an irresistible attraction for each other. According to the newspaper article, this phenomenon occurs more often among family members. People who are blood-related but do not know this can feel strongly attracted to each other.[15] This syndrome carries a scientific name—genetic sexual attraction, or GSA.

Marieke describes the power of this attraction.[16] She explains what she felt when she first met her half brother and fell in love with him at first sight. "It was as if everything around me disappeared—there was only him and me. There was a tidal wave of emotions, and we felt the need to touch each other. I didn't understand what was happening." After experiencing many problems in other relationships, they now live happily together.

There are many examples of GSA, according to Dr. Maurice Greenberg,[17] advisor for the Post-Adoption Centre in London. He studied the phenomenon and analyzed forty cases, interviewing people who said they experienced such feelings. Two-thirds of the people he interviewed said they ended up in sexual relationships with their blood-related significant others.

The experiences of others varied from erotic feelings toward the other family member to sexual behavior such as intimate caressing. When they first met their lost family members, all experienced overwhelming and complex rushes of feelings and almost uncontrollable sensations of being in love. They all said they felt unusual forms of closeness and intimacy toward their relatives, who felt the same way.

This does not only occur between twins but also between parents and offspring who lived separate lives from birth and were not even aware of each other's existence.

This reminds me of a case in my practice. About four years ago, Peter, age twenty-nine, took part in a constellation. From the introductory discussion, it was put forward he did not know his father because his mother strictly refused to reveal his father's name. In his constellation he was able to physically see and hug the representative of his (until then unknown) father. This clearly did him a lot of good—to know he had a father and that his father loved and supported him.

Two years ago he called me and told me in an excited voice about a recent experience. He was waiting at a supermarket checkout when he noticed an older man with whom he felt an immediate and strong connection. They started conversing, and it soon became clear it was his biological father standing next to him. He said his joy at that moment was indescribable.

The remarkably strong sense of attraction these people feel is undeniable. As a constellation therapist, I know all members of a family system feel special connections with each other. As long as they grow up together, they recognize it as a usual and normal family connection. However, if they meet coincidentally as adults (unaware of their blood relationship) and consequently feel this force of attraction, it is very understandable that they interpret this attraction as being in love, and they want to embark on an intimate relationship.

However, what brings about this special attraction for one another, and what are the forces operating in this process? The scientific theory behind GSA states that the genetic connection between blood relatives leaves a kind of blueprint on the genes. Since the blueprints resemble each other so strongly, it seems on meeting they both feel perfectly matched. As yet I have not found an explanation that accounts for how people can sense this special blueprint connection.

The phenomenon of GSA shows the existence of a strong connection between family members—a connection so strong that family members can even feel attracted to one another without knowing they are blood-related. The connections with Marcus Pembrey's epigenetics and Rupert Sheldrake's morphologic field theory are easy to make.

We now leave the arena of genetics and look at how the science of quantum physics can help further the quest for a scientific explanation regarding the perceptions of the representative.

Quantum Physics

Information is the fundamental building block of the universe.
—A. Zeilinger[18]

To avoid misunderstanding I will not attempt to explain all quantum physics. This subchapter will only look at certain phenomena in the world of very small particles. This might help illuminate how the perceptions of representatives operate. They are, in fact, due to transfers of information. These transfers occur during constellations. The detailed perceptions of a family member's representative are examples of this information transfer. In hindsight these specifics are verified as clearly accurate, even though at times the client was not aware of this knowledge.

This can be seen in forty-year-old Jerry's constellation. His grandfather lost a leg in the war, but Jerry did not know whether it was his right or left leg. The representative of the grandfather spontaneously knew it was the left leg that was amputated. When Jerry returned the next day, he confirmed the perception of the representative. He had called his father, who verified the information.

If we look closely at what presents itself at the moment this information is revealed, we see the information transfer takes place beyond space and time. A comparable phenomenon in quantum theory is known as entanglement and nonlocality. When two (or more) particles (photons that are quantum-mechanically entangled, for example) are taken apart, they always react simultaneously in an identical manner. This is irrespective of distance.

The entanglement is formed by particles colliding with each other.[19] The particles are then sent off in different directions a long distance away from each other. If the movement of one of the particles is measured, the other entangled particle reacts in an identical manner. The measurement in one location, therefore, gives the same result at the other location. Because quantum physicists found this simultaneous reaction in different particles in multiple locations, they used the term *nonlocality* to describe this phenomenon. This transfer of information takes place beyond space and time and is one of the most important discoveries in quantum physics. Classic physics theory was turned on its head with this discovery.

Is something similar occurring when the knowing field is created in a constellation? Could it be that an exchange of entangled particles is taking place among the participants, which causes this information transfer? How does this entanglement come into life?

One theory is that the information comes from the knowing field, which is intricately connected to and forms part of the seeker's conscience and memory system. The information is spontaneously and immediately present in the space in which the constellation takes place.

Then there is the question of what the field actually is. A prime example of one of the many fields physics recognizes is gravitation. The gravitational field (gravity) makes all objects move in a downward direction and is responsible for keeping everything on Earth. This field is invisible but influences everything in the environment.

Radio and television stations also create fields. Every receiver within range can tune into a channel to receive the available broadcast. Mobile phone networks operate in a similar way. Fields, therefore, operate invisibly but can influence individuals. In constellations the client's family field is laid out. It is selective and limited to the family, as the perceptions concern only the members who are part of his or her family system. In this field, does the information transfer take place as per the principles of nonlocality and entanglement?

Quantum physics describes phenomena on the level of subatomic particles. The question is, can these phenomena simply be transferred in order to interpret human and social systems? There are obvious parallels. However, I suspect the real answer is some way off.

Further in my quest, thanks to Franz Ruppert,[20] I came across the operation of mirror neurons. This was a special revelation.

Mirror Neurons

When people use the expression "I feel your pain" they may not realize how literally it could be true.[21]
—"Mirrors in the Mind", Rizzolati, Fogassi, and Gallese

In 1996 Giacamo Rizzolatti, head of the physiological institute at the University of Parma, made a remarkable discovery. A veteran researcher into how brains coordinate targeted actions, he studied monkeys with a focus on how their brains strongly resemble those of humans. During one of his tests, something interesting happened. Two monkeys were connected to a brain-scanning device that showed which brain cells (neurons) were active during an activity.

One of the monkeys grabbed a nut while the other monkey watched. Surprisingly the device displayed that the monkey watching had activity in the same area of the brain as the monkey that actually picked up the nut. Further investigation revealed that each time one monkey observed an action of the other, the same physiological effect was observed in the brain of both the performing and the watching monkeys. When this study was later repeated on humans, it became clear the same thing happened. The brain cells responsible for this process are called *mirror neurons*. What happens when you see someone eating an apple? Your mouth starts watering. Your mirror neurons are letting you taste and enjoy the sensation along with the person eating the piece of fruit.

The observing monkey in Rizzolatti's follow-up research could only see parts of the movements of the other monkeys, such as the paw grabbing the nut and not the entire monkey. In the observing monkey, all mirror neurons required for the whole sequence of movements were activated.[22] Researchers concluded humans only have to see a part of the whole picture in order to understand the meaning of what is happening. It is, therefore, sufficient to see only a wide-open mouth and an apple to initiate the mouthwatering response. With the activation of mirror neurons, a person does not actually have to see the apple being eaten. It even goes a lot further than this, as these neurons do not only mirror operations of movement but also of emotional states. When people observe others, they can perceive their emotional and mental states.[23] This happens spontaneously and involuntarily—without having to do anything or even having to think about it.[24]

Through the discovery of mirror neurons, we have for the first time a scientific theory to explain humans' ability to empathize. This discovery has shown how humans understand and perceive the moods and intentions of others. It is mirror neurons that enable people to understand and trust others. The whole content of consciousness is being mirrored within people, allowing them to feel and reconstruct similar feelings in themselves.

The more a person is connected with another individual, the stronger the resonance of mirror neurons is. With the aid of these mirror neurons, people are able to construct inner pictures of fellow humans, and this gives people the feeling they can understand and share others' feelings. Mirror neurons enable people to connect with each other in a nonverbal manner.

People can now understand how we naturally know and sense if someone is honest and his or her communication is congruent Via mirror neurons people feel which areas of the brain are active. When another person communicates and conflicting areas of the brain are activated, mirror neurons observe this as a conflict situation. In that case people can sense that there is more to a given situation and that the communication is not congruent.

Is it then possible that mirror neurons are responsible for the operation of the knowing field? How does this occur? I provide here my hypothesis subject to further scientific research.

During introductory discussions with seekers, I try to make inner connection with my clients while we discuss themes and facts. My mirror neurons are in operation at this time. The client chooses his or her representatives intuitively and places them accordingly. During the ritual of setting up the constellation, the client is asked to stay closely in touch with his or her theme. When this is done, the mirror neurons can reflect the necessary information. In this way every representative subconsciously knows the family history relating to that theme. Information is also being passed to the representatives when the seeker places them. Mirror neurons make no distinction between the conscious and subconscious, and all information is universally present within the subconscious.

This is my hypothesis presently, but do we have sufficient proof and explanation concerning the perceptions of the representatives?

A family constellation provides a wonderful context for people to find answers in a very deep and respectful way. I use constellations just like I continue to use electricity—even though there is currently no one explanation for what electricity really is. We only have theories. This helps me to view constellations as a phenomenon I do not need to prove. The popularity of constellations verifies that people are convinced of their value. People can experience the benefits for themselves. When it becomes clear that with relatively little effort a person can achieve major results, it will be widely recognized as an effective therapeutic method. John, who managed to increase revenue by 28 percent through his organizational constellation, and Nancy, who was afraid of commitment but now has a steady boyfriend one year after her constellation, are just two of many people who do not insist on a scientific explanation.

The first flying pioneers were also confronted with scientific theory that tried to tell them what they were attempting was impossible. Yet these pioneers trusted their own perceptions and did what they felt they had to. Only later did science find an explanation in the laws of aerodynamics.

10
Preparing for One's Own Constellation

Men climb mountains
because where the mountain ends
the sky begins.
But the point is
at every point on the mountain
the sky begins.
All you have to do
is to jump.
—Michael Barnett[1]

This chapter provides a questionnaire as well as some guidelines about how to prepare for one's own constellation. Various testimonials will show how constellations operate and what they have meant for those who have set up their own.

Questionnaire and Preparation

If, after reading this book, you would like to use constellations to improve your personal life, relationship, or health, then it is necessary to find as much relevant information as possible about your family. All facts from the family's history are important. The most important facts relate to difficult fates of family members.

Please note constellations can still be very beneficial—even for people with very little knowledge of their family histories. This includes cases of adoption. Below is an overview of the most common difficult fates.

Difficult fates

o The early death of a sibling, before he or she or you turned twenty-eight to thirty years of age

o The early death of one of the parents, before the child turned twenty-eight to thirty years of age

o Miscarriages after the third month of pregnancy

o Maternal death

o Major accident or illness

o Victims of natural and other disasters

o Physical abuse or incestuous relationships

o Physical or mental disabilities

o Suicide or murder

o Artificial insemination

o Victims or perpetrators of a crime in the family

o Imprisonment (jail, concentration camps, confinement to reservations, etc.)

o All kinds of war-related experiences

o Homosexuality

o Exclusion from the family

o Nuns, monks, or priests in the family

o Psychiatric patients in the family

o Bankruptcies

o Emigrants

o Forefathers involved in slavery (as slaves or masters)

o Native forefathers

o Colonial rulers

o Extramarital births (in the past and causing social disturbance)

o Children who were passed on to foster parents or relatives at a young age

o Adoption

o Family members sent without necessary reason to a boarding school at a young age

o Family members forced to move or flee from their home country

o Family members with parents of different nationalities

o Family members never allowed to leave the parental home

To make it easier, find some questionnaires about you and your family below.

Personal facts from your childhood
o   Were there complications regarding your birth?
o   Was your mother ill, or did she have permanent injury as a result of your birth?
o   Were you hospitalized early or later on in life due to a sudden or heavy illness?
o   How many siblings do you have?
o   Were there miscarriages or children who died at a young age?
o   Do any of your siblings have a difficult fate?

Personal facts from your adolescence/adulthood
o   Were there important partners (first great loves) before the current relationship?
o   Were there special reasons for the premature end to an earlier relationship such as parental influence or interference?
o   Were there any abortions?
o   Were there any miscarriages or children who died at a young age?
o   Were there extramarital births?
o   Were there children from an earlier relationship?

Facts on the level of the parents
o   How did your parents meet?
o   Did one of them have a relationship earlier, or was he or she married before?
o   Were there important reasons why an earlier relationship of either parent could or should not continue?
o   How old were they when they were married?
o   Were you born before or after they were married?
o   Were you the reason they married?
o   If they were not married, was there a special reason for this?

Facts from your maternal/paternal family of origin (mother/father)
o   How many siblings did he or she have, and what was his or her place?
o   Were there miscarriages or children who died at a young age?
o   Was there a difficult fate?

Maternal grandmother/paternal grandmother
o   How many siblings did she have, and what was her place?
o   Were there miscarriages or children who died at a young age?
o   Did she as a child or adult undergo a difficult fate?

Maternal grandfather/paternal grandfather
o   How many siblings did he have, and what was his place?
o   Were there miscarriages or children who died at a young age?
o   As a child or adult did he undergo a difficult fate?

Maternal great-grandparents/paternal great-grandparents and former ancestors on both sides
o   Were there any difficult fates or notable events?

Once all these facts have been collected, you need to ask yourself where and with whom it is best to set up a family constellation.

Personally I suggest you look for someone with some years of experience as a facilitator/therapist before he or she started to work with family constellations. Ensure your chosen facilitator/therapist or coach is a well-trained, seasoned professional. By checking online, for example, at www.isca-network.org, you will certainly be able to find a suitable facilitator/therapist or coach in your neighborhood.

After One's Constellation

Try to talk as little as possible in the first half hour after your constellation, and give yourself the necessary time and space to integrate your new insights and solutions. Take all the time you need. Avoid questions out of curiosity from others about how things went or why the constellation took a particular course. This will disrupt the process and only serve to distract you. It is better to give yourself time to allow everything to sink in.

Most facilitators advise the seeker to forget about the constellation and not ponder it any further. What you can do, however, is recall or recollect the end sensation of the constellation—the feeling and relief you experienced.

This will give you the chance to resonate with the final family image that the constellation presented. If you do this in the days after your constellation—without becoming compulsive—you will actually enhance the integration process.

The integration of experiences from your constellation needs time. The amount of time needed will vary from person to person. One person might feel direct changes, while the next might go through a period of worsening symptoms before things change for the better. This is a phenomenon also known in classic homeopathy, in which the symptoms first become worse when the right substance is administered.

The patient goes through a healing process, as his or her immune system apparently finds balance on a fundamental level. If this is the case for you, have patience. Do not immediately look for another facilitator. Instead, make another appointment with the facilitator who guided you in the constellation. He or she knows what happened in the constellation and can best guide you through the readjustment process. Of course, this process can never be a substitute for required medical treatment.

After a successful constellation in which significant issues were resolved, a client sometimes wants to engage in another constellation shortly thereafter. He or she starts to see all kinds of deep unresolved issues and wants to clear them away as soon as possible. Although this is very understandable, I would advise against it. If you do constellations too frequently over a short period of time, you hamper the integration process. You also risk only partial resolution and manifestation of constellation solutions into your life. The best thing to do is wait a few months before you do another constellation—or at least until clear results start to emerge.

Do not forget that you might need months or sometimes a year for a complete integration process to take place. So relax. Let your soul do the work for you.

Testimonials

To give you an idea of the possible outcomes of family constellations, here are various testimonials that clients have sent me.

Petra, age twenty-nine

"I recently did a constellation on finding my own place. Much has stayed with me from the constellation. It became clear to me that I was strongly connected with my sister, who died at three years of age. The remarkable thing was that when I visited my mother a few days after having done the constellation, among pictures of my siblings and me on display, there was for the first time a picture of my little sister, who had passed away as a young girl. I said to my mother, 'She belongs here too.' She replied, 'Indeed, she has a place in my heart.' It was just like in the constellation, it was a little like a miracle."

Martine, age thirty-eight

"In January 2002 I constellated my family situation together with my partner. My theme concerned my difficulties raising my eldest daughter. The consequences were far-reaching. Everyone is now a lot more relaxed. There is no more complaining about who sits where at the table. Without having to say anything everyone just sits where they should. Also, your advice to hang up a substitute picture of a toddler in order to give our miscarriage a place had a positive impact on us. He was the twin brother of our eldest daughter. Her style of clothing changed drastically; she spontaneously asked me to buy her skirts, when previously all she wanted to wear were trousers."

Sarah, age forty-three

"My relationship constellation has triggered many changes in my life. You might remember my theme was that there was no more pleasure in my relationship. Now the enjoyment has returned. For the first time, I look back with gratitude on my previous relationships. I now feel there is more space in my current relationship with my husband. Something that was in the way is now gone. We feel closer to each other. Before the constellation, I sometimes felt better being apart from him, but now I desire to be with him more."

Jerry, age forty-seven

"The constellation about my father has brought about many changes. It was not clear to me how much I stood above him. What a relief it was to come away from this and to meet my real dad. I still feel to this day the strength of all those men who stood behind me at the end of the constellation. It is a constant source of energy. For the first time, I felt safe and secure in my masculinity."

Tom, age thirty

"I asked for a constellation because I had the feeling of being trapped in family issues. I read Hellinger's book *Love's Hidden Symmetry* and his method of working seemed special to me. Even though sometimes I found what happened during the constellation a bit odd, I have to admit in hindsight that the constellation has given me clear insights and a structure to help me move forward. The moment I replaced my own representative at the end of the constellation, I remember feeling strong and clear-minded. From the new insights offered, I started feeling and behaving differently toward my family, as well as generally loosening up. As a result, I started looking deeper into other peoples' lives. One of the very concrete consequences was that within two weeks after the constellation my father came to spend a day with me without my mother! I really enjoyed it because, since I left home eleven years ago, this has never happened!"

Elizabeth, age forty-two

"I was amazed when I came home after my first constellation. My theme was to know how to deal with my children when they were arguing. I couldn't believe my eyes when I got home. My son was chatting with his sister in her room! I hadn't seen that in years. I even went so far as to call my ex-husband, without mentioning the constellation. I didn't feel the usual anxiety about doing this. For the first time since our divorce, it was possible to really communicate. All problems have not been solved, of course, but at least a new start has been made."

Maria, age fifty-one

"I woke up this morning with a happy feeling, a feeling of being free. A realization that I am free—free of guilt, free of fear, and free of melancholy. It's lovely to be myself and I am thankful to be able to experience this sensation. All situations, experiences, and people I have met in my life have led to this wonderful experience, and my family constellation definitely belongs among them. I am thankful that I am now able to connect with the feeling of freedom. I realize more that I have the space to exist and that I create my life via my thoughts, and that all my feelings, thoughts, and deeds are in line with each other; it's fantastic. Thank you for your insights. Thank you for organizing consciousness expansion sessions (through your constellation work) and thank you for the warmth and support that I experienced during the workshop in Ostend. Keep up the good work!"

Working on Personal Aspects

Not knowing is true knowledge.
Presuming to know is a disease
First realize that you are sick;
then you move toward health.
—Lao-Tzu[2]

As has been shown, people carry over a great deal from their family systems. However, there are also problems that come into existence through negative personal experiences acquired during childhood or infancy.

Parents have given their children what they could. Humans cannot give more than they have received if they have not been through transforming processes. For example, if someone has received too little attention during his or her childhood, then he or she most likely passes this on to the following generations. It is well-known among therapists that all things that remain unfulfilled in childhood are stored or remembered as unprocessed experiences.

On the intellectual level, this storage occurs in the form of beliefs. If people received too little attention, they might believe, "They do not want me." Although this might have only been an issue with parents while the children were still toddlers, people later project this onto society, social environments, and relationships. Subconscious patterns of belief come into existence. People are strongly convinced that reality is just the way subconscious patterns of thinking make us believe it to be. The limited experience of a person's youth arises from the limited opportunities the parents had themselves. These limited opportunities might have been passed to the child and thus become the basic idea about life and reality.

Through the pain people have experienced (for example, receiving too little attention), people put up inner walls on the emotional level. This is because the little child needed to be protected from the pain, as this was too much to bear. Small children, therefore, make inner decisions. "I will not let this happen again. I don't ever want to be that vulnerable again." This decision then becomes part of their subconscious patterns of thinking, or mind-sets.

On the physical level, people manifest their thinking patterns and the emotional walls as chronic muscle tension. Wilhelm Reich calls this "character armor."[3] This is reflected in the inner body. For example, shoulders hanging forward show a fear about opening up. A forward and pumped-up chest (macho attitude) shows a wall around the heart. In the pelvic area a person collects all sorts of tensions around the theme of sexuality. Stiff necks usually represent suppressed anger. Through all these tensions, people become stiff. For the experienced therapist, the body and its chronic tensions are like an open book that reveals much of its story of suppressed and unprocessed emotions and fears.

These chronic muscle tensions are ways to protect oneself from the potentially hostile world. If a person then meets and falls in love with someone, he or she cannot or does not dare open up out of fear of triggering pain from the past. At the same time, a person obviously really wants a partner to give him or her what has always been wanted. However, old experiences haunt people, and that keeps them suspicious.

People prefer hiding behind walls because, as they allow affection in from newfound love, they subconsciously come in contact with their histories of pain and loss during childhood. They tend to stay behind safe walls to avoid reliving these experiences. Partners love each other and would like to share love, but they keep hitting walls and cannot get through. They are kept at safe distances.

As general rule, people cannot allow more love and attention than what they were used to in their childhoods. People keep their loving partners at the same distance and re-create the same experiences as in childhood. This is the vicious circle in which most people are trapped.

There is a way to get out of this. However, to do so people have to be prepared to bring up hurtful experiences and feelings. An example of doing this in a safe way is by taking rebirthing-breath work sessions or doing bioenergetic exercises originally taught by Alexander Lowen.[4]

These methods, among others, help bring up all trapped and suppressed emotions layer by layer. Expressing and sometimes even acting out emotions relaxes the body. It's freeing. The chronic muscle tension clears up, and the limited beliefs and patterns of thinking become conscious.

People relive key moments of their lives that had strong impacts on them or were traumatizing. This might have been birth, a terrifying moment at school with a bully, or the nights as a baby left totally alone in the bassinet.

Through this awareness process, people are able to see their beliefs in context. They start to see and understand that they have been there for certain reasons and within certain contexts, but in another context many other experiences are possible.

This purification or healing process relaxes the body, whereby the chronic tensions resolve and a person becomes suppler. The person learns how to open up to new experiences, and as a consequence fixed patterns of thinking dissolve. Step by step, a person learns it is safe again to open his or her heart to the world.

Consequences of Constellation Therapy

Anyone who has participated in a constellation, either by being the seeker or acting as a representative, will change as a result of the experience. Participants can clearly see how strongly people are all connected and how strong the power of family connections and the collective conscience really are. They understand that many ideas, beliefs, and attitudes are not their own but rather ones that have been carried over from ancestors. This insight helps to put beliefs and attitudes into perspective.

Through constellation work many people are beginning to realize they pass on their unprocessed burdens and issues to their children, and all exclusions will burden the following generations. As a result of this understanding, people are changing by taking the necessary steps to be more aware, conscious, and responsible when relating to each other.

Respect, love, and a sense of worth gain a new and lively meaning through constellation work. This is not possible when the systemic order is imposed externally as a new moral system. Integrating the wisdom of constellation work will work better as an individual and collective learning and consciousness changing process. It then becomes a natural transition that creates a new inner attitude. In this regard constellations reveal the consequences of actions and the associated responsibility for them. If people do not wish to carry these and be responsible for them, their children will do this for them. This applies not only to families but also to nations, cultures groups, religions, and organizations.

Through the work of constellations, we are able to clearly see the costs involved when a nation starts a war. The extent of trauma that World War II has caused German families and the high price they and their offspring have had to pay is clearly visible. Take the war in Vietnam, where American casualties were about 250,000 compared to about 2 million Vietnamese deaths. The extent of pain and suffering that many traumatized veterans from Vietnam and (more recently) Afghanistan and Iraq have been subject to has led many individuals to suicide, drug abuse, criminality, divorce, and so forth.

The burdening of their offspring as a result of such traumatic states seems to evoke further pain and suffering in order to attain a balance. It appears as if the collective conscience once again seeks recompense. (See "War" in chapter four.) Bearing these consequences in mind, it becomes clear that wars are just as destructive for both the perpetrating nation as the victimized nation.

If people on a large scale understand there is no escape from nature's compensatory effect—the balance of give and take—then current and future generations will look for other solutions rather than trying to dominate and conquer other nations by force.

The social and material costs for the perpetrating nation are simply too high. The same applies to life itself. If people understand that murder, theft, deceit, and exclusion always have an influence on the life and happiness of their children, they would look for other ways to solve their problems.

You can do whatever you want, but you have no control over the consequences.
—Bert Hellinger

Indra Torsten Preiss

From an early age, Indra developed an interest in social psychology. He quickly came to the conclusion that society cannot be changed from the outside. Real change, he discovered, comes about primarily through an individual awareness process.

This is how Indra's own journey of self-discovery began. Rebirthing and bodywork became his main foci after beginning with gestalt. What started off as psychotherapy gradually developed into an intense spiritual purification and initiation journey. After training as a rebirthing counselor, he opened up his first practice in Germany in 1983.

He went on to take training courses in bodywork, NLP, and voice dialogue, and the spiritual teacher Osho inspired him. Meeting with the spiritual teacher Michael Barnett marked a turning point in his life. It was clear that even deeper spiritual dimensions awaited him. In an intensive period of study and learning, he broke away from restraining patterns and discovered the beauty of living in the here and now and looking at things as a whole.

After this time of intensive learning, he established himself in Antwerp in 1992. He became a father to three children. In his practice he continued to develop and refine his own ways of working with the inner child and energy. Alongside individual sessions he worked with groups and initiated annual intensive residential workshops titled "Being Yourself."

During this period in 1998, Indra made the inner move away from being a therapist to becoming a spiritual teacher. In his ongoing quest to improve and refine his work, he followed tantra workshops and accredited courses by Margot Anand, René Koopmans, and others. This is when he came into contact with family constellations. He followed an annual training course conducted by Berthold Ulsamer in 2001 and attended seminars by Bert Hellinger, Albrecht Mahr, and other well-known constellators.

The genius of this method had such an impact that the kernel of his first book was soon in the pipeline. It was a book he felt he had to write. Published in Dutch in 2004 and titled *Familieopstellingen in de Praktijk (Family Constellations in Practice)*, it was followed in 2008 by his second book, *Gezonde verhoudingen*, translated into English as *Family Constellations Revealed* and soon to be published in Korean and Bulgaria. In 2015 he published *Heal Your Relationship*.

This is the path Indra has taken to be the accomplished spiritual teacher he is today—experienced, resolute, and loving. Indra stands apart through his constant quest for a deeper truth as well as his candor, encompassing consciousness, and wisdom. He conducts an extensive range of courses in his Art of Life Studio and on tour.

Notes

Acknowledgments

1. B. Ulsamer, The Healing Power of the Past, A New Approach to Healing Family Wounds, The Systemic Therapy of Bert Hellinger (Nevada City, California: Underwood Books, 2005).

2. I. Boszormenyi-Nagy, Invisible Loyalties (New York: Harper & Row, 1973).

1 Introduction

1. For more information about rebirthing-breath work, see http://en.wikipedia.org/wiki/Rebirthing-breathwork.

2. For more information about inner child work on my site, see http://www.the-systemic-view.com.

3. For more information about the energy work by Michael Barnett, see http://www.michaelbarnett.net.

4. B. Hellinger, G. Weber, and H. Beaumont, *Love's Hidden Symmetry*: *What Makes Love Work in Relationships* (Phoenix: Zeig, Tucker and Theisen Inc., 1998).

5. Lao-Tzu, *Tao te Ching*, trans. S. Mitchell. http://genius.com/Lao-tzu-tao-te-ching-annotated#note-3580911

6. C. G. Jung, *Collected Works of C. G. Jung* (New York: Princeton University Press, 1981).

7. M. Barnett, *The Arrow of Man: The Search for Meaning Beyond Enlightenment* (Zurich: CEC, 1991).

8. B. Hellinger, *Ordnungen der Liebe*, (Heidelberg: Carl-Auer-Systeme Verlag, 2001).

9. I. Boszormenyi-Nagy and B. Krasner, *Between Give and Take: A Clinical Guide to Contextual Therapy* (New York: Brunner/Mazel Inc., 1986).

10. R. Sheldrake, *Seven Experiments That Could Change the World*: *A Do-It-Yourself Guide to Revolutionary Science*, Ed. 2 (Rochester, Vermont: Park Street Press, 2002).

11. U. Franke, *In My Mind's Eye: Family Constellations in Individual Setting and Consultation* (Heidelberg: Carl-Auer-Systeme Verlag, 2003).

2 The Method

1. B. Hellinger, *Ordnungen der Liebe* (Heidelberg: Carl-Auer-Systeme Verlag, 2001).

2. B. Ulsamer, *The Art and Practice of Family Constellations, Leading Family Constellations as Developed by Bert Hellinger* (Heidelberg: Carl-Auer-Systeme Verlag, 2003).

3. H. Döring-Meijer (Hrsg), *Leiden ist leichter als lösen, Ein Praxiskurs mit Bert Hellinger, Familieaufstellungen mit Suchtkranken* (Paderborn: JunfermannVerlag, 2000).

4. B. Hellinger, G. Weber, and H. Beaumont, *Love's Hidden Symmetry: What Makes Love Work in Relationships* (Phoenix: Zeig, Tucker and Theisen Inc., 1998).

5. Information about bowing and the working of muscle chains can be found:

Godelieve Struyf-Denys:

http://www.prodim.be/ictgds.html

Françoise Méziéres:

http://www.mezieres.eu/anglais/hist_fm.php

See also: B. Hellinger, G. Weber, and H. Beaumont, *Love's Hidden Symmetry: What Makes Love Work in Relationships* (Phoenix: Zeig, Tucker and Theisen Inc., 1998).

6. Lao-Tzu, *Tao te Ching*, trans. S. Mitchell: http://genius.com/Lao-tzu-tao-te-ching-annotated#note-3580911.

7. B. Hellinger and B. Ulsamer, *Das Handwerk des Familienstellens, Eine Einführung in die Praxsis der systemischen Hellinger-Therapie* (Munich: Wilhelm Goldmann Verlag, 1999).

8. B. Ulsamer, *The Art and Practice of Family Constellations, Leading Family Constellations as Developed by Bert Hellinger* (Heidelberg: Carl-Auer-Systeme Verlag, 2003).

9. Lao-Tzu, *Tao te Ching*, trans. S. Mitchell: http://genius.com/Lao-tzu-tao-te-ching-annotated#note-3580911.

10. B. Hellinger, *Ordnungen der Liebe* (Heidelberg: Carl-Auer-Systeme Verlag, 2001).

11. I. Maso and A. Smaling, *Kwalitatief onderzoek: praktijk en theorie* (Amsterdam: Boom, 1998).

12. Bert Hellinger, *Praxis der Systemaufstellung* (Munich: DGfS, 2001).

13. I. Boszormenyi-Nagy and B. Krasner, *Between Give and Take: A Clinical Guide to Contextual Therapy* (New York: Brunner/Mazel Inc., 1986).

14. Bert Hellinger, *Praxis der Systemaufstellung* (Munich: DGfS, 2001).

3 Order of Love

1. B. Hellinger, *Ordnungen der Liebe* (Heidelberg: Carl-Auer-Systeme Verlag, 2001).

2. B. Hellinger, J. Neuhauser, and C. Beaumont, *Supporting Love: How Love Works in Couple Relationships* (Phoenix: Zeig, Tucker & Co, 2001).

3. B. Hellinger, G. Weber, and H. Beaumont, *Love's Hidden Symmetry, What Makes Love Work in Relationships* (Phoenix: Zeig, Tucker & Co., 1998).

4. B. Ulsamer, spoken statement during my training, Freiburg, 2001.

5. For more information see http://en.wikipedia.org/wiki/Systems_theory.

6. Michielsen, Van Mulligen, and Hermkens, *Leren over Leven in loyaliteit* (Leuven: Acco, 2002).

7. B. Hellinger, *De wijsheid is voortdurend onderweg, een rijke oogst aan teksten* (Groningen: Het Noorderlicht, 2002).

8. *Op Pelgrimage Naar Ground Zero*, De Morgen Antwerpen: De Persgroep, July 6, 2002.

9. I. Boszormenyi-Nagy and B. Krasner, *Between Give and Take: A Clinical Guide to Contextual Therapy* (New York: Brunner/Mazel Inc., 1986).

10. B. Hellinger, *Praxis der Systemaufstellung* (Munich: DGfS, 2001).

11. B. Hellinger, *Praxis der Systemaufstellung* (Munich: DGfS, 2001).

12–13. B. Hellinger, *Religion, Psychotherapie, Seelsorge* (Munich: Kösel Verlag, 2000).

4 Entanglements within the Family System

1. H. Döring-Meijer (Hrsg), *Leiden ist leichter als lösen, Ein Praxiskurs mit Bert Hellinger, Familieaufstellungen mit Suchtkranken* (Paderborn: JunfermannVerlag, 2000).

2. B. Ulsamer, *The Healing Power of the Past, A New Approach to Healing Family Wounds, The Systemic Therapy of Bert Hellinger* (Nevada City: Underwood Books, 2005).

3. Lao-Tzu, *Tao te Ching*, trans. S. Mitchell: http://genius.com/Lao-tzu-tao-te-ching-annotated#note-3580911.

4. Michielsen, Van Mulligen, and Hermkens, *Leren over Leven in loyaliteit* (Leuven: Acco 2002).

5. M. Weggemans, *Broederziel alleen* (Utrecht: Kok, Kampen 2006).

6–7. H. Döring-Meijer (Hrsg), *Leiden ist leichter als lösen, Ein Praxiskurs mit Bert Hellinger, Familieaufstellungen mit Suchtkranken* (Paderborn: JunfermannVerlag, 2000).

8. For more information see http://en.wikipedia.org/wiki/Maternal_death.

9. B. Hellinger, G. Weber, and H. Beaumont, *Love's Hidden Symmetry, What Makes Love Work in Relationships* (Phoenix: Zeig, Tucker and Theisen Inc., 1998).

10–11. A. R. Austermann and B. Austermann, *The Surviving Twin Syndrome* (Berlin: Königsweg-Verlag, 2009).

12. B. Hellinger, *Die Quelle braucht nicht nach dem Weg zu fragen, Ein Nachlesebuch* (Heidelberg: Carl-Auer-Systeme Verlag, 2002).

13. B. Hellinger, G. Weber, and H. Beaumont, *Love's Hidden Symmetry, What Makes Love Work in Relationships* (Phoenix: Zeig, Tucker and Theisen Inc., 1998).

14–16. B. Hellinger, *Ordnungen der Liebe*, (Heidelberg: Carl-Auer-Systeme Verlag, 2001)

17. Lao-Tzu, *Tao te Ching*, trans. S. Mitchell: http://genius.com/Lao-tzu-tao-te-ching-annotated#note-3580911.

18. B. Hellinger, *Wo Ohnmacht Frieden stiftet, Familien-Stellen mit Opfern von Trauma, Schiksal und Schuld* (Heidelberg: Carl-Auer-Systeme Verlag, 2000).

19. F. Ruppert, *Verwirrte Seelen, Der verborgene Sinn von Psychosen* (Munich: Kösel Verlag, 2002).

See also: F. Ruppert and V. Broughton, *Trauma, Bonding and Family Constellations: Healing Injuries of the Soul* (Somerset: Green Balloon Publishing, 2008).

20. B. Ulsamer, Freiburg, 2001.

21. "Suicide Epidemic among Veterans," CBS News, February 11, 2009.

22. Dr. Jonathan Shay, *Achilles in Vietnam, Combat Trauma and the Undoing of Character* (New York: Scribner, 1994).

23. B. Hellinger, *Wo Ohnmacht Frieden stiftet, Familien-Stellen mit Opfern von Trauma, Schiksal und Schuld* (Heidelberg: Carl-Auer-Systeme Verlag, 2000).

24. B. Ulsamer, *The Healing Power of the Past, A New Approach to Healing Family Wounds, The Systemic Therapy of Bert Hellinger* (Nevada City: Underwood Books, 2005).

25. B. Hellinger, *Ordnungen der Liebe* (Heidelberg: Carl-Auer-Systeme Verlag, 2001).

26. B. Ulsamer and H. Hohnen (Hrsg), *Mit der Seele gehen* (Freiburg: Herder Verlag, 2000).

27. B. Hellinger, *Ordnungen der Liebe* (Heidelberg: Carl-Auer-Systeme Verlag, 2001).

28. B. Hellinger, *Bonding and Balancing in Close Relationships*, trans. Maureen Oberli-Turner and Hunter Beaumont (Phoenix: Zeig, Tucker and Theisen Inc., 2001).

29. I. Precop and B. Hellinger, *Wen Ihr wüsstet wie ich euch liebe* (Munich: Kösel Verlag, 1998).

30. For more information see http://en.wikipedia.org/wiki/Rebirthing-breathwork.

31. B. Hellinger, G. Weber, and H. Beaumont, *Love's Hidden Symmetry: What Makes Love Work in Relationships* (Phoenix: Zeig, Tucker and Theisen Inc., 1998).

5 Family Constellations and Relationships

1. Lao-Tzu, *Tao te Ching*, trans. S. Mitchell: http://genius.com/Lao-tzu-tao-te-ching-annotated#note-3580911.

2. J. R. Schneider, *Praxis der Systemaufstellung* (Munich: DGfS, 2002).

3. B. Hellinger, J. Neuhauser, and C. Beaumont, *Supporting Love: How Love Works in Couple Relationships* (Phoenix: Tucker & Co., 2001).

4. I. Boszormenyi-Nagy and B. Krasner, *Between Give and Take: A Clinical Guide to Contextual Therapy* (New York: Brunner/Mazel Inc., 1986).

5. B. Hellinger, J. Neuhauser, and C. Beaumont, *Supporting Love: How Love Works in Couple Relationships* (Phoenix: Zeig Tucker & Co., 2001).

6. The inner child meditation can be found on my website: http://www.the-systemic-view.com.

7. B. Hellinger, J. Neuhauser, and C. Beaumont, *Supporting Love: How Love Works in Couple Relationships* (Phoenix: Zeig Tucker & Co., 2001).

8. B. Hellinger, *Wo Ohnmacht Frieden stiftet, Familien-Stellen mit Opfern von Trauma, Schiksal und Schuld* (Heidelberg: Carl-Auer-Systeme Verlag, 2000).

9. B. Hellinger, *Was in Familien krank macht und heilt, Ein Kurs für Betroffene* (Heidelberg: Carl-Auer-Systeme Verlag, 2001).

10. B. Hellinger, *Ordnungen der Liebe* (Heidelberg: Carl-Auer-Systeme Verlag, 2001).

11. *Die Kinder von der Samenbank*, Der Spiegel, (Hamburg: R. Augstein GmbH & Co, 31/2002).

12. For more information see http://childrenhaverights-saynotoreprotech.blogspot.com/2007/02/doron-blake-genius-designer-baby.html.

See also
http://www.slate.com/articles/life/seed/2001/03/the_nobel_sperm_bank_celebrity.html.
Since his birth, brilliant, precocious Doron Blake has symbolized the Repository for Germinal Choice. Now the *super baby* is an eighteen-year-old college freshman, and he's longing to be normal.

13. B. Ulsamer, *The Healing Power of the Past, A New Approach to Healing Family Wounds, The Systemic Therapy of Bert Hellinger* (Nevada City: Underwood Books, 2005).

14. B. Hellinger, *Ordnungen der Liebe* (Heidelberg: Carl-Auer-Systeme Verlag, 2001).

6 Family Constellations and Children

1–2. S. Schneider, *Kindliche Not und kindliche Liebe, Familien-Stellen und systemische Lösungen in Schule und Familie*, Gomez Pedra, S. (Hrsg), Hellinger, B., Schneider, S., Franke-Gricksch, M. (Heidelberg: Carl-Auer-Systeme Verlag, 2000).

3. For more information see http://www.darndivorce.com/divorce-rates-around-the-world.

4. For more information see http://en.wikipedia.org/wiki/Jay_Haley.

5. B. Hellinger, *Kindliche Not und kindliche Liebe, Familien-Stellen und systemische Lösungen in Schule und Familie*, Gomez Pedra, S. (Hrsg), Hellinger, B., Schneider, S., Franke-Gricksch, M. (Heidelberg: Carl-Auer-Systeme Verlag, 2000).

6. S. Schneider, *Kindliche Not und kindliche Liebe, Familien-Stellen und systemische Lösungen in Schule und Familie*, Gomez Pedra, S. (Hrsg), Hellinger, B., Schneider, S., Franke-Gricksch, M. (Heidelberg: Carl-Auer-Systeme Verlag, 2000).

7. S. Schneider, *Kindliche Not und kindliche Liebe, Familien-Stellen und systemische Lösungen in Schule und Familie*, Gomez Pedra S. (Hrsg), Hellinger, B., Schneider, S., Franke-Gricksch, M. (Heidelberg: Carl-Auer-Systeme Verlag, 2000).

8. Sosan in *Waking Up!,* M. Barnett, (Zurich: CEC 1991).

See also http://www.peterrussell.com/Odds/FaithMind.php.

9–10. B. Hellinger, *Kindliche Not und kindliche Liebe, Familien-Stellen und systemische Lösungen in Schule und Familie*, Gomez Pedra, S. (Hrsg), Hellinger, B., Schneider, S., Franke-Gricksch, M. (Heidelberg: Carl-Auer-Systeme Verlag, 2000).

11. For more information see http://en.wikipedia.org/wiki/Single_parent.

12. De Morgen (Antwerpen: De Persgroep 15/10/2005).

7 Family Constellations and Disease

1. A. Mahr, *Family Constellation and Illness,* (Amersfoort, the Netherlands, 2003).

2. G. Weber (Hrsg) *Praxis des Familien-Stellens, Beiträge zu Systemischen Lösungen nach, Bert Hellinger* (Heidelberg: Carl-Auer-Systeme Verlag, 2000).

3. B. Hellinger, *Ordnungen der Liebe* (Heidelberg: Carl-Auer-Systeme Verlag, 2001).

4–5. A. Mahr, *Family Constellation and Illness,* (Amersfoort, the Netherlands, 2003).

6. B. Hellinger, *Ordnungen der Liebe* (Heidelberg: Carl-Auer-Systeme Verlag, 2001).

7. B. Hellinger, *Ordnungen der Liebe* (Heidelberg: Carl-Auer-Systeme Verlag, 2001).

8. B. Willems, De Bijgedachte: *Domweg Gelukkig in Belgie*, De Morgen, (Antwerpen: De Persgroep 25/07/02).

9. BDB, *Een op de vier Vlamingen ooit depressief,* De Morgen, (Antwerpen: De Persgroep 26/07/02).

10. For more information see http://www.cdc.gov/Features/dsDepression.

11. For more information see http://www.mentalhealth.org.uk/help-information/mental-health-statistics/common-mental-health-problems/?view=Standard.

12. For more information see http://www.mentalhealth.org.uk/help-information/mental-health-a-z/S/suicide.

13–14. For more information see www.wikipedia.org/wiki/Zelfmoord.

15. For more information see http://www.nimh.nih.gov/health/publications/suicide-in-the-us-statistics-and-prevention/index.shtml.

16. H. Döring-Meijer (Hrsg), *Leiden ist leichter als lösen, Ein Praxiskurs mit Bert Hellinger, Familieaufstellungen mit Suchtkranken* (Paderborn: Junfermann Verlag, 2000).

See also: Stephan Hausner, *Even If It Costs Me My Life: Systemic Constellations and Serious Illness* (New York: Routledge 2015).

17–19. F. Ruppert, *De verborgen boodschap van psychische stoornissen* (Eeserveen: Akasha, 2008).

See also: Franz Ruppert and Vivian Broughton, *Trauma, Bonding and Family Constellations: Healing Injuries of the Soul* (Somerset: Green Balloon Publishing, 2008).

20. B. Hellinger, *Ordnungen der Liebe* (Heidelberg: Carl-Auer-Systeme Verlag, 2001).

21. H. Döring-Meijer (Hrsg), *Leiden ist leichter als lösen, Ein Praxis-kurs mit Bert Hellinger, Familieaufstellungen mit Suchtkranken* (Paderborn: Junfermann Verlag, 2000).

22–24. M. Wiendl and U. Ostermeier-Sitkowski, *Beter Zien, systemische oog-therapie* (Den Haag: De Driehoek, 2008).

8 Other Types of Constellations

1. Lao-Tzu, *Tao te Ching*, trans. S. Mitchell: http://genius.com/Lao-tzu-tao-te-ching-annotated#note-3580911.

2. U. Franke, *In My Mind's Eye: Family Constellations in Individual Setting and Consultation* (Heidelberg: Carl-Auer-Systeme Verlag, 2003).

3–5. G. Weber, *Het succes van Organisatieopstellingen* (Haarlem: Altamira-Becht, 2003).

6–8. I. Sparrer and M. Varga von Kibéd, *Het succes van Organisatieopstellingen* (Haarlem: Altamira-Becht, 2003).

See also: Insa Sparrer and Matthias Varga von Kibéd, *Miracle, Solution and System: Solution-focused Systemic Structural Constellations for Therapy and Organizational Change* (Cheltenham, UK: Solutions Books, 2007).

9. M. Franke-Gricksch, *Jij hoort bij ons!, systemisch denken en handelen voor ouders, leraren en leerlingen* (Groningen: Het Noorderlicht, 2006).

10. For more information see http://www.delos-inc.com.

11. For more information see http://www.wikipedia.org/wiki/Gestalttherapie.

12. For more information see http://www.wikipedia.org/wiki/Carl–Gustav–Jung.

13. For more information see http://en.wikipedia.org/wiki/Jungian_archetypes.

14. Lao-Tzu, *Tao te Ching*, trans. S. Mitchell: http://genius.com/Lao-tzu-tao-te-ching-annotated#note-3580911.

15. For more information see http://www.prb.org/Publications/PopulationBulletins/2010/immigrationupdate1.aspx.

16–17. B. Hellinger, *Hart tegen hard* (Haarlem: Altamira-Becht, 2006).

18. Michielsen, Van Mulligen, and Hermkens, *Leren over Leven in loyaliteit* (Leuven: Acco, 2002).

19. B. Hellinger, *Hart tegen hard* (Haarlem: Altamira-Becht, 2006).

20. For more information see http://www.hiddensolution.com/peace1.htm.

21. B. Hellinger, *Hart tegen hard* (Haarlem: Altamira-Becht, 2006).

22. Videos about constellations with the "Movement of the Soul" can be ordered on the Bert Hellinger Institute USA website. See http://mn8.net/hellingerUSA/color3.html.

23. B. Hellinger, *Praxis der Systemaufstellung* (Munich: DGfS, 2007).

24. M. Mossel, *Praxis der Systemaufstellung* (Munich: DGfS, 2007).

25. W. Nelles, *Praxis der Systemaufstellung* (Munich: DGfS, 2007).

9 Science and Constellations

1. For more information see:
http://nl.wikipedia.org/wiki/Wetenschapsfilosofie#Karakter_van_wetenschappelijke_ui tspraken_en_concepten.

2. For more information see:
Deutsche Gesellschaft für Systemaufstellungen DGfS:
http://www.familienaufstellung.org/.

International Systemic Constellations Association (ISCA): http://isca-network.org/.

The knowing field: http://www.theknowingfield.com/.

Praxis der Systemaufstellung: http://praxis-der-systemaufstellung.de/.

3. G. Höpper, *Heilt Demut: wo Schiksal wirkt? Eine Studie zu Effecten des Familie-Stellens nach Bert Hellinger* (Munich: Profil-Verlag, 2001).

The book can be purchased in PDF format via www.carl-auer.de.

4. P. Schlötter, *Vertraute Sprache und ihre Entdeckung, Systemaufstellungen sind kein Zufallsprodukt—ein empirischer Nachweis* (Heidelberg: Carl-Auer Verlag, 2004).

5. For more information see http://www.e-r-langlotz.de/familientherapie/familientherapie_publikationen.php.

6. Lao-Tzu, *Tao te Ching*, trans. S. Mitchell: http://genius.com/Lao-tzu-tao-te-ching-annotated#note-3580911.

7. R. Sheldrake, *Seven Experiments That Could Change the World: A Do-It-Yourself Guide to Revolutionary Science*, Ed. 2 (Rochester, Vermont: Park Street Press, 2002).

Also see: http://www.sheldrake.org/homepage.html.

8. The story of the "Hundredth Monkey": http://www.wowzone.com/monkey.htmwww.enealand.nl/aapjeskijken.htm.

9. H. Beaumont, *Praxis der Systemaufstellung* (Munich: DGfS, 2000).

10. For more information see http://www.bbc.co.uk/sn/tvradio/programmes/horizon/ghostgenes.shtml.

11. For more information see http://nl.wikipedia.org/wiki/Epigenetica

and http://en.wikipedia.org/wiki/Epigenetics.

12–13. G. Vines, "Hidden Inheritance," *New Scientist* 28 (1998): 27–30.

14–15. De Morgen, (Antwerpen: De Persgroep 14/01/08).

See also: http://www.dailymail.co.uk/news/article-507588/Shock-married-couple-discovered-twins-separated-birth.html.

16. For more information see http://www.ad.nl/familie–en–relaties/article1291038.ece.

17. For more information see http://www.geneticsexualattraction.com.

18–19. A. Zeilinger, *Einsteins Spuk* (Munich: Bertelsman, 2005).

20. F. Ruppert, *Praxis der Systemaufstellung* (Munich: DGfS, 2006).

21. G. Rizzolati, L. Fogassi, and V. Gallese, "Mirrors in the Mind," *Scientific American* 59 (2006).

22. M. Iacoboni, I. Molnar-Szakas, V. Gallese, G. Buccino, J. C. Mazziotta, and G. Rizzolatti, "Grasping the Intentions of Others with One's Own Mirror Neuron System," *PLOS Biology* (2005).

See also: http://journals.plos.org/plosbiology/article?id=10.1371/journal.pbio.0030079.

23. V. Gallese, *Embodied Simulation: From Mirror Neuron Systems to Interpersonal Relations* (Parma: University of Parma, 2006).

24. J. Bauer, *Warum ich fühle, was du fühlst* (Hamburg: Hoffmann und Campe, 2005).

10 Preparing for One's Own Constellation

1. M. Barnett, The Arrow of Man: The Search for Meaning Beyond Enlightenment (Zurich: CEC, 1991).

2. Lao-Tzu, Tao te Ching, trans. S. Mitchell: http://genius.com/Lao-tzu-tao-te-ching-annotated#note-3580911.

3. W. Reich, Die Funktion des Orgasmus, Wien, 1927

and A. Lowen, Leven zonder angst, (Utrecht: Servire,1995).

4. For more information see http://en.wikipedia.org/wiki/Alexander_Lowen.

Recommended Literature

Heal Your Relationship: A New Way of Improving Your Relationship Skills, Indra Torsten Preiss, The Systemic View Series, Antwerp, 2015.

Art and Practice of Family Constellations: Leading Family Constellations as Developed by Bert Hellinger, Bertold Ulsamer and Colleen Beaumont, Carl-Auer-Systeme-Verlag, 2003.

Images of the Soul: The Workings in Shamanic Rituals and Family Constellations, Daan Van Kampenhout, Carl-Auer-Systeme-Verlag, 2001.

Acknowledging What Is: Conversations with Bert Hellinger, Bert Hellinger, Gabriele Ten Hoevel, and Colleen Beaumont, Zeig, Tucker & Co., 1999.

Farewell: Family Constellations with Descendants of Victims and Perpetrators, Bert Hellinger and Colleen Beaumont, Carl-Auer-Systeme-Verlag, 2003.

Peace Begins in the Soul: Family Constellations in the Service of Reconciliation, Bert Hellinger and Colleen Beaumont, Carl-Auer-Systeme-Verlag, 2003.

Connecting to Our Ancestral Past: Healing through Family Constellations, Ceremony, and Ritual, Francesca Mason Boring, North Atlantic Books, 2012.

Miracle, Solution and System: Solution-focused Systemic Structural Constellations for Therapy and Organizational Change, Insa Sparrer and Matthias Varga von Kibéd, Solutions Books, 2007.

Even If It Costs Me My Life: Systemic Constellations and Serious Illness, Stephan Hausner, Gestalt Press, 2011.

No Waves without the Ocean: Experiences and Thoughts, Bert Hellinger, Carl Auer International, 2006.

Supporting Love: How Love Works in Couple Relationships, Bert Hellinger, Neuhauser Johannes, and Colleen Beaumont, Zeig, Tucker & Co, 2001.

Trauma, Bonding and Family Constellations: Healing Injuries of the Soul, Franz Ruppert and Vivian Broughton, Green Balloon Publishing, 2008.

Splits in the Soul: Integrating Traumatic Experiences, Franz Ruppert and Vivian Broughton, Green Balloon Publishing, 2011.

Symbiosis and Autonomy: Symbiotic Trauma and Love Beyond Entanglements, Franz Ruppert and Vivian Broughton, Green Balloon Publishing, 2012.

Mummy's Boy Daddy's Girl, Anna Zanardi Capon and Rachel Standring, E-book, 2012. (available on Kindle and online stores)

Recommended Websites

Indra's website and blog:
http://www.the-systemic-view.com

International Systemic Constellations Association (ISCA):
http://isca-network.org

The Knowing Field International Constellations Journal:
http://www.theknowingfield.com

Bert Hellinger Institute USA:
http://mn8.net/hellingerUSA/color3.html

Deutsche Gesellschaft für Systemaufstellungen (DGfS):
http://www.familienaufstellung.org

Information about the energy work by Michael Barnett:
http://www.michaelbarnett.net

Information about rebirthing-breath work:
http://en.wikipedia.org/wiki/Rebirthing-breathwork

Made in United States
Troutdale, OR
02/16/2024

17727192R00184